# Inside
# XENIX®

## Christopher L. Morgan

*ffff*
## SAMS

A Division of Macmillan Computer Publishing
11711 North College, Carmel, Indiana 46032 USA

© 1986 by The Waite Group, Inc

FIRST EDITION
FIFTH PRINTING—1990

International Standard Book Number: 0-672-22445-3
Library of Congress Catalog Card Number: 86-61875

Acquisitions Editor: *James S. Hill*
Designer: *T. R. Emrick*
Illustrator: *Ralph E. Lund*
Cover Designer: *Keith J. Hampton*
Cover Illustrator: *Debi Stewart, Visual Graphic Services*
Compositor: *Shepard Poorman Communications, Indianapolis*

Printed in the United States of America

**Trademark Acknowledgments**

AT&T is a registered trademark of American Telephone and Telegraph Corporation.

CP/M and Digital Research are registered trademarks of Digital Research Corporation.

DEC, PDP, and VAX are registered trademarks of Digital Equipment Corporation.

IBM, IBM PC, IBM AT, and IBM XT are registered trademarks of International Business Machines Corporation.

Intel is a registered trademark of Intel Corporation.

Microsoft, MS, and XENIX are registered trademarks of Microsoft, Inc.

UNIX is a trademark of AT&T Bell Laboratories, Inc.

# Contents

**Foreword**                                                    v

**Preface**                                                     vi

**1  Preliminaries**                                            1

XENIX System V □ What Is an Operating System? □ A Short History of UNIX □ A Short History of Microcomputers □ XENIX Today □ Our Approach to XENIX □ Summary □ Questions and Answers

**2  Organization of XENIX**                                   13

A Guided Tour □ Logging In □ The Environment □ Some Key Directory and File Commands □ Combining Commands □ DOS Commands □ Security □ Processes □ The Kernel □ Summary □ Questions and Answers

**3  Programming Tools in XENIX**                              47

Overview □ Editing with Vi □ Writing Shell Programs □ Compiling with the C Compiler □ Developing Programs for PC-DOS and MS-DOS □ Debugging □ Automating Program Development □ Summary □ Questions and Answers

**4  Filters**                                                 89

What Is a Filter? □ Redirection of I/O □ Programming Filters □ Summary □ Questions and Answers

**5  System Variables**                                        121

The Environment □ Shell Variables □ Using Shell Variables in Scripts □ Summary □ Questions and Answers

**6  XENIX Screen and Keyboard: Curses and Termcap**  **141**

Screen Routines □ String I/O □ Terminal Capabilities □ Summary □ Questions and Answers

**7  Files and Directories**  **167**

Files, Directories, and File Systems □ Physical and Logical Organization of Files □ Paths, Trees, and Directories □ Exploring the Super Block □ I-Nodes □ Modifying File Attributes □ Fundamental File Reading and Writing Routines □ Summary □ Questions and Answers

**8  Process Control**  **205**

Processes □ The Fork Function □ A First Warmup Example □ Using Semaphores □ Example Program □ Signals □ Example Program □ Pipes □ Example Program □ Summary □ Questions and Answers

**9  Device Drivers**  **225**

Overview □ The Kernel □ System Calls □ Hardware Interrupts □ Device Driver Routines □ Block and Character Drivers □ The Device Tables □ Special Device Files □ File Operation Routines for Devices □ Routines in the Kernel Used by Device Drivers □ Structures in the Kernel Used by Device Drivers □ Block Oriented Devices □ Example: a Terminal Driver □ Installing Device Drivers □ Summary □ Questions and Answers

**10  Advanced Tools for Programmers**  **269**

Yacc □ Lex □ Comparison Between Lex and Yacc □ An English Analogy □ Parts of a Yacc Program □ Compiling a Yacc Program □ How Yacc Works □ Lexical Analysis with Lex □ Refining Our Example of Simple English □ A Numerical Example □ Summary □ Questions and Answers

**Index**  **320**

# Foreword

XENIX enjoys the lion's share of the multiuser market today. This operating system has been installed on more computers worldwide than all other UNIX systems combined. Over 85 percent of all microprocessor-based computers running any version of UNIX are running XENIX.

In 1980, Microsoft Corporation released their commercially enhanced version of UNIX—the XENIX Operating System—for microprocessor-based computers. In 1982, The Santa Cruz Operation (SCO) became Microsoft's co-development partner and alternate source for XENIX. SCO and Microsoft have continued to work together cooperatively to develop and enhance XENIX as UNIX has moved into System V and microprocessor technology has moved up to the 80286 and beyond.

The SCO XENIX Operating System features the XENIX Development System, which includes a C compiler and a complete DOS support library. This, coupled with the standard XENIX capability to copy files to and from a DOS partition, makes XENIX an excellent choice for a DOS development system. The XENIX approach to shared information and resource computing for PCs integrates UNIX and DOS, multiuser and LAN, and PC and mainframe into a unified environment unprecedented in its power, productivity, and price performance per user.

With *Inside XENIX,* Christopher L. Morgan has created an excellent and much needed reference work for the serious C programmer who wants to use the XENIX Operating System Development System to create new software solutions specifically for the XENIX and DOS environments. *Inside XENIX* is worthy of being a college course text on "XENIX and the Multiuser Developer," and soon may find itself in that role.

We at SCO recognize and appreciate the painstaking work that has resulted in this comprehensive book and are proud to be able to welcome the reader to explore the future of shared information and resource computing by taking a close look at *Inside XENIX.*

Doug Michels, Vice President
The Santa Cruz Operation

# Preface

The XENIX operating system and its attendant development system bring the power of minicomputers and mainframes to desktop microcomputers. XENIX is a direct descendant of the popular UNIX operating system and is a full-blown multitasking system for single users.

XENIX has an extensive set of software development tools developed at AT&T's Bell Labs, the University of California at Berkeley, and Microsoft Corporation. With these tools programmers can develop sophisticated application programs that run under XENIX, UNIX, or PC-DOS.

This book is for programmers who have had experience with other microcomputer program development environments, such as PC-DOS, MS-DOS, CP/M, BASIC, or Pascal. It is also for people who have had some UNIX experience. They will gain from this book because we present some material that even experienced UNIX programmers may not be acquainted with. This book will also be of benefit to XENIX system administrators who need to understand how XENIX works and who must write an occasional program for it.

This book is designed to help a new user/programmer quickly learn what XENIX is, what it can do, and how to develop programs with the XENIX system. We help you get started with the system as a whole and learn the various major programming tools. You will learn the general philosophy of XENIX applications in which large programs are built of small general purpose pieces.

We introduce XENIX programming tools including:

- ☐ editing programs
- ☐ debugging tools
- ☐ compilers
- ☐ text processors
- ☐ program generators

We also explain:

- ☐ XENIX's file system
- ☐ general layout
- ☐ how jobs are run
- ☐ how devices such as terminals, printers, and disk drives are connected
- ☐ how to install new devices

This book assumes that you have access to a microcomputer that has the XENIX operating system. Typically this is an IBM XT, IBM AT, or equivalent to one of these. A number of different manufacturers make machines of these classes.

The first three chapters are introductory. The first chapter explains XENIX in terms of its history and role in computing, relating it to operating systems in general, to UNIX (which was developed for the larger timesharing minicomputers), and to the smaller microcomputer operating systems such as PC-DOS and CP/M. The second chapter takes a tour through a typical XENIX system, providing an overview of the system and introducing many of the topics that are covered in the rest of the book. The third chapter describes the programming tools, starting with the main editing program and ending with a discussion of debugging tools.

The last seven chapters cover major topics with examples. These examples are usually short illustrations of features of the system or demonstrations of programming techniques that are possible with the system. They consist of system commands and programs written in the C programming language or in the language of one of the programming tools.

Chapter 4 introduces filters. These are text processing tools that perform many of the basic jobs in the system. This chapter introduces the XENIX standard I/O functions and several kinds of system files including library files.

Chapter 5 introduces screen and keyboard I/O, an important part of the system because it controls the efficiency with which humans can communicate with the computer.

Chapter 6 discusses system variables. These control the way the system is set up for each of its users. Users can adjust these variables to make the system behave in a number of different useful ways.

Chapter 7 describes XENIX file systems. It discusses how files are stored and organized within the system. It covers file management variables that control such things as file security.

Chapter 8 elaborates on how XENIX breaks its work into processes that compete with each other in the system for the CPU, memory, and other resources such as terminals. This chapter shows how processes can communicate with each other and exchange data.

Chapter 9 delves into the kernel, the innermost part of the system, and describes how devices such as terminals, printers, disk drives, and local area networks are connected to the system. It shows how a XENIX system can be reconfigured to handle a different set of devices.

Chapter 10 concludes the book with a discussion of advanced programming tools that can be used to create programs such as compilers and interpreters that understand human language. Our examples demonstrate how to use these tools to write programs that understand a simple subset of English and programs that understand algebraic expressions.

This book takes a "special topics" approach to XENIX, surveying the major areas, but concentrating on a few major parts of the system. The hundreds of system commands and library functions simply cannot be thoroughly covered in a book of this size. However, their nature and use can be understood by sampling certain key commands. These key commands either provide information about the system or perform useful programming functions.

The book is designed to be read sequentially by beginners. However, because some beginners may want to skip some discussions that rely on the C programming language, we have included plenty of material using system commands to describe the system. In fact, we show how to write simple "scripts" in the system command languages. Advanced readers may want to quickly go through Chapters 2 and 3, then choose topics to study from the remaining chapters. All readers will benefit by trying the examples on their own XENIX system.

We hope that you enjoy and profit from this book. Happy XENIXing!

## Acknowledgments

I would like to thank a number of people for their help and support with this book. At the Waite Group, Mitchell Waite initiated the project and provided much appreciated feedback on Chapter 10. Jerry Volpe served as editor at first, providing valuable comments on several chapters. Corey Kosak also reviewed portions of the first drafts, nipping some serious errors in the bud. I am especially indebted to James Stockford, who was the editor in the final stages when encouragement and support were vital.

I am grateful to Santa Cruz Operation for rushing their versions of XENIX to me and reviewing the manuscript. Eric Griswald, August Mohr, Brian Moffit, Doug Michaels, and Bruce Steinberg checked the manuscript for accuracy and provided suggestions. Brigid Fuller expedited the process, rushing suggestions to us under very tight deadlines.

At Howard W. Sams & Co., I thank all who participated in the production of this book, and especially Kathy Ewing for quickly and efficiently preparing the manuscript for typesetting.

Two of my students, Craig Leres and Edward James, provided insight about the inner workings of UNIX on larger machines. Ronald Warren provided clerical assistance, a tremendous help under tight deadlines.

My wife Carol, my daughter Elizabeth, and my son Thomas have patiently endured the long periods that I worked on this book.

# 1

# Preliminaries

- XENIX System V
- What Is an Operating System?
- A Short History of UNIX
- A Short History of Microcomputers
- XENIX Today
- Our Approach to XENIX
- Summary
- Questions and Answers

# Preliminaries

XENIX System V brings minicomputer and mainframe capabilities to desktop machines. Its hundreds of system commands and library functions provide a rich programming development environment.

In this chapter we introduce the XENIX operating system and program development system and explain our relationship to it as application programmers who are new to XENIX, but who have had experience with other program development environments.

We trace the ancestry of XENIX back through AT&T's System V to the earlier versions of the UNIX operating system for these larger timesharing machines. We discuss powerful XENIX programming tools developed at the University of California at Berkeley. We also explain how XENIX maintains a kind of upward compatibility with earlier microcomputer operating systems.

This chapter puts XENIX in perspective with smaller and larger systems and sets the stage for the rest of the book in which we explore specific features of XENIX.

## XENIX System V

In this book we explore XENIX System V from the point of view of a programmer who has had experience with other program development systems, such as CP/M, PC-DOS, BASIC, or Pascal, but who now needs to understand XENIX. We take a "special topics" approach in which we explore major programming subsystems, such as shell scripts or C programming; components of the system, such as file I/O and device drivers; and tools, such as system commands that act as text processors. By going into some depth in these areas, you gain working knowledge of some of the key commands and structures in the system and learn basic approaches that extend throughout XENIX.

XENIX opens up the world of minicomputer and mainframe computing to 16-bit microcomputers. It is a powerful operating system that brings multitasking, a large repertoire of system commands, and an extensive set of system libraries to 16-bit microcomputers, for example, the IBM XT, IBM AT and newer 32-bit machines such as the IBM PS/2 Model 80. At the same time it allows development for and file transfers with the most popular 16-bit operating systems, MS-DOS and PC-DOS.

The heart of XENIX System V largely conforms to AT&T's standards for UNIX System V. In fact, its success depends partly on its conformance with this standard. However, XENIX also includes some very valuable enhancements from the University of California at Berkeley and some additional features from its developers, Microsoft and Santa Cruz Operation (SCO).

The Berkeley enhancements to XENIX include such features as its visual screen editing program (see Chapter 3), its software routines for connecting intelligent terminals (see Chapter 6) and its program generator tools (see Chapter 10).

The Microsoft enhancements to XENIX include a set of DOS commands to read and write to MS-DOS or PC-DOS formatted disks. Also included in the XENIX enhancements are libraries of functions that allow development of MS-DOS and PC-DOS applications while in XENIX. These extensions allow programmers to work in the more powerful UNIX-like environment, then transfer their work to the smaller, more established microcomputer operating systems.

The SCO enhancements include multiple console screens, device drivers for peripheral devices, and some administrative programs.

Exceptions to the AT&T standard include lack of virtual memory and lack of ability to temporarily stop jobs from the keyboard. The default choice of the erase character and kill line keys also is improved in XENIX to use the control keys, **control h** (backspace), and **control u**, rather than the original pound sign (#) and at sign (@). These exceptions are minor compared with the extensive set of features that are in total conformity with the AT&T standard.

## What Is an Operating System?

XENIX is an *operating system,* but what does that really mean? Because this book is aimed primarily at programmers and the like, you as a reader should be already familiar with the basic functions of an operating system, having used one or more. Perhaps you could even come up with several definitions of this term. However, we need a common understanding that also helps beginning readers place XENIX within the context of such systems, small and large.

We can draw an analogy between what operating systems do for computer systems and what governments do for people. Governments come in all sizes and provide a wide variety of *services* for people, but their main function is to provide management so that people can safely share resources.

Operating systems also come in all sizes, but their function is to *man-*

*age* and provide *support* for computer systems, allowing computer software to *share* a computer system's *resources.*

Basically, an operating system consists of *software* that allows people to use computer *hardware.* Without software, a computer system cannot be effectively controlled to do useful work.

The most basic tasks of an operating system are to *load programs* into memory, *start* them up, and *provide support* routines for input from such devices as keyboards and card readers and output to such devices as printers and terminal screens. The first generation of operating systems allowed early mainframe computers to read programs from decks of punch cards and/ or from reels of paper tape in "batch" processing fashion. The first cassette tape and floppy disk microcomputer operating systems didn't do much more, but in some cases displayed the contents of the tape or disk.

More recent operating systems also provide facilities for developing new programs. Thus they also normally include *editors, assemblers,* and *debuggers.* Small single user microcomputer operating systems, such as CP/M and MS-DOS, provide such facilities.

Still larger operating systems, such as those for timesharing mainframe and minicomputers, provide the necessary management for many simultaneous users to share the computer system's resources. System resources include devices, such as its CPU, memory, disk drives, keyboards, screens, terminals, and printers, as well as more abstract objects, such as its programs and data. For example, management is needed because users have to have exclusive access to some resources, such as printers, but can share other resources, such as some program code. Other resources, such as CPU's, have to be quickly shuttled from user to user.

XENIX provides this kind of management. It allows single users to run a variety of different jobs that *simultaneously* compete for the computer system's resources. With XENIX, a single user can run a number of different tasks at the same time, perhaps several editing sessions and some background tasks all at once.

Still larger systems often provide extensive tools for program development, including sophisticated screen editors, compilers, libraries of routines, linkers, symbolic debuggers, program generators, and program maintenance systems. XENIX has a rich set of such tools including the `vi` screen editor, its C compiler that automatically invokes an assembler and linker as needed, its `adb` symbolic debugger, program generators such as `lex` and `yacc`, and its `make` program maintenance systems.

Even larger systems protect programs and data from unauthorized access and from crashing the system. As we shall see in Chapter 2, XENIX provides many of the protection techniques, such as passwords and permission bits, used in much larger systems. However, XENIX's ability to provide complete protection from crashes is limited by the hardware that it runs on. For example, the hardware configurations of an IBM XT allow one program to accidentally clobber another program's memory and even bring down the entire operating system. However, with well-test. l software, this is not a problem.

5

Multiuser systems require accounting systems that keep track of system usage and allow system managers to monitor and tune system performance and detect unauthorized use. This is important when a large number of users share the same system. XENIX provides such an accounting system. However, the accounting information that is produced tends to overwhelm the smaller (10 to 20 megabyte) hard disks currently used on microcomputers, so XENIX users may prefer to turn off this feature. Larger hard disks (40 to 80 megabytes) are becoming popular. These can easily accommodate full use of XENIX's accounting systems.

## A Short History of UNIX

XENIX traces its history back to 1969 when Ken Thompson at AT&T's Bell Laboratories in Murray Hill, New Jersey, developed the first version of UNIX on a PDP-7, a small minicomputer.

UNIX was developed at a time when computer managers, users, and programmers were reeling from the complexities of large operating systems with complicated job control languages. Thus, Thompson tried to keep the system small and simple. The first versions of UNIX were single user systems.

Although the first version of UNIX was written in assembly language, Thompson began writing parts of the system in a programming language that he called *B*. Later, Dennis Ritchie joined Thompson to develop the C programming language and rewrite most of the system in this new programming language, providing one of the most important reasons for UNIX's success, namely portability. Moving the system to a new central processor can, to a large extent, be reduced to writing a C compiler for the new machine.

Because the system was used to develop itself, an extensive set of programming tools was produced as the system grew and matured. Instead of developing large general purpose tools, smaller tools were constructed. The system was developed to make it easy to interconnect these tools to create larger special purpose programming tools quickly. During this period, UNIX was used largely by researchers within Bell Laboratories at AT&T.

A C compiler was included with the system so that the entire system can recompile itself. Editors, debuggers, tools for extracting information, and tools for producing documentation added to the self sufficiency of the system.

For a long time UNIX stayed within AT&T because AT&T was barred by federal regulations from the computer business. However, during the middle 1970s special arrangements were made with universities, for example, the University of California at Berkeley. In 1976, the first public version (version 6) was distributed, and in 1978, version 7 was publicly released, both with special licensing agreements. These versions are the basis for most current versions of UNIX, including XENIX System V (see figure 1-1).

**Figure 1-1**
**Ancestry of XENIX**

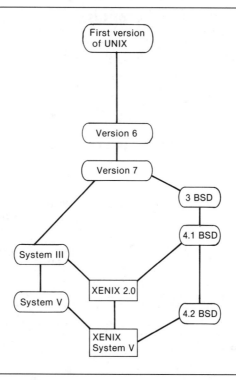

Version 7 was moved by the University of California at Berkeley to Digital Equipment Corporation (DEC) VAX supermini computers. At Berkeley, the VAX version of UNIX developed into what is called version 3 BSD (Berkeley Standard) in 1979, then version 4.1 BSD in 1981, and version 4.2 BSD in 1984. Many features, such as virtual memory, were added for these larger computers. However, many other features and tools were developed, for example, the vi editor and the terminal I/O routines, and are of universal interest. These are the so-called Berkeley enhancements that have been incorporated within XENIX. The Berkeley versions have been installed on powerful supermini computers. These machines use modern reduced instruction-set architectures to provide high performance for UNIX users. Meanwhile AT&T, after the release of version 7, moved responsibility for UNIX from the Research Group to the UNIX Support Group. This group produced System III in 1981 and System V in 1983.

XENIX was originally based on System III, but in 1985, it switched to System V and is now almost totally compatible with AT&T System V.

## A Short History of Microcomputers

At the same time UNIX was being developed, microcomputers came into being. At first (mid 1970s), they were considered to be mere toys created by hobbyists.

Based around the first 8-bit microprocessors, the first microcomputers consisted of table-top boxes filled with integrated circuit boards that connected to such peripheral devices as keyboards, video screens, and cassette tape recorders. Often microcomputers were programmed via toggle switches on a front panel, at least to get them started.

Microcomputers soon developed into useful machines for applications like word processing, games, and education, and business uses such as inventory and accounting. These machines were called personal computers because they provided individuals with their own stand-alone computers for about the cost of an automobile. A large number of people began writing programs for these machines, which revolutionized the computer industry, bringing it much closer to the average citizen.

Some of the first operating systems for microcomputers were development systems that were loaded from paper tape or cassette tape into the memory of the machine. These usually included an editor, assembler, and debugger/command interpreter. Programs were saved on cassette tape.

Later, ROM-based systems were introduced. The most popular ones ran an interpreter for the BASIC programming language. For these machines, the operating system consisted of the BASIC interpreter, with perhaps a special machine level monitor or debugger mode. With this system, BASIC programs could be edited, tested, then run as application programs on the system.

The advent of the floppy disk facilitated the development of more sophisticated operating systems, for example, CP/M by Digital Research. This operating system consists of a central core that is automatically loaded into the computer's memory when the machine is first turned on. The central core contains an I/O system (BIOS) and a manager program (BDOS), both of which stay in memory while the machine is on, and a command interpreter (CCP) that is often overlayed (replaced) by application programs loaded from the floppy disk. The command interpreter used simple but effective syntax for the time, much like that used on minicomputer operating systems by Digital Equipment Corporation.

CP/M soon became the most popular operating system in the world with an extensive software base of applications for business, education, and personal use. Because it had a separately configurable I/O section, it was portable to a wide class of 8-bit machines. Later, versions were developed for the newer 16-bit microcomputers. A multiuser version (MP/M) was also developed with 8-bit, 16-bit, and hybrid versions.

Microsoft Corporation of Bellevue, Washington, became a large supplier of software for microcomputers by developing FORTRAN and BASIC compilers that ran under CP/M. Microsoft's BASIC interpreter served as an industry standard with a version that ran under CP/M and other versions and that served as complete operating systems for many other machines.

In the early 1980s, IBM introduced their personal computer, the IBM PC. This computer was and is based on the Intel 8088 microprocessor chip, a transition from the earlier 8-bit microprocessors to the more modern 16-bit, then 32-bit microprocessors. IBM's operating system for this machine, PC-DOS, was developed by Microsoft at IBM's request. Microsoft also offers its own version, MS-DOS, for compatible machines made by other manufacturers.

The first version of MS-DOS and PC-DOS was very much like CP/M, but the second version introduced some of the fundamental features of UNIX. These features, including I/O redirection and tree-structured directory systems, are quite independent of whether the system supports a single user or many and show the strong influence of UNIX.

An example of a UNIX-like feature found in MS-DOS is redirection through the use of less-than (<) and greater-than (>) symbols. These symbols allow a programmer and ordinary users to specify any destination, for example, the screen, printer, communications line, or even a disk file for the output of programs. The symbols also allow input to programs that come from any source, including the keyboard, communications line, or an ordinary file. In addition, we can use the vertical bar symbol (|) to set up "pipelines" in which the output of one program is fed as the input to another. These pipelines conveniently combine small stand-alone programs to form larger programs that accomplish complex tasks, such as report generators; word processing tools, such as spelling and grammar checkers; and program generators.

Tree-structured directories also are familiar to MS-DOS and PC-DOS programmers. These directories allow users to organize information in terms of categories within categories. At each point in the tree, subdirectories can be given meaningful names according to the information they contain.

Microcomputers are still evolving. The recent availability of inexpensive hard disks on machines like the IBM XT made possible and indeed reasonable the installation of large operating systems such as XENIX.

Newer machines use 32-bit microprocessors and a million bytes or so of main memory. Hard disks allow these machines to handle tens of millions of bytes of secondary storage. Desktop machines offer much larger capacities than the early minicomputers on which UNIX was first developed and are able to easily handle the demands of today's versions of XENIX. Still newer architectures for microcomputers use reduced instruction-set architectures to boost performances of personal work stations beyond minicomputers and mainframes of the past. For these systems, a UNIX-like operating system such as XENIX is the system of choice because of its portability and configurability.

## XENIX Today

In the context of machines like the IBM XT, XENIX represents a step up in microcomputer operating systems over CP/M and MS-DOS because it brings the minicomputer and mainframe UNIX operating system to desktop machines that are used by individuals. XENIX is larger and more sophisticated than the earlier microcomputer operating systems, but it is smaller than the large mainframe operating systems.

In fact, XENIX can be a multiuser system for individual users. It allows a number of users to log onto the same console screen and keyboard at once. A couple of keystrokes allows one to flip from user to user. In that spirit, one person usually logs onto the system as several users, perhaps opening a copy of the editing program for a number of different files that all belong to the same project.

The user can attach two ordinary terminals to the two serial communications lines, but a machine like the IBM XT does not support intensive activity by more than one user at a time. Newer, faster XT compatibles and AT-type computers can comfortably support much more activity. Several implementations of XENIX, including the SCO version, are licensed for up to 16 work stations.

No matter what the performance is, it is extremely convenient for a single user to "open" a number of windows into the system, perhaps editing several files at once and flipping to another screen to compile the results every once in a while. This saves time and keystrokes without putting a strain on the system. In addition, the user and the operating system can easily run light tasks in the background, perhaps checking a calendar or monitoring system activity.

XENIX has some structural similarities with single user microcomputer operating systems like CP/M and MS-DOS in that it has a central program that remains in memory at all times and a command interpreter that can be replaced by an application program or other system utilities like editors and compilers when they are invoked. In XENIX, the central program is called the *kernel* and the command interpreter is called a *shell*. Like these other systems, commands can be built into the command interpreter or contained in system files. However, both the shell commands and file commands that come with XENIX are much more extensive. Of course, a wide variety of useful programs has been written to run under PC-DOS and MS-DOS on the IBM PC, XT, AT, and compatible computers, but most are larger applications: editors, spreadsheets, and data base programs.

XENIX is actually compatible with MS-DOS and PC-DOS via a collection of special XENIX "DOS" commands including `dosls` and `doscp` that imitate the more general `ls` (list files in a directory) and `cp` (copy) commands. These commands allow XENIX users to list directories of and copy files to and from MS-DOS and PC-DOS diskettes and hard disk partitions. It is also possible to use the excellent facilities of XENIX to develop programs that run under MS-DOS.

## Our Approach to XENIX

In this book, we demonstrate the wide·variety of programming environments available within the XENIX operating system. We write *shell scripts* in a command language of the operating system. These correspond to batch files in PC-DOS and "submit" files in CP/M. However, the XENIX shell languages are much more powerful and complete. We also create C programs and *special programs* in languages that are used for special utilities, such as the string processing tool awk, the lexical analyzer generator lex, and the parser generator yacc. With these last two tools we are able to build programs that translate human language into actions a machine can perform.

In each case, we take advantage of existing software and try to write the minimum amount of code to accomplish the job or illustrate the point. Using existing software has many advantages, including shorter development time, reduced effort, and smaller programs. The results are more uniform and thus easier to understand and maintain.

We are not able to cover each of the hundreds of commands and library functions in detail in a book this size. Rather, we survey the entire system and present certain representative areas in detail. Some of the major areas are: *string processing* commands that sort, search, and transform strings; *terminal I/O* routines that help bridge the gap between users and the machine, *file I/O* routines to manage the secondary storage; and *process control* commands and routines to control how work is managed within the system. We also delve into the *kernel* of the XENIX system, again studying terminal I/O routines but at a much lower level. We finish with some very useful *advanced programming tools* that generate programs which recognize language and thus help to bridge the gap between humans and machines.

We will see that XENIX is a system which allows new users to get useful work done after a few hours of training. It normally takes a few weeks for users to know confidently their way around the system and perhaps a few months to become expert, but even after years of experience, a persistent user can learn something new about XENIX every day.

## Summary

In this chapter, we have introduced the XENIX operating and development system as a powerful program development environment, complete with a full set of program development tools.

We have described XENIX's history, starting with the first single user version of the UNIX operating system in 1969 and extending through the latest versions of UNIX for timesharing supermini computers that led to today's versions on XENIX. We have discussed also the history of microcomputers from their humble beginnings to today's powerful machines that are fully capable of supporting XENIX.

We have related XENIX to operating systems in general, other versions of UNIX, and other microcomputer operating systems. Finally, we have discussed our basic approach to XENIX in this book.

## Questions and Answers

### Questions

1. What is an operating system and what does it do?
2. How does XENIX compare to the CP/M operating system?
3. In what ways is XENIX compatible with UNIX and PC-DOS?

### Answers

1. An operating system is a set of computer programs that helps control a computer to make it useful. At a minimum, it allows users to load and run programs and gives them I/O support. Often, operating systems include program development tools, such as editors, assemblers, and debuggers. More advanced systems include multitasking, which allows computer resources such as CPUs, main memory, and secondary storage to be shared among several users.

2. Both XENIX and CP/M are designed to run on microcomputers. However, XENIX is considerably more complex and sophisticated than CP/M. XENIX is a multiuser system designed for modern and more powerful microcomputers, whereas CP/M is a single-user system developed for the earlier, smaller computer systems. XENIX has an extensive set of system utilities, including a C compiler, a screen editing program, a debugging program, and various text processing programs. CP/M comes with a minimal set of utilities, including a line editing program, an assembler, and a debugger. XENIX has other features, such as a tree-structured directory system, password security, and I/O direction, that CP/M doesn't have.

3. XENIX is very compatible with UNIX. XENIX is a direct descendant of UNIX. It is a microcomputer implementation of UNIX, having the same directory structure, the same extensive set of utilities, and the same system calls. XENIX is compatible with PC-DOS in that it has DOS commands to transfer files between it and PC-DOS. The XENIX C compiler has an option that compiles programs to run under PC-DOS.

# 2

# Organization of XENIX

- A Guided Tour
- Logging In
- The Environment
- Some Key Directory and File Commands
- Combining Commands
- DOS Commands
- Security
- Processes
- The Kernel
- Summary
- Questions and Answers

# Organization of XENIX

This chapter provides an overview of a typical XENIX system in operation. We approach the system as a new user who sits down at a terminal and is given a guided tour by a more experienced user. This is a scouting trip that exposes most of the major areas we explore in the rest of the book.

Our tour begins with logging in, then uses specific examples of useful commands and their resulting output to explain how the system is set up and how we can use it to develop and run our own programs as well as take advantage of what the system can do for us.

We will see such commands as env (short for *environment*) to display the basic assumptions that the system makes about us. This env command shows such key information as our "home" directory, our "path," our "shell," and the directory for mail. We discuss each of these in detail.

Our tour explores XENIX's tree-structured directory system, using such basic commands as the pwd command to show our current location, the lx command to display what's there, the cd command to move around, and the more command to display the contents of long files. We also use the cat command to display the contents of particular files and to illustrate how programs work in cooperation in this system through I/O redirection and pipelining.

Our tour continues into the system's security, including passwords, file permissions, and the superuser. Next, we see how XENIX organizes its work into separately running "processes." We use the ps command to display all the currently active processes and see how they also form a tree. Finally, we explore the innermost part of the system, namely its kernel, and see how devices are connected to the system via "device drivers" in the kernel.

This chapter serves as a second level introduction to the XENIX system by showing details of the system in operation. Most of the commands and terms introduced here are explored more thoroughly in subsequent chapters of this book.

## A Guided Tour

Let's take a tour of a XENIX system, introducing commands that help you, as a user, understand the what, why, and where of the system. This tour should be of interest even to experienced users of other UNIX-like systems because we present commands that check the system out, revealing the particulars of how it is set up. In subsequent chapters we explore in much greater detail many of the concepts introduced on this tour.

## Logging In

Suppose we, as new users/programmers, have been given an account on a microcomputer system running XENIX System V. This particular computer system happens to be an IBM XT with four active console screens and an additional (dumb) terminal connected to a serial communications line, but any XENIX System V behaves in a similar manner. The differences are not in the commands that we issue, but only in the details of the outputs that we see.

We have been given an account named `iamnew` and a secret password. Usually, accounts are given names that are related to users' own names, such as their first or last names, nicknames, or initials. However, people often use names like `wombat` and `shark`. We can use any name we wish with the following restrictions: it must be at least three but not more than eight characters long, begin with a lowercase letter, consist of only lowercase letters and numbers, and not be already in use. The password follows much the same rules.

Let's sit down at the "dumb" terminal and learn the ropes. We begin with the login. When we step up to the terminal, we see the login prompt `xenix86!login:`. The first part `xenix86` is the name of our system, and the second part `login:` invites us to log in:

*Note:* The ◂┘ symbol signifies that you press **return**. This symbol is used at the end of lines that you type.

```
xenix86!login: iamnew◂┘
Password:
```

We type our assigned password and press **return,** then we see:

```
                      Welcome to XENIX System V
                        for personal computers

                          Brought to you by
                      The Santa Cruz Operation

     TERM = (ansi) dumb◄┘
     Terminal type is dumb
     %
```

After giving the login name, we give our assigned password (that's hidden from view). Next the system asks for the type of terminal. We respond, giving dumb as the terminal type. The prompt % indicates that the system is ready for normal input. Different prompts normally indicate different user "environments" in XENIX. For example, while the system is in maintenance mode, a pound sign (#) appears at the beginning of each command line. However, any user can change the current prompt with the prompt command.

## The Environment

Let's begin with the env command. The reason for introducing this command first is that it shows many of the basic assumptions the system is making about you, thus it introduces many of the assumptions that we can make about it.

On many systems a command like env is unnecessary because the system behaves essentially in one way all the time. However, XENIX, like any other type of UNIX system, can be initially configured in a wide variety of ways that control how the system first responds to you, then as you work with it, you can gradually modify your environment.

Here is the output from the env command:

```
     % env◄┘
     HOME=/usr/iamnew
     PATH=:/usr/iamnew/bin:/bin:/usr/bin
     TERM=dumb
     HZ=20
     TZ=PST8PDT
     SHELL=/bin/csh
     MAIL=/usr/spool/mail/iamnew
     TERMCAP=su¦dumb¦un¦unknown:co#80:os:am
```

Each line of the output displays a different *environmental* variable. We go through environmental variables in detail in this chapter. In Chapter 5, we discuss *system variables* in general.

## HOME

The first variable, namely HOME, gives us a place to start when we first log in. It is our home directory. The directories form a tree (see figure 2-1). The line HOME=/usr/iamnew specifies a *path* through the tree by listing a series of subdirectories starting from the *root* of the tree and ending at our HOME directory.

**Figure 2-1**
**The HOME directory**

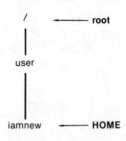

Our HOME directory happens to be at the third level: below the directory usr, which is below the *root* of the entire system. The root itself is indicated by a slash (/), and each level is separated by a slash (/). A user's home directory can be placed anywhere in the tree, but it is customary to place user home directories under the usr directory.

Let's demonstrate how the lx command displays the contents of HOME. At first a user's home directory contains only *hidden* files, so we use a special *option* of the lx command to display *all* files. If we don't use this option, we see nothing. The all option is indicated with a −a after the command name.

```
% lx -a◄┘
. .. .cshrc .login
```

Four files ., .., .cshrc, and .login now appear (see figure 2-2). The first two names automatically occur as *hidden* files in every XENIX directory. The first one . is a reference to the directory itself, and the second one .. is a reference to the *parent* directory that, in this case, is usr. These directories allow *relative* references to be made within the directory system.

The third and fourth files .cshrc and .login are script files containing a series of operating system commands. They are included normally in a user's HOME directory when that user is added to the system. They can be modified subsequently by the user. These scripts are executed when the user logs in, which causes automatic initialization of the user's environment.

**Figure 2-2**
**The contents of HOME**

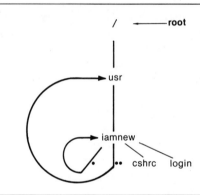

The name lx is unique to XENIX. It is part of a family of slightly differing commands that are used to list directories, including l, lc, and the familiar UNIX ls command.

## The Root

Let's apply the lx command to the root directory of the whole system. This time, we follow the lx command name with the name of the desired directory, namely a slash (/):

```
% lx /⏎
bin    boot   dev    etc    lib    lost+found
mnt    once   tmp    usr    xenix
```

This shows the top of the directory tree (see figure 2-3).

**Figure 2-3**
**The top of the tree**

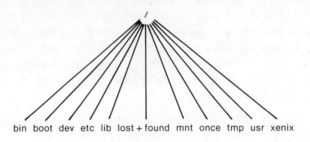

bin boot dev etc lib lost+found mnt once tmp usr xenix

All these entries have special meaning to the system, and some have particular interest in this book. The directory bin contains operating system commands. The directory dev contains special files connecting the system to its peripheral devices, such as disk drives, terminals, and printers. The memory of the system is even represented as a file called mem in this directory. The directory etc contains commands and data files that are especially useful to system managers. The directory lib contains object code *library* files that can be *linked* to other programs. The directory lost+found contains recovered files that get disconnected from the tree. The directory tmp contains temporary files created by various system utilities. The directory usr contains our HOME directory.

## Finding Commands

When we look in the bin directory, we see some of the system commands. The name bin is short for *binary files*. These are files that contain executable machine code. That is, they contain programs already compiled and thus those that can run directly on the system.

We give the pathname /bin to the lx command:

```
% lx /bin◄┘
STTY      [         adb       adb286   adb86    ar      as     asm
asx       awk       backup    banner   basename cal     cat    cb
cc        chgrp     chmod     chown    chroot   cmchk   cmp    comm
copy      cp        cpio      csh      csplit   date    dc     dd
df        diff      diff3     dircmp   dirname  disable dtype  du
dump      dumpdir   echo      ed       edit     egrep   enable env
ex        expr      false     fgrep    file     find    fsck   getopt
gets      grep      grpcheck  hd       hdr      head    id     ipcrm
ipcs      join      kill      l        lc       ld      lf     line
ln        lr        ls        lx       make     masm    mkdir  mv
```

| | | | | | | | |
|---|---|---|---|---|---|---|---|
| ncheck | newgrp | nice | nl | nm | nohup | od | passwd |
| pr | printenv | ps | pstat | pwadmin | pwcheck | pwd | ranlib |
| red | regcmp | restor | restore | rm | rmdir | rsh | sddate |
| sdiff | sed | setkey | settime | sh | size | slee | sort |
| strings | strip | stty | su | sum | sync | tail | tar |
| tee | test | time | touch | tr | true | tset | tsort |
| tty | uname | uniq | vedit | vi | view | wc | who |
| whodo | xargs | yes | | | | | |

This long list contains just some of the XENIX commands that are directly available to ordinary users.

To see some other commands, look at the environmental variable PATH. This contains a list of directory paths (separated by colons) that the system uses to search for commands that the user types in. In this case PATH is:

```
PATH=:/usr/iamnew/bin:/bin:/usr/bin
```

Thus, the first directory searched is /usr/iamnew/bin, then /bin, then /usr/bin. The first is a subdirectory (if it exists) of iamnew's account, but the others are standard system directories filled with system commands.

## Terminal Control

Let's return to the environment. The next environmental variable is TERM=dumb.

When we logged on, we specified a dumb terminal. In Chapter 6, we learn about connecting *intelligent* terminals that allow cursor control on the screen, such as those used in screen editors like vi. The last environment variable TERMCAP tells the system exactly how to communicate special screen commands with such a terminal.

The file ttys in the /etc directory specifies the most fundamental things about how all the system's terminals are connected. You can obtain a listing by using the more command followed by the pathname etc/ttys:

```
more /etc/gettydefs
```

The more command is useful for displaying large files (more than one screenful). It displays a page at a time. Use the prompt at the bottom of the screen to indicate when you wish to proceed (just press the **space bar** when you are ready). With this prompt, you can also ask for help to get directly into such features as an editor or a search routine. More is a Berkeley enhancement of System V.

Here is the result on our system:

```
% more /etc/ttys◄┘
1mconsole
1mtty02
1mtty03
1mtty04
0mtty05
0mtty06
06tty11
1ktty12
01tty13
01tty14
```

Each line lists information about a different terminal. The first character is either a 0 (meaning not enabled) or a 1 (meaning that the terminal can be used). The second character specifies a particular type of configuration for that terminal. The configurations are defined in a file called `gettydefs` that is also in the `/etc` directory. The remaining characters name the particular device driver to be used (discussed later in this chapter and in Chapter 9).

The configuration information in `gettydefs` specifies such things as initial baud rate, login prompt, and login program for each terminal communications line. You can use the `more` command on the pathname `/etc/gettydefs` to list these `tty` definitions.

Our particular terminal is connected to `tty12` (line 8 in the `ttys` file). It uses `tty` definition *k,* which has a 2400 baud rate among other things.

Once you are logged in, the `stty` command allows you to change the settings of your terminal line. Typing this command with the option `-a` (for *all* ) displays all current settings:

```
% stty -a◄┘
speed 2400 baud; line = 0; intr = DEL; quit = ^¦; erase = ^h;
kill = ^u; eof = ^d; eol = ^'
parenb -parodd cs7 -cstopb hupcl cread -clocal
-ignbrk brkint ignpar -parmrk -inpck istrip -inlcr -igncr icrnl
-iuclc
ixon ixany -ixoff
isig icanon -xcase echo echoe echok -echonl -noflsh
opost -olcuc onlcr -ocrnl -onocr -onlret -ofill -ofdel tab3 ff1
```

Here we see among other things that the speed is 2400 baud, the interrupt key is **del**, the erase key is **control h** (backspace) the kill line key is **control u**, and the end of file (end of text) key is **control d**. We also see that parity is enabled and is even ignored for input, the word length is 7, and we are using the X-ON/X-OFF protocol.

## Keeping Time

The next two environmental variables HZ and TZ help keep time:

```
HZ=20
TZ=PST8PDT
```

The first one tells the system how often a timer interrupts the system to manage events that happen on a periodic basis, such as switching control from user to user to achieve timesharing. In this case, it's 20 times a second. In larger systems, this rate is usually higher so that the system is interrupted more often.

The second one specifies the time zone. We happen to be using Pacific Standard Time with Pacific Daylight Savings, which is eight hours different from Greenwich time.

## The Shell

The next variable specifies the shell. A *shell* is an operating system command interpreter. It sits between the user and the *kernel* of the operating system (see figure 2-4). The kernel forms the heart of the operating system and contains routines to manage the resources of the system, including its memory, CPU, disk drives, terminals, and printers.

**Figure 2-4**
**The shell and the kernel**

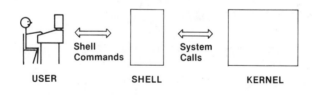

The shell understands human-generated commands, whereas the kernel only understands function calls called *system calls,* which can only be invoked by programs running in the system.

In our case, the shell is

```
SHELL=/bin/csh
```

The shell is a program located in the directory /bin and is named csh. This is the famous University of California, Berkeley C-Shell (pronounced like sea shell).

XENIX provides a number of different shells including the standard Bourne shell sh, a visually oriented shell vsh, a restricted shell rsh, and a special shell for machine to machine communications. However, in this book we use the C-Shell. It is particularly well suited to programmers because of its many interactive features, such as its ability to remember previous commands, and its rich programming structures.

Different shells have different prompts. For example, the Bourne shell normally displays a dollar sign ($) and the C-Shell normally displays a percent sign (%). However, most shells allow you to change the prompt. Special system accounts also often have distinctive prompts.

The Berkeley C-Shell has a *history* feature that allows users to recall previous commands and parts of commands, editing them and combining them to form new commands. For example, if you have just typed a very long pathname as the argument to one command, then just a couple of characters, namely an exclamation point and a dollar sign (!$) invoke this pathname as the argument to the next command. Programmers can also use the history feature to short cut typing repetitious edit, compile, and testing commands. For example, once a command to edit a file with the vi editor has been issued, then the full form need not be used again. Just typing an !v on a command line recalls an entire previous command line that began with the letter v.

The csh can be used as a powerful operating system command language with syntax like a higher level language. In Chapter 3, we write programs called *scripts* in this language. System administrators use scripts to set up complicated account systems and to monitor system behavior on a regular basis. Programmers can use it to process their files according to complicated rules.

## MAIL

Finally, let's look at MAIL:

```
MAIL=/usr/spool/mail/iamnew
```

This variable tells the system where to store unopened electronic mail for this user. Electronic mail allows users to leave notes for each other on the system. It is valuable on larger systems where lots of users are working together. It is particularly valuable when you need to communicate system problems to the system administrator.

## Some Key Directory and File Commands

Some commands are built into the shell, and some are contained in the system directories listed in the PATH variable. To read about the built-in shell commands, read the documentation for the csh. To learn about the other commands, read about them individually in the documentation provided with your system. We now look at a number of these *external* file commands.

## The Pwd Command

The XENIX command `pwd` gives your current directory. It stands for *print working directory*. For us, right now, this command yields:

```
% pwd◀┘
/usr/iamnew
```

In general, directory paths can either begin with the root (/) or they can begin at the current directory (as displayed by the `pwd` command). That is, if you don't begin a pathname with a slash, the system in effect *prefixes* it with the output of `pwd`. For example

```
/usr/iamnew/.login
```

is a long way to specify `iamnew`'s login file, and currently

```
.login
```

is a short way to indicate the same path.

The C-Shell permits a third method that specifies paths which begin with somebody's home directory. With this method you begin the pathname with a tilde (~). If the tilde is followed by a slash (/), the path begins at *your* home directory. If the tilde is followed by somebody else's login name, the path starts from their home directory. For example:

```
~/.login
```

and

```
~iamnew/.login
```

both also specify `iamnew`'s login file.

## The Cat Command

The `cat` command is useful for displaying the contents of a file. It stands for *concatenate* and is designed to combine a number of files into one. However, it is most often used to print a single file on the terminal screen.

The `cat` command allows us to demonstrate the important idea of I/O *redirection*. This is a powerful notion that extends far beyond this command and allows a programmer or even an ordinary user to send output to and receive input from any specified file or device.

Without any parameters, the `cat` command expects input from the standard input, which is normally the user's keyboard, so whatever you type becomes input for the `cat` command. The `cat` command sends whatever it gets from input to the standard output, which is normally the user's terminal screen. The system usually saves input in buffers until you press the **return** key. This causes the `cat` command to get its input a line at a time.

Here is a sample:

```
% cat◄┘
This is what I type.◄┘
This is what I type.
Here is another line.◄┘
Here is another line.
<control d>
```

Each line appears twice: once as each character is typed and again after you press **return**. A **control d** at the end of the input terminates the `cat` command.

In the text in the remainder of this book, we continue to show the ◄┘ symbol at the end of every line that is typed in.

The less-than (<) and greater-than (>) symbols help direct where the standard input is coming from and where it is to go. Other variations are possible, but let's stick to the basics in this chapter.

The greater-than symbol (>) followed by a name causes the output to go to a file by that name. For example

```
% cat >xxx◄┘
This is what I type.◄┘
<control d>
```

sends the characters to a file called `xxx`.

If we use the `lx` command to display our directory, we see this new file:

```
% lx◄┘
xxx
```

There are two ways to use the `cat` command to display the contents of this file. The first uses *redirection of output* like this

```
cat <xxx
```

and the other uses its natural default syntax:

```
cat xxx
```

Here is the result of typing the second version

```
% cat xxx◀┘
This is what I type.
```

As we said previously, the `cat` command is designed to combine several files into one. Thus, it expects a list of files as its parameters. For example

```
% cat xxx xxx xxx◀┘
This is what I type.
This is what I type.
This is what I type.
```

produces three copies of the line. We can store that in a file yyy with the following command.

```
% cat xxx xxx xxx >yyy
```

Applying `cat` to the file yyy shows the three lines:

```
% cat yyy◀┘
This is what I type.
This is what I type.
This is what I type.
```

## Changing Directories

The `cd` command is used to change the current working directory. For example

```
% cd / ←┘
```

changes to the root directory. Then the pwd command gives

```
% pwd←┘
/
```

and the lx command without any parameters gives

```
% lx←┘
bin   boot   dev   etc   lib   lost+found
mnt   once   tmp   usr   xenix
```

Typing cd without any parameters returns us HOME:

```
% cd←┘
% pwd←┘
/usr/iamnew
```

## Making New Directories

The mkdir command allows ordinary users to make their own directories. For example

```
% mkdir book←┘
```

makes a new directory called book that resides under the current directory, namely /usr/iamnew (see figure 2-5).

**Figure 2-5**
**A new directory in our HOME**

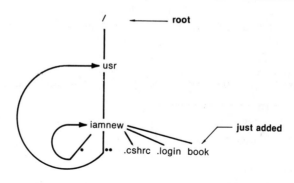

Then we could use cd to go to this new directory and make new directories there (see figure 2-6).

```
% cd book◄┘
% mkdir chap2◄┘
```

**Figure 2-6**
**Another new directory**

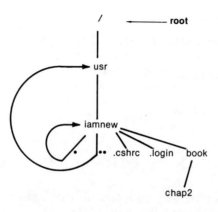

## Combining Commands

Notice that the output for the `lx` command is a simple unadorned list, placing the file names on the screen six per line. Some variations of this command, such as the more traditional `ls`, output the file names one per line.

There is good reason for the simplicity of the XENIX commands. It allows us to combine a series of simple commands to form compound commands that allow us to do some very sophisticated things.

In Chapter 3 we write scripts that put commands together. In Chapter 4, we describe how filtering programs can be hooked together in pipelines so that the output of one command is fed as input to another. This allows us to create large special purpose programs using small, general purpose programs.

One of the basic philosophies of XENIX is to provide the right pieces and convenient methods for putting these pieces together so that programmers and other users can efficiently process textual information.

## DOS Commands

As we mention in Chapter 1, XENIX is compatible with PC-DOS in that it can read and write diskettes formatted for PC-DOS. The commands `dosls`, `doscp`, and `doscat` allow us to perform similar functions to the normal XENIX `ls`, `cp` (copy), and `cat` commands.

For example, the command

```
dosls b:
```

displays a directory of the PC-DOS files on a floppy diskette in drive B:, and the command

```
doscat b:myfile.txt
```

displays the contents of the PC-DOS file `myfile.txt` on drive B:.

The command `doscp` allows you to save XENIX files on PC-DOS diskettes and get them back again later. For example

```
doscp myfile.c b:
```

copies the XENIX file `myfile` to a PC-DOS file on drive B:, and the command

```
doscp b:myfile .
```

copies that file back to the current working XENIX directory.

Other "DOS" commands are available to add directories and remove files and directories. As we show in Chapter 3, it is also possible to compile programs so that they run under PC-DOS once they are moved to a PC-DOS diskette.

# Security

Security is an important consideration in any computer system. Single user systems can be physically locked to restrict access to them, but larger systems require more elaborate measures.

In larger systems we have the competing requirements of sharing resources (both equipment and data) and protecting these resources from getting into the wrong hands.

Although XENIX is usually implemented on machines that have one or only a few users (usually one at a time), it has the security measures of much larger systems that might support as many as several hundred different users (although probably not at one time).

## Password Security

The first stage in security occurs at login. Here, users are required to supply login names (account names) and passwords. The passwords are all stored in a *public* file /etc/passwd that anyone can read who can get onto the system. However, the passwords themselves are encrypted in secret codes that nobody should be able to read, not even the system. To see the password file, type:

    cat /etc/passwd

For example:

```
% cat /etc/passwd←┘
root:iwk3uUi0Uj2bU:0:0:The Super User:/:/bin/sh
cron:NOLOGIN:1:1:Cron Daemon for periodic tasks:/:
bin:NOLOGIN:3:3:The owner of system files:/:
uucp::4:4:Account for uucp
program:/usr/spool/uucppublic:/usr/lib/uucp/uucico
asg:NOLOGIN:6:6:The Owner of Assignable Devices:/:
sysinfo:3xWE3eclmYowA:10:10:Access to System Information:/:
network:NOLOGIN:12:12:Account for mail program:/usr/spool/micnet:
lp:NOLOGIN:14:3:The lp administrator:/usr/spool/lp:
morgan:j9JijX7ztTR1E:201:51:C shell account:/usr/morgan:/bin/csh
iamnew:j9N4GrbiRnh/6:202:52:Demonstration :/usr/iamnew:/bin/csh
```

```
guest:j9c2.gYbQBzkE:203:52:Guest Account:/usr/guest:/bin/rsh
smith:j9c2.gYbQBzkE:204:50:John Smith:/usr/smith:/bin/sh
```

You can see that this file contains a number of entries, each with a number of fields (separated by colons). Many of these entries belong to the system itself. For example, root is the login name of the superuser (normally the system administrator) and bin is the owner of the system files. There are also entries for normal users such as morgan and iamnew. The entries in this file list the user's *login name,* the *password* (encrypted), the user's *identification number,* the user's *group* identification number, a *comment* (limited to 20 characters), the user's *home directory,* and login *shell.*

The system encrypts the user's original password to give a sequence of characters that are stored in the password file right after the user's login name. When the user logs in, the system encrypts the password that the user gives in response to the password prompt. It compares the result with the encrypted password in the password file. If these two encrypted passwords agree, the user is permitted to use the system. A delay is built in so that an unauthorized user cannot easily use programs (as, for example, one used in the movie *War Games*) that repeatedly try different combinations to get into the system.

If more security is needed, the password can be set up so that the user is forced to change it periodically.

## Groups

Each user belongs to one or more groups. A group is a collection of users who needs special access to a set of common files. For example, all programmers working on the same software project might belong to the same group. Groups can be created by the system administrator.

The user's primary group is specified in the password file, but a user can belong to a number of different groups. A public file /etc/group specifies group memberships. That is, this file gives each group and the login names that belong to it. You can view this file with the command:

```
cat /etc/group
```

Here is the result:

```
% cat /etc/group←┘
root:x:0:root
cron:x:1:cron
bin:x:3:bin,lp
uucp:x:4:uucp
asg:x:6:asg
sysinfo:x:10:uucp
network:x:12:network
```

```
group::50:demo,cdemo,vdemo,smith
morgan::51:morgan
learner::52:iamnew,guest
```

Groups may be given passwords (the second field), but this is not really necessary, nor is it desirable. Each group has a group identification (id)
number (third field). The fourth field specifies the members of that group.

## File and Directory Security

Each file and directory on the system is assigned a special computer word
that contains *protection bits.* Each file and directory is also assigned an
owner and a group membership. In Chapter 7, we see how these protection
bits, ownerships, and membership information are stored within the file
system.

To view the protection bits and ownerships, we use the −l option (*l* for
long display) of the ls command. Let's use the cd command to move back
to our HOME directory and see how the −l option of the ls command displays this information. This time we type both commands on the same line,
separating them with a semicolon:

```
% cd; ls -l◀┘
total 6
drwxr-xr-x  3 iamnew  learner     48 Apr 6 19:59 book
-rw-r--r--  1 iamnew  learner     28 Apr 6 19:51 xxx
-rw-r--r--  1 iamnew  learner     84 Apr 6 19:54 yyy
```

The first column contains a ten-letter string that displays the file type
and protection bits in human readable form. The file type indicates which
files are directories and which files contain actual information. For the first
character, the d represents directories and a hyphen (−) represents ordinary
files. The next three characters give *read, write,* and *execute* permissions (r,
w, and x) for the *owner* of the file. After that come three characters giving
the *read, write,* and *execute* permissions for members of the file's *group,*
and the last three characters for all others. A hyphen (−) means no permission and the corresponding r, w, or x means that permission is granted.

The third column gives the ownership of the file, and the fourth column gives its group membership. For example, the file xxx belongs to user
iamnew and to the group learner. The file xxx has read and write permissions for the owner (in this case iamnew), but only read permission for
members of the file's group learner and all others.

For ordinary files, read, write, and execute permissions are fairly obvi-
ous. That is, read permission allows one to read and copy the file, write
permission allows one to modify it or delete it, and execute permission allows one to execute it as a command. When you try to use a file that you
don't have access to, the usual response is permission denied.

For directories, read permissions allow the `lx` or `ls` type of commands to work, write permissions allow commands like `mkdir` and `cat >xxx` to work within that directory, and execute permissions allow the `cd` command to work on that directory and allow you to use that directory in a path to a command.

Here are some more observations. If you own a file that has permissions like `---rwxrwx`, you do *not* have read, write, or execute permissions to it, even if you belong to the same group that it belongs to. Likewise, if you do not own a file whose permissions are `rwx---rwx`, but belong to the group that it belongs to, you don't have any access to it.

You might wonder why so many different kinds of permissions are necessary. The answer is that just about everything in XENIX, including text files, binary files, directories, and devices, appears as a file within one big tree. This permission scheme gives us the flexibility we need to individually control the various types of access by the various types of people to all of these kinds of files.

Here are some examples: files that contain programs for system commands should be executable by all, but readable and writeable only by a system account (`root` or `bin`). Public files that contain system data should be executable by nobody, writeable by a system account, and readable by all. My private text files should be readable and writeable only by me, executable by nobody, and so on.

When you create files and directories, several things determine their ownership, membership, and permissions. One is the corresponding ownership, membership, and permissions for the directory in which the file or directory sits, another is the identity of the person making the change, and another is that person's `umask`.

## The Umask

The `umask` is a variable that controls the protection bits. It determines which protection bits get automatically turned off when you create a new file or directory. The `umask` command allows a user to display his or her `umask` variable. The command

```
umask
```

by itself displays the user's `umask` variable as three octal digits, the first of which controls the user's permissions, the second of which controls the group permission, and the third of which controls the permission of all others. Octal digits are used because they encode bits in threes corresponding to the three kinds of permissions (namely, read, write, and execute) for each class of user. The nine bits in these three octal digits correspond to the nine different permissions for the file. For each bit, a one in the `umask` turns off permission, and a zero leaves it alone.

For example:

```
% umask◄┘
022
```

The 0 on the left indicates that directories and binary files are created with full permissions, nothing turned off. The two 2s (binary 010) indicate that write permissions are turned off for both group members and others.

When followed by an octal number, the umask command also allows the user to change his or her umask. For example

```
umask 077
```

causes files and directories to be created with no permissions for group members or others, and

```
umask 624
```

causes files and directories to be created with no read or write permissions for the owner, no write permission for the group, and no read permission for others. Although the system allows this last choice, it is unlikely that anybody would use it.

## The Chmod Command

The chmod command allows users to change permissions for files. It can be used in a variety of ways to add, subtract, or simply specify owner, group, and other permissions for a specified file. However, only the owner (and the superuser) can use this command.

Here are some examples of its use. The command

```
chmod +x myscript
```

gives execute permissions to the owner, group, and all others. The command

```
chmod o-x myscript
```

(that's the letter *o* for others) takes execute permission away from others. The command

```
chmod g-x myscript
```

takes execute permission away from the group. The command

```
chmod u= myscript
```

takes all permissions away from the user, whereas the command

```
chmod u=wx myscript
```

gives just write and execute permissions to the user. The permissions can also be given as three octal digits. For example, the command

```
chmod 700 myscript
```

gives all permissions to the user, but none to anybody else.

### The Superuser

There is a special login name `root` that has very special privileges on the system. The password to this account should be guarded very carefully because the superuser has permission to read or write any file or directory in the entire system. The superuser can also shut down the system at any time.

The superuser account is created when the system is first set up. If you know the superuser's password, you can either log in as the superuser in the ordinary way, log into maintenance mode as the system is booted up, or use the `su` (switch user) command to become the superuser from any ordinary account.

## Processes

Every job that XENIX does is broken up into *processes*. These are running programs that are directly managed by the system. Processes are normally associated with the execution of a particular command.

To see the processes that are currently running, type the `ps` (process status) command. This command has a number of useful options. The `e` option shows *every* process, and the `f` option shows a *full* listing. Here is the result:

```
% ps -ef◄┘
      UID  PID PPID  C   STIME TTY TIME COMMAND
     root    0    0  3  Dec 31   ? 0:01 swapper
     root    1    0  0  Dec 31   ? 0:02 /etc/init
     root   31    1  0 13:11:33 co 0:11 -sh
   morgan   32    1  0 13:11:34 02 0:17 -csh
     root   18    1  0 13:11:04   ? 0:04 /etc/update
       lp   23    1  0 13:11:20   ? 0:02 /usr/lib/lpsched
     root   27    1  0 13:11:27   ? 0:03 /etc/cron
```

```
morgan    33     1   0 13:11:34 03 0:18 -csh
  root    64     1   0 13:45:26 04 0:04 - tty04 m
iamnew    56     1   0 13:39:57 2a 0:17 -csh
  root    78    31   0 13:56:04 co 0:05 view /etc/passwd
morgan    42    32   0 13:15:33 02 0:02 sh
morgan    80    33   0 13:58:40 03 0:02 more /usr/sys/conf/c.c
iamnew    86    56  14 14:00:57 2a 0:13 ps -ef
```

This particular form of the ps command shows the login names of
each process, the identification number of each process (PID), the identification number of the process' parent process (PPID), and what command
is being executed.

Let's trace the ancestry of these processes (see figure 2-7). Process
number 0 is running the *swapper* and belongs to the root (superuser). It is
the first process created in the system when it is "booted up." The next
process (id number 1) runs the program /etc/init. This process parents
many other processes including ones that run such system tasks as the printer lpsched and the master calendar cron as well as user shells. For example, process number 23 is running the printer, process number 27 is running
cron, process number 31 is running the standard shell for root on the console, process number 32 is running the C-Shell for morgan on the second
console screen (TTY 02), process number 33 is running the C-Shell for
morgan on the third console screen (TTY 03), and process number 56 is running the C-Shell for iamnew on the serial port (TTY 2a).

**Figure 2-7**
**Ancestry of some processes**

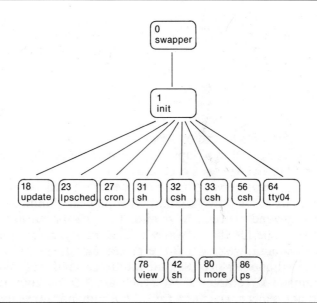

Some of the shell processes have launched other processes. For example, process 31 has a child number 78, which is using `view` on the password file. The `ps` command itself is being run by process number 86, which belongs to process number 56.

It is possible for a user to launch a number of processes from the same terminal screen by creating background tasks. To launch a background task, just type an ampersand (&) at the end of the command line. For example, the command line:

```
% cc myprogram.c &←┘
```

causes the C compiler `cc` to compile a program in the background, allowing you to run the shell in the foreground. Here is a sample of how that works:

```
% cc showenv.c &←┘
114
% ps←┘
showenv.c
   PID TTY TIME COMMAND
    40 2a  0:22 csh
   114 2a  0:01 cc
   115 2a  0:12 ps
   120 2a  0:02 ld
% ps←┘
   PID TTY TIME COMMAND
    40 2a  0:22 csh
   114 2a  0:01 cc
   121 2a  0:12 ps
   120 2a  0:18 ld
% ps←┘
   PID TTY TIME COMMAND
    40 2a  0:22 csh
   122 2a  0:10 ps
```

We first type the command `cc showenv.c &` to compile a C program that is presented in Chapter 5. Because we finished the line with the ampersand (&), that line was executed as a background task. As soon as `cc` started, its process id was printed on the screen and the shell prompt `%` appeared, letting us know that we could type the next command. Then we typed `ps` as a foreground process to monitor the system. Meanwhile, the `cc` command reported the file that it was working on. Then looking at the output of the `ps` command, we saw that the `cc` command was still running. In fact, it had launched another process (pid 120) to run the `ld` (linker). As soon as the `ps` command is completed, we typed another `ps` command, but the situation had not really changed. A third `ps` command shows us that `cc` has finished.

In Chapter 8, we discuss processes in more detail, showing how any process can spawn new processes and how one process can synchronize with another one.

# The Kernel

As its name implies, the *kernel* of XENIX is the central program of the operating system. It consists of a collection of routines and data structures that are permanently housed in the computer's main memory and perform XENIX's most basic business. This includes allocating and scheduling resources, such as the CPU, the memory, and the floppy and hard disks. It also contains device drivers that perform lower level tasks, such as transferring data between the computer and its peripheral devices.

## Entry Points

One way to understand the kernel is through its "entry points" (see figure 2-8). These provide access to the majority of its functions and thus define the kernel in terms of the services that it performs.

**Figure 2-8**
**Entry points to the kernel**

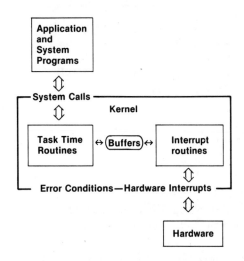

The kernel's entry points fall into three major categories: system calls, hardware service requests, and error conditions. All three types of entry points are handled by *interrupts*. An interrupt is an event that causes the computer to stop what it is doing and perform some special processing task.

Because its entry points are handled by interrupts, the kernel can be thought of as an *event-driven* or *interrupt-driven* program.

## System Calls

Let's begin with the system calls. XENIX has about 70 system calls. They include: exit, stat, ustat, chmod, open, close, write, geteuid, getuid, getgid, getegid, execve, fork, getpid, kill, wait, pause, and signal. We use these directly in our C programs throughout the rest of this book. XENIX has a host of other calls that support other commands at higher levels in the system.

System calls allow applications and systems programs to request such services as file transfers and program control.

System calls serve as an interface between "outer" parts of the system, namely user and system programs, and the "inner" parts of the operating system, namely the kernel. That is, they provide entry points from applications and system utility programs to routines that sit within the kernel of the operating system. An application program connects to these system calls via libraries that are automatically linked to the program when it is compiled.

To see a list of all the routines and tables in the kernel, use the nm command on the file /xenix. This file contains a machine code copy of the kernel. The command name nm stands for *print name list*. It extracts symbol names from object files. Such files are not directly readable by humans, but the nm allows you to "peek" inside in spite of this. The −n option places the output in increasing numerical order according to its address:

```
nm −n /xenix
```

Some of the output of this command is

```
003f:19ba  T start
003f:1c8c  T __idle
003f:1ca6  T __waitloc
003f:1cb1  T __save
003f:1d0d  T __resume
003f:1d56  T __setjmp
003f:1d83  T __longjmp
003f:1da4  T __gctime
003f:1da8  T __spl0
003f:1da8  T __tasktime
003f:1dae  T __spl1
003f:1db4  T __spl2
003f:1dba  T __spl3
003f:1dc0  T __spl4
003f:1dc6  T __spl5
```

```
003f:1dcc  T  __spl6
003f:1dd2  T  __spl7
003f:1de0  T  __splx
```

## Hardware Interrupts

Under XENIX (as with most multiuser systems), the majority of devices pass data to and from the computer via hardware interrupts. These are hardware signals that alert the CPU when a device is ready for attention. Having the devices signal for attention in this way provides a convenient method for allowing the various user devices to function independently while the computer goes about its normal business.

## An Example

Let's see what happens when a user presses a key on a keyboard. (A similar thing happens when a printer, disk, or communication line is ready to make a transfer of data.) Suppose that we are running a program which is expecting a line of input from the keyboard (having made a system call). This program could be a shell or some application program.

While the program waits for our input, it "sleeps," allowing other processes in the system to do their work. When we press the **a** key on the keyboard, the keyboard hardware generates an interrupt that causes the CPU to stop whatever it is doing and execute a special interrupt service routine. This routine moves the ASCII code for this key from a keyboard hardware register to a keyboard buffer (actually a series of buffers). The CPU then returns to what it was doing before it was interrupted. This happens each time you press a new key until you press **return**. At that point, the interrupt service routine "wakes" up the program that was waiting for the input. Our program then grabs the entire line of input from the system's buffers and begins to process it.

## Hardware Entry Points to the Kernel

These hardware interrupts provide another set of entry points to the kernel. That is, when the CPU receives such an interrupt signal, it immediately begins to execute some code that sends it into the kernel.

Whenever a device is ready to transfer data, a hardware interrupt is generated that causes the CPU to stop what it is doing (perhaps in the middle of another user's program) and begin to execute a special service routine to handle the transfer. This service routine resides within the kernel and usually belongs to a particular *device driver*. When the action is completed, the CPU normally returns to what it was doing before the interrupt.

While the interrupt is being serviced, the system is in what is called *interrupt time*. During this time it is in the kernel but not under control of any particular user. As a rule, the process that is responsible for the interrupt is not the process that was interrupted.

Interrupt service routines should act quickly and only when work can actually be performed. If a buffer is too full or if the device is otherwise busy, the service routine returns (quits) instead of actively waiting or even sleeping. This allows other routines in the kernel and other user processes to proceed, perhaps emptying buffers or performing other useful work while the devices recover from their last actions. Once they have cleared, these other routines can directly call the interrupt routine to finish its business.

In addition to the peripheral devices that may generate hardware interrupts, a *clock* (actually a timer) interrupts the CPU on a regular basis. This entry point allows XENIX to manage a number of different activities, such as scheduling processes and updating internal statistics, that have to be done on a regular basis. This prevents any single process from "hogging" the CPU. Without such an interrupt, multiuser timesharing would not be possible.

## Devices

For our purposes, a *device* is a piece of hardware that generates and/or consumes data. Examples include terminals, printers, modems, and disk drives.

Each device that is to work with a XENIX system requires a device driver. A device driver consists of a set of routines and structures that handle the lowest or most device-dependent parts of the job of exchanging data between the device and the more central parts of the computer, namely the memory and CPU. As we see in Chapter 9, you can install your own set of device drivers to customize the system to suit your own needs.

A XENIX system often comes with a rather complete set of device drivers. With the SCO distribution of XENIX for an IBM XT, there are drivers to handle four console screens on the monochrome or color display, a printer on the parallel port, other printers, two terminals or two modems on the serial ports (or one each), two floppy disks, and two hard disks.

A XENIX system has two types of device drivers: *block*-oriented device drivers and *character*-oriented device drivers. The file /usr/sys/conf/c.c contains a list for each in the form of a table. These tables are stored as separate structures within the kernel and contain the addresses of certain key routines and data structures belonging to these drivers. You can obtain a listing by using the more command followed by this pathname:

```
more /usr/sys/conf/c.c
```

Block-oriented device drivers are those for which data is transferred to applications and system programs in fixed size blocks. For example, a floppy or hard disk normally is organized as an array of physical blocks (see figure 2-9). Any read or write operation is physically implemented, at least at the lowest levels, as transfers of entire sectors between memory and the disk. That is, even to transfer a single byte, a whole sector must be moved.

Character-oriented device drivers allow arbitrary numbers of bytes to be transferred at one time (see figure 2-10). Character-oriented drivers are

**Figure 2-9**
**Sectors on a disk**

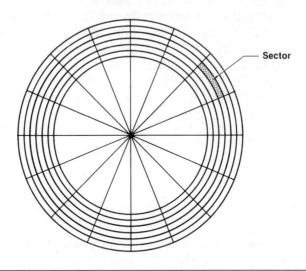

Sector

normally used for such devices as printers and terminals, but with the proper buffering, even disks can be handled by character-oriented drivers in addition to their more fundamental block-oriented drivers.

**Figure 2-10**
**Character-oriented devices**

Each installed device is connected to the system via a special file in the directory system. These device files are normally kept in the /dev directory, right under the root of the directory system. Each special file has permissions, an owner, a group, a date of creation, a date of modification, and so on, just like an ordinary file. However, instead of having a byte count, it has two special device numbers: a major device number and a minor device number. Also, it has a file type of either b for block-oriented device drivers or c for character-oriented drivers.

The major number corresponds to the row position of the device driver in the device table specified by the configuration file c.c. The minor number is used by the driver routines themselves to determine which particular copy of the device is being referenced.

For example, applying the ls -l command to the path /dev/tty11 might yield the following output on the screen:

```
crw-rw-rw-   2 root     root       5,  0 Oct 21 22:18 tty11
```

The c in column 1 indicates that this is a special device file that connects a character-oriented device with the system. The 5 toward the middle where the byte count normally appears is the major number, and the 0 following it is the minor number.

Likewise, applying the ls -l command to the path /dev/tty12 might yield:

```
crw--w--w-   2 iamnew   learner    5, 8 Apr 8 16:35 tty12
```

Here, the file type is c (for character-oriented), the major number is 5, and the minor number is 8.

In Chapter 9, we study the kernel and its device drivers in more detail and show how you can develop and install your own device driver.

## Summary

In this chapter, we have taken a tour of the system to introduce you to the general "lay of the land" and given you practical experience with actual XENIX commands. We began with how to log in and explored such topics as the environment, the tree-structured directory system, the command shell, I/O redirection, system security, the kernel, and device drivers.

In subsequent chapters, we explore many of these issues in detail. We explore system variables (including the environment) in Chapter 5, screen and keyboard I/O in Chapter 6, files and directories in Chapter 7, process control in Chapter 8, and device drivers in Chapter 9.

## Questions and Answers

### Questions

1. How long can a XENIX login name be?
2. How can you find out how a XENIX user has configured his or her environment?
3. How can you see what files and directories are located directly under the root?
4. How can you see the name of your current directory?
5. Can an ordinary XENIX user make new directories? If so, how?
6. What does `cat` stand for? What can you do with this command?
7. How can you see what processes are running on a XENIX system?
8. How can you see what devices are connected to your XENIX system?

### Answers

1. A XENIX login name can be as long as eight characters.
2. Typing the `env` command shows your current environment. You can also examine a user's `.login` and `.cshrc` script files to see how his or her environment is initialized.
3. Typing `lx /` displays the files and directories directly under the root. For more information about these files and directories, type `l /`. This gives a "long" listing.
4. The `pwd` command prints the path to your current directory. This path is a list of directories through the directory tree from the root to your current directory.
5. Yes, an ordinary user can make a new directory. If you are currently in a directory for which you have write permission,

   ```
   % mkdir name◄┘
   ```

   creates a new subdirectory with the name `name`.

6. `Cat` stands for *concatenate*. This command can be used to display the contents of text files. As the name implies, it concatenates the contents of one or more files, sending the result to the standard output. With I/O redirection this command can be easily used to

save text from the keyboard to a specified file or send the concatenation of several files to one file.

7.  The ps command can be used to display information about processes currently running on the system. The -ef option shows a fair amount of information about each process on the system.

8.  The command

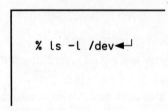

```
% ls -l /dev↵
```

displays a long listing of the device directory that contains files which represent each active device driver on the system.

# 3

# Programming Tools in XENIX

*DOS format*

① # dosformat - /dev/fd0 135 ds 18 / for 3,5 HD dsk.
  To read from 3,5"(?)
② # dosdir - /dev/fd0 135 ds 18 /

- Overview
- Editing with Vi
- Writing Shell Programs
- Compiling with the C Compiler
- Developing Programs for PC-DOS and
  MS-DOS
- Debugging
- Automating Program Development
- Summary
- Questions and Answers

③ # Tar - tv6 / File will be displayed on the Screen

Look for   /usr/abies/rum/ Pat/REG - GEN

/usr/abies/rum/ Pat/ NOT - GEN

/usr/abies/ rum/ Pat/ med - GEN

& check the date

# cd - ch/~~default~~ to read Boot Directory

# Programming Tools in XENIX

This chapter introduces the excellent fundamental programming tools provided by XENIX. XENIX programmers can use these tools to good advantage to edit, compile, debug, and manage their program development in the C programming language. XENIX programmers can also use the C-Shell as a powerful command interpreter and even develop sophisticated applications programs using it.

Editing programs is essential to a good programming environment. In this chapter we introduce the vi screen-editing program with a subset of its most powerful commands so that you can create and modify your programs.

The operating system itself should be programmable. In this chapter we show how to write script files that consist of operating system commands housed within modern program control structures.

Debugging is also important. Often the fastest way out of a programming mess is to see exactly what the program is doing at the lowest levels. In this chapter, we show an example of this for the adb debugging tool.

Developing large programs often involves putting together a number of different source files that generate a number of intermediate files. Sometimes the situation becomes complicated, involving repetitious actions. In this chapter, we introduce the make program manager that automates the process of putting together large programs.

## Overview

The XENIX System V is a very powerful programming environment. With it, a single user can have a number of screens open into various parts of a programming project and use sophisticated tools to control the project, such as editors, compilers, interactive and batch command interpreters, debuggers, language analyzers, and updating mechanisms.

From the main keyboard, we can use function keys to select instantaneously among four or more screens. This multitasking approach is very useful when you have a number of different files that are being put together to form an entire program. A good example of this occurs when you use several different compilers on different files that comprise the entire job. In that case you can open a separate screen for each source code file and another to run the compilers and test the results. As we see in Chapter 10, this situation is quite possible even for small programs because of the rich variety of different and yet interrelated programming tools available with the XENIX programming environment.

## Editing with Vi

An editing program is one of the most important tools that a programmer has. It should allow the programmer to display and enter and modify program and data text.

The main editor on the XENIX system is called vi, which is short for *visual editor*. Vi is a screen editor. It displays a portion of the text on the screen and allows the user to move a cursor around to edit any part of it. Furthermore, vi has a rich set of commands (more than are needed even by experienced users). We examine a subset of all these commands in enough detail to edit files in an efficient manner.

Vi is an extension of a line editing program called ex. There is another line editing program called ed. However, we wish to take advantage of the screen editing available with today's microcomputer systems.

Vi has three or so modes of operation, including a screen command mode, an ex command mode, and an insertion mode. You can tell when you're in the ex mode because a special command line appears at the bottom of the screen with a colon at the extreme left side. However, immediate recognition between the other two modes is a problem because no visual clues distinguish them. Pressing **escape** safely takes you to command mode when you lose track of which of the two modes you are in.

Vi can be configured via system files to work with most any terminal or terminal emulator to take advantage of arrow keys and screen commands, such as clear screen, clear line, insert line, and cursor movement.

### Entering and Exiting

To edit a file under vi, type the line from the shell:

```
% vi filename◀┘
```

where filename is the name of the file that you want to edit. It is also possible to enter vi without giving a file name.

```
┌─────────────────────────────────────────────────────────┐
│                  entering and exiting vi                 │
│                                                          │
│   vi ◄─┘               enter vi, editing no file         │
│   vi filename ◄─┘      enter vi, editing filename        │
│   escape              return to command mode             │
│   :q ◄─┘              exit vi, making no changes         │
│   :q! ◄─┘             exit vi, forgetting all changes    │
│   :wq ◄─┘             save changes, then exit            │
│   ZZ                  save changes and exit              │
│                                                          │
└─────────────────────────────────────────────────────────┘
```

You can exit vi in a few different ways, but you must be in command mode first. (Just press **escape** first). To quit without changing anything, press the colon (:) key, then the **q**, then **return**. This won't work if you have changed anything in the file. If you really want to quit and ignore all changes, then type :q!, then **return**. Incidentally, pressing : puts you into the ex line editor mode (for one command line's worth of commands).

To save your work and quit, type ZZ (two uppercase zs). If you see ZZ on the screen, you are in insert mode, not command mode. If this happens, press **backspace** a couple of times to remove the ZZ, press **escape** to return to the command mode, then type ZZ. ZZ won't appear on the screen, but you eventually see the familiar % or $ prompt indicating that you are back in the csh or sh shell program.

## Cursor Commands

Once in vi you are in the screen command mode. That is, you can move the cursor around the screen (and the file) and you can invoke various other modes such as the ex and insert modes.

```
┌─────────────────────────────────────────────────────────┐
│                     cursor commands                      │
│                                                          │
│   h             character left                           │
│   l             character right                          │
│   j             line down                                │
│   k             line up                                  │
│                                                          │
│   4h            four characters left                     │
│   4l            four characters right                    │
│   4j            four lines down                          │
│   4k            four lines up                            │
│                                                          │
│   backspace     character left                           │
│   space         character right                          │
│   ─             line up (to beginning of line)           │
└─────────────────────────────────────────────────────────┘
```

| linefeed | line down |
|----------|-----------|
| return | beginning of next line |
| w | word right |
| b | word left |
| e | end of word |
| 0 | beginning of line |
| $ | end of line |
| H | upper left corner of screen |
| L | lower left corner of screen |
| control f | forward one screen |
| control b | backward one screen |
| 23G | go to line 23 |
| control g | display current line number |

The four keys **h**, **j**, **k**, and **l** (lowercase) are the standard way to move the cursor. In the screen command mode, **h** moves the cursor left, **j** moves it down, **k** moves it up, and **l** moves it right. However, the system often can be programmed to allow the arrow keys to be used as well. Other keys help, too. For example, **backspace** moves the cursor to the left, **space** moves it right, the - key moves it up a line, **linefeed** command moves it down a line, and **return** moves it to the beginning of the text on the next line.

Some keys give word-oriented cursor motions. For example, **w** moves the cursor forward to the beginning of the next word in the file, **b** moves the cursor backwards one word in the file. In both cases the cursor lands on the first letter of the word. To get to the end of the next word, use an **e**.

The keys **0** (zero) and **$** move the cursor to the beginning and end, respectively, of the current line.

Some keys are page-oriented. For example, **H** moves the cursor to the "home" position (upper left corner of the screen) and **L** moves the cursor to the lower left corner of the screen. **Control f** moves forward one screenful and **control b** moves backward one screenful.

The **G** key (uppercase) moves to a designated line in the file. Just type the line number first, then a **G**. The cursor moves to the beginning of that line. **Control g** displays the current line number at the bottom of the screen.

## Entering Text

When you first enter vi, you cannot immediately begin entering text, but there are a number of keys you can press to get into text entry mode. The **i** key causes text to be inserted before the character where the cursor is now. The **a** key causes text to be appended after the character where the cursor is now. Capitalizing these commands causes text to be inserted (in the case of **I**) or appended (in the case of **A**) with respect to the whole current line.

**entering text**

| | |
|---|---|
| i | insert before current character |
| a | append after current character |
| I | insert at beginning of line |
| A | append after end of line |
| o | open line after current line |
| O | open line before current line |
| escape | exit insert mode |

The **o** and **O** keys open up new lines. In the case of **o**, the new line is appended after the current one. In the case of **O**, a new line is inserted before the current one. In both cases, you enter the insert mode in which the keys you press are entered directly into the file.

To exit the insert mode, press **escape**. If you don't want to be in insert mode but are not sure whether you are, you can always press **escape** to get back to the screen command mode.

## Removing and Copying Text

**removing and copying text**

| | |
|---|---|
| x | remove cursor character |
| 10x | remove ten characters forward |
| X | remove previous character |
| 10X | remove ten previous characters |
| dw | remove rest of word |
| dd | remove current line |
| d0 | remove beginning of line |
| d$ | remove end of line |
| yw | yank rest of word |
| yy | yank current line |
| y0 | yank beginning of line |
| y$ | yank end of line |
| 4dw | remove four words |
| 4dd | remove four lines |
| 4yw | yank four words |
| 4yy | yank four lines |
| 4"adw | remove four words and put in buffer a |
| 4"bdd | remove four lines and put in buffer b |

```
4"ayw    yank four words into buffer a
4"byy    yank four lines into buffer b

ma       mark position a
d'a      delete from current position to a
y'a      yank from current position to a

cw       change word

r        replace character

u        undo changes
p        put text
```

Vi maintains some hidden buffers where it holds text that you have removed. You can also copy text into these buffers without removing the text from your file.

From screen command mode, you can remove the character on the cursor by pressing **x** or the character before the cursor by pressing **X**. If you type a number first, the system removes that many characters.

To remove a word, place the cursor on the first letter of the word, press **d**, then **w**. To remove the current line, press **d**, then **d**. To remove the beginning of a line, press **d**, then **0** (that's zero). To remove the rest of the line, press **d**, then **$**. This is part of a larger picture in which the letter **d** is followed by a command to move the cursor.

The **y** key stands for *yank*. This key places text in the delete buffer without removing it from the file. Just like the **d** key, it is followed with a second key that specifies the range of characters affected. For example, **yy** yanks the line, **yw** yanks the rest of the word, and **y$** yanks the rest of the line.

Both the **d** and **y** keys may be preceded by a count that multiplies their effect, and they can be directed to place their text into any one of 26 special buffers labeled by the letters *a* through *z*. For example:

        2"add

deletes two lines and stores them in buffer a. Furthermore, successive (unlabeled) deletes (and yanks) are stored in a queue of buffers labeled 0 through 9 so that they can be recovered later (as we shall see through the use of the p command).

The **m** command marks a position in the text. For example **ma** places a hidden mark **a** at the current cursor position. You can go back to this position later by typing

        'a

However, **m** is perhaps more useful in conjunction with a **d** or **y** command. For example, moving the cursor to the beginning of a block of text, marking it with an **ma**, then moving to the end of the block and typing

    d'a

deletes it.

The **c** key stands for *change*. It works in a similar way to that of the **d** and **y** keys as far as the range of text that is affected. For example, to change a word, place the cursor at the beginning of the word, type **c**, then **w**. A **$** sign appears at the end of the area that is to be changed. You can finish your changes by pressing **escape**.

To remove the effects of the last insert or delete command, press **u**. To replicate the last insert or delete command, press **.** (that's a period).

The **p** key is used to *put* text back into the file that has been removed or yanked previously. Pressing **p** places the most recently removed or yanked text into the file at the position starting after the cursor.

You can use the **p** command to place text from the labeled buffers into the file. Thus, you can use the **d** or **y** commands to save a section of text into a labeled buffer, then use the **p** command to place text wherever you want (just move the cursor there first).

## Reading or Writing to Other Files

The commands **r** and **w** allow text to be read and written from and to other files. They are ex commands, so you type a colon first, which appears at the bottom of the screen, as does the rest of the command.

| reading and writing to other files | |
|---|---|
| :r xxx◄┘ | read in contents of file xxx |
| :w ◄┘ | save current file |
| :w xxx ◄┘ | save current file in file xxx |
| :20, 30 w xxx◄┘ | save lines 20-30 in file xxx |

For example, **:r xyz** reads the contents of the file xyz into the current file at the current cursor position, and the command **:w xxx** writes the contents of the current file to the file xxx. You can precede the **w** with a range of line numbers such as **3, 6**. For example

    :3, 6 w xxx◄┘

saves lines 3 through 6 in file xxx.

The cursor commands do not work with these commands because they are strictly ex commands.

### Searching and Replacing

The slash (/) command searches for string patterns (regular expressions with ordinary and special command characters such as *, [, ], +, and \). See Chapter 4 for a discussion of regular expressions.

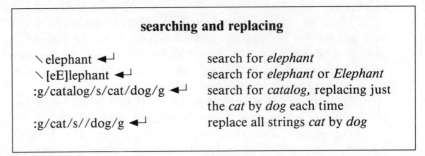

| searching and replacing | |
|---|---|
| \elephant ◄┘ | search for *elephant* |
| \[eE]lephant ◄┘ | search for *elephant* or *Elephant* |
| :g/catalog/s/cat/dog/g ◄┘ | search for *catalog,* replacing just the *cat* by *dog* each time |
| :g/cat/s//dog/g ◄┘ | replace all strings *cat* by *dog* |

When you press the slash (/), it appears at the bottom of the screen just like the colon does (although you are *not* in the **ex** mode). Type in the pattern, press **return**, and **vi** begins the search. Once the pattern is found, you can search for the next instance by pressing the **n** key.

To do global search and replacements, you can use the **ex** command, **:g/**, to specify the string to search for and the string to replace it. For example, suppose you type:

```
:g/catalog/s/cat/dog/g◄┘
```

This rather complicated instruction finds all lines that contain *catalog,* then substitutes *dog* for *cat* each time that *cat* occurs on that line. More often, you might type

```
:g/cat/s//dog/g◄┘
```

to replace all instances of *cat* by *dog* in the file. Here, the second specification of *cat* on the command line (after the **/s/** for substitute) is not explicitly given but is understood as a default choice.

Many variations of the **:g/** command are possible, but this is enough to start, and it should last most people a very long time.

## Writing Shell Programs

As we mentioned in previous chapters, a XENIX shell is really a command interpreter. It's like having a BASIC interpreter that has all the system commands built into it.

A shell reads and executes operating system commands written in a special shell language. Each shell has its own language for these commands. Two major shells come with XENIX: the Bourne or standard shell `sh` and the C-Shell `csh` (pronounced like sea shell), developed at the University of California, Berkeley.

To write a shell program, use an editor, such as `vi`, to write the commands into an ordinary text file, then use `chmod` to change the permissions of this file to make it executable. For example, suppose we wish to write a shell program called `mystatus` that prints the date, the current working directory, and the current environment. We begin by entering the `vi` editing program with the command

```
% vi mystatus◄┘
```

then type **i** to enter the insert mode. We type the lines

```
date◄┘
pwd◄┘
env◄┘
```

ending each line with a **return**. Next, we press **escape** to get to the `vi` command mode, then **ZZ** to exit the editor and return to the shell prompt. Finally, we type

```
% chmod +x mystatus◄┘
```

to add "execute" permission for all users to the file `mystatus`.

Such a shell program is called a *script* file. When you type

```
% mystatus◄┘
```

the system tries to execute the commands listed within the file.

### Selecting the Shell

You can force a script to run under a shell of your choosing by typing a command line consisting of the shell name followed by the script name. For example from the shell prompt, the command

```
% csh myscript◄┘
```

executes the script `myscript` under the Berkeley `csh`. That is, its commands are interpreted according to Berkeley's rules.

If you execute a script directly, the first line determines which shell it runs under. If it is a comment, it runs under `csh`, but if it is not a comment, the script runs under `sh`. Comment lines begin with a pound sign (**#**). For example, if `myscript` consists of the following two lines

```
#This runs under the Berkeley shell
set
```

and has execute permission, then

```
% myscript◄┘
```

runs the `set` command under `csh`. However, if the (executable) file `myscript` consists of the single line

```
set
```

then

```
% myscript ◄┘
```

runs the `set` command under `sh`.

The reason why we choose the command `set` in these examples is that it produces distinctively different output depending on which shell it runs under. See Chapter 5 on system variables for a discussion of what this output means.

When you wish to run a script directly, remember to use `chmod` to make it executable. For example

```
chmod u+x myscript
```

makes the file `myscript` executable for the file's owner.

## Passing Parameters

It is often useful to pass parameters to a script. This allows you to write general purpose scripts that work on arbitrary files.

Within the script file, we can designate the values of these parameters as the variables $0, $1, $2, and so on, or as $argv[0], $argv[1], $argv[2], and so on. The first one is the name of the script (designated by $0 or $argv[0]).

### passing parameters

$0    name of script
$1    first parameter
$2    second parameter
$3    third parameter

Here is a script file called `myecho` that demonstrates parameter passing. It uses the `echo` command that displays whatever string parameters you give it. Double or single quotes group a series of words into a single parameter.

```
#example of parameter passing to a script
echo "The script parameters are:"
echo " zero =" $0
echo " one  =" $1
echo " two  =" $2
```

You can use `vi` as described in the preceding discussion to enter these lines in a file called `myecho`, then use `echo` to give it execute permissions. If we run it with parameters `alpha`, `beta`, `gamma` like this

```
% myecho alpha beta gamma⏎
```

we get the following results:

```
The script parameters are:
    zero = myecho
    one  = alpha
    two  = beta
```

Let's see how this script works. The first line is a comment. Thus, this script runs under the C-Shell. The next line contains the `echo` command. It simply prints its single string parameter as the message
`The script parameters are:`.

The next line also contains an `echo` command. Its first parameter is the string     `zero =` and its second parameter is the string variable $0. It prints the line

```
    zero = myecho
```

in which the first parameter is printed literally and the second causes the name of the script file to appear. Similarly the next two lines "echo" a literal string, followed by the value of a parameter. The value *alpha* is substituted for $1 and the value *beta* is substituted for $2. Notice that *gamma* is ignored because $3 is never used in the script.

Here is a more practical example. Suppose that you have written a program called `myprogram`, and you wish to test it against data files `test00` through `test17` that are in a directory called `~ morgan/pascal`. Suppose that you wish to test the files one by one with a minimum of typing.

One solution is to use `vi` or `cat` to write a script file. Let's use `cat` to make this file and name it `r`:

```
% cat >r◄┘
#Script to test myprogram against test files
myprogram  ~ morgan/pascal/test$1
<control d>
```

We use `chmod` to make the file executable:

```
% chmod +x r◄┘
```

Then typing the short command

```
% r 00←
```

has the effect of executing the long command line

```
myprogram  ~morgan/pascal/test00
```

and typing the command

```
% r 01←
```

has the effect of executing the command line

```
myprogram  ~morgan/pascal/test01
```

In both cases, running the script causes the command line to be executed with the parameter substitution for $1.

## Expressions and Control Structures

The Berkeley C-Shell gets its name because its syntax is much like that of the C language. In particular it has a number of control structures, such as `if`, `while`, and `switch`. There is even a kind of `for` loop called `foreach` that implements counting loops.

**Expressions**—These control structures use expressions just as any control structure does in an ordinary programming language. However, these expressions are made up from strings.
  Here are some binary operators:

|  |  |
|---|---|
| == | equal |
| != | not equal |
| =~ | matches |
| !~ | does not match |

The last two operators match a string expression on their left to a regular expression on their right.

Here are some unary operators that operate on a file name to their right.

| | |
|---|---|
| -e | does the file exit? |
| -r | does the file have read permission? |
| -w | does the file have write permission? |
| -x | does the file have execute permission? |
| -d | is the file a directory? |

There are also the pathname modifiers that can be placed immediately after pathname variables:

| | |
|---|---|
| :r | extract the root |
| :h | extract the head |
| :t | extract the tail |

The next section gives examples of these expressions.

**If**—There are two possible ways to write the if control structure. One way is:

```
if (expression) command
```

This first one is quite limited because it resides on a single line of the file. You cannot have any further control structures within it. Another form of the if is:

```
if (expression) then
   command
   command
   ...
   command
endif
```

This second form is very general. Here the if must begin the line. It must be followed by the expression (in parentheses) and that is followed by then. Any number of commands can come between the if line and the endif. The endif must be at the beginning of the line.

A further variation includes one or more else clauses. Each else must be at the beginning of the line:

```
if (expression) then
   command
   ...
   command
else if (expression) then
   command
   ...
```

```
    command
else if ...
    ...
else
    command
    ...
    command
endif
```

With an example script, let's illustrate how some of this works. When applied to a pathname, this script first checks to see whether the file exists. If the file exists, the script prints the root, head, and tail, then various permissions. The *root* of a pathname is everything but its extension, the *head* is everything but the file name, and the *tail* is the file name itself, including any extension. The following script file, which we call f, illustrates what these terms mean:

```
# script to illustrate expressions and if statements
if (-e $1) then

    echo root: $1:r
    echo head: $1:h
    echo tail: $1:t

    if (-r $1) echo "read permission"
    if (-w $1) echo "write permission"
    if (-x $1) echo "execute permission"
    if (-d $1) echo "is a directory"
    if (-f $1) echo "is an ordinary file"
    if (-z $1) echo "has zero size"
    if (-o $1) echo "belongs to you"

else
    echo $1 does not exist
endif
```

The first line is a comment, forcing the script to be run under csh. The next line is an if clause that tests whether the first parameter is a pathname leading to an actual file. The next two blocks are executed if the expression is true because they come after the if...then line and before the else line. The first block consists of three lines to display the root, head, and tail of the pathname, and the second block checks various conditions such as read, write, and execute permissions, and whether it's a directory or ordinary file or has zero length. The last part of the script contains an else clause that proclaims that the file doesn't exist (in case the if fails).

Here are some examples of this script's use. We give it the very short name f for convenience. Let's apply it first to a file x.c in our current directory.

```
% f x.c◀┘
root: x
head: x.c
tail: x.c
read permission
write permission
is an ordinary file
belongs to you
```

In this first case, the root of the path x.c is just x, the head and the tail are both the file's name x.c. This file has read, write, but not execute permissions, and is an ordinary file that belongs to the user. Let's try again:

```
% f x◀┘
x does not exist
```

In this case, we gave a pathname to a file that doesn't exist. Now let's use it to explore some system files:

```
% f /bin/who◀┘
root: /bin/who
head: /bin
tail: who
execute permission
is an ordinary file
```

This third case checks out the who system command. Its pathname is /bin/who of which /bin is the head and who is the tail. This file has only execute permissions for us and is an ordinary file that does not belong to us.

```
% f ~◀┘
root: /usr/morgan
head: /usr
tail: morgan
read permission
write permission
execute permission
is a directory
belongs to you
```

In this fourth case, the tilde (~) signifies our home directory. In this example, it expands as the path /usr/morgan to a directory that belongs to us and for which we have read, write, and execute privileges.

```
% f ~/book/chap3/x.c◄┘
root: /usr/morgan/book/chap3/x
head: /usr/morgan/book/chap3
tail: x.c
read permission
write permission
is an ordinary file
belongs to you
```

The last case illustrates a longer pathname ~/book/chap3/x.c. The root is everything but the last .c, the head is everything but the last x.c and the tail is just the name x.c. We have already discussed its read, write, and execute permissions and ownership.

**Foreach**—The foreach statement implements a counting loop. This is especially valuable for running through lists such as parameters or pathname expansions.

The foreach statement has the following form:

```
foreach name (list)
   command
   ...
   command
   end
```

Here is an example script of how this works

```
#example of foreach

foreach item($argv)
   if (! -d $item) file $ item
   end
```

The first line is a comment forcing the script to run under the Berkeley C-Shell csh. The second line contains the foreach statement. The shell variable item is created and is ready to be loaded with the items in the list $argv (the arguments that are passed to this script). The third line applies the file command to the pathname in item provided that the file is not a directory. Note the $ before item gives its string value. The file command was designed to report as much information as possible about a given file.

Here is a sample run in which this file is applied to the files under the root.

```
% for /* ↵
/boot: cannot open for reading
/xenix: separate standalone executable not stripped, Middle model
```

From this we learn that the root directory contains two files that are not directories themselves. The file boot does not give us permission to read it, and the file xenix contains machine code. We study this second file in Chapter 9.

**While Loops**—The while statement allows you to execute a block of commands as long as a condition is true. The general form is:

```
while (expression)
  command
  ...
  command
  end
```

Here is an example of how to implement a for loop with a while statement:

```
#example of while loop

while ($1 != "")
  echo $1
  shift
  end
```

The conditional expression for this while is $1 != "". That is, argument number one is not the empty string. Thus the while loop continues as long as argument one is nonempty. In the body of the loop, we simply echo that argument. This is done just to test and demonstrate the loop control. It is a good idea to start programming this way to test your ideas before too many extraneous issues cloud whatever basic syntax problems you might have.

The shift statement shifts all the arguments to the left so that argument two is now argument one, and so on. Thus we are really looking at the second argument, the second time through the loop, and so on. The shift statement can be applied to other lists besides the list of arguments. This is just the default case.

The while statement can be used with break and continue statements to stop the loop prematurely or move onto the next interaction of the loop prematurely.

Here, we apply it to the argument list /usr/sys/*, which is a list of all files in the directory /usr/sys. It just gives us a listing of that directory.

```
% wloop /usr/sys/* ←┘
/usr/sys/conf
/usr/sys/h
/usr/sys/io
/usr/sys/mdep
/usr/sys/sys
```

**Switch**—The switch statement is like the switch statement in C or the *case* statement in Pascal.
It has the form:

```
switch (string)

   case string1:
     commands
     breaksw
   case string2:
     commands
     breaksw
   ...
   default:
     commands
     breaksw
endsw
```

Here is an example:

```
#example of switch

foreach item($argv)
  switch($item)
    case "*.c":
      echo $item " is a c file."
      breaksw
    case "*.h":
      echo $item " is an include file."
      breaksw
    case "*.o":
      echo $item " is an object file."
      breaksw
    case "*.s":
      echo $item " is an assembly language file."
```

**67**

```
                        breaksw
                    default:
                        echo $item " is not a c, include, object, or assembly file."
                        breaksw
                endsw
            end
```

This script has a `foreach` loop that runs the `switch` statement through all the pathnames in the argument list. For each item in the list, we check to see whether it matches one of the cases `*.c`, `*.h`, `*.o`, or `*.s`, which are files with special file extensions. For each of these cases, we print the pathname with a short message.

Each case ends with a `breaksw` command. This is different from `break` that is used in C. The *default* case handles all items not caught by the regular cases. The entire `switch` statement ends with an `endsw`.

Let's try it on the files in a directory that we study in Chapter 9 which has a variety of different file types.

```
% cases /usr/sys/conf/* ←┘
/usr/sys/conf/KMseg.o is an object file.
/usr/sys/conf/Klibc.a is not a c, include, object, or assembly
   file.
/usr/sys/conf/README is not a c, include, object, or assembly
   file.
/usr/sys/conf/c.c is a c file.
/usr/sys/conf/c.o is an object file.
/usr/sys/conf/config is not a c, include, object, or assembly
   file.
/usr/sys/conf/hdinstall is not a c, include, object, or assembly
   file.
/usr/sys/conf/link_xenix is not a c, include, object, or assembly
   file.
/usr/sys/conf/makefile is not a c, include, object, or assembly
   file.
/usr/sys/conf/master is not a c, include, object, or assembly
   file.
/usr/sys/conf/oemsup.o is an object file.
/usr/sys/conf/picmask.c is a c file.
/usr/sys/conf/picmask.o is an object file.
/usr/sys/conf/rkseg is not a c, include, object, or assembly
   file.
/usr/sys/conf/space.c is a c file.
/usr/sys/conf/space.o is an object file.
/usr/sys/conf/termsw.c is a c file.
/usr/sys/conf/termsw.o is an object file.
```

```
/usr/sys/conf/xenixconf is not a c, include, object, or assembly
    file.
```

## Controlling I/O

Let's now look at how to make scripts interactive, how to make them send input to commands, and how to use output from command.

---

**script I/O**

|  |  |
|---|---|
| line | get a line of input |
| << | send input to a command |

---

To get input from the user, use the `line` command. It expects from the keyboard a line of input that ends with a newline character. Here is an example:

```
#example of input from the user

echo "What is your name? \c"
set name='line'
echo "Hi," $name
```

First, the script uses `echo` to print the message "What is your name?" on the screen. The `\c` at the end of the line causes the cursor to stay at the end of the line, waiting for input. The next line gets the answer from the user. The backward single quotes around the `line` command causes it to be executed and get its output so that it can be temporarily assigned to the variable `name`. On the last line, we echo the name back with the usual salutation.

Here is a typical run:

```
% input◄┘
What is your name? Christopher◄┘
Hi, Christopher
```

Sometimes you might have to send input to a command that is invoked from the script. A special form of redirection is used in that case. It is specified by << followed by a word that appears later in the file. Everything between the <<word and word is sent to the command.

Here is an example:

```
#example of sending input to a command
tr "[a-z]" "[A-Z]" <<EOF
This line was in upper- and lowercase.
EOF
echo "ok"
```

The first command is `tr`, which is short for *translate*. It is a classic filter. That is, it is a program that takes input from the standard input, transforms it in some way, then sends it out the standard output. In this case, it replaces each character in the string `abc...z` with the corresponding character in the string `ABC...Z`. See Chapter 4 for more on filters. The `<<EOF` at the end of this line introduces the text to be sent to the `tr` command as its input. The EOF on a line by itself ends this special text. The `echo` on the next line helps verify when the text ends.

Here is the result when we run this script:

```
% send◄┘
THIS LINE WAS IN UPPER- AND LOWERCASE.
ok
```

You can see that the text sent to the `tr` command has been capitalized, but the ok on the line after the magic word `EOF` is not.

## Compiling with the C Compiler

Most of the programs that make up the XENIX system are written in C. That is, C is the basic development language for this operating system. Although the basic XENIX system does not include the C compiler, the development system is built around it.

Throughout this book we use examples of C programs along with other kinds of programs, such as scripts and specialized programs such as `lex` and `yacc`.

This book does not attempt to teach you the C programming language. We recommend *C Primer Plus* by Mitchell Waite, Stephen Prata, and Donald Martin to get started and, once you know the basics, *The C Programming Language* by Brian W. Kernighan and Dennis M. Ritchie as a reference.

C acts both as a higher level and a lower level language. It acts like a modern higher language because it supports control structures such as subroutines, blocks (complex statements), `if-then-else` statements, and while loops. It also supports a variety of data structures, including arrays and programmable structures like Pascal's records. It acts as a lower level language because it has operations that correspond to the way central processors tend to handle data. For example, you can directly increment a variable or add any number to it.

If you are familiar with Pascal, learning C is not that hard. All the basic structures are there, although they are implemented a bit differently, so it might take you a few weeks to get used to the differences. When you see how these work, you will be pleasantly surprised because C's many extra features allow you to do things that you have always wanted to but weren't allowed to do in Pascal.

## Developing Programs for PC-DOS and MS-DOS

The ability to use XENIX to develop programs for PC-DOS and MS-DOS is an important reason for using the XENIX Development System. In this section we show how to invoke the XENIX C Compiler to compile a C program into a file that runs as a command under PC-DOS or MS-DOS.

Let's begin with an example C program that can be compiled to run under either XENIX or PC-DOS. Programs that use special features of XENIX, such as pathnames for files, would have to be modified (at the source code level) to run under PC-DOS or MS-DOS. Our program just uses "standard I/O" (see Chapter 4) and thus does not have to be modified to run under either system.

We used the XENIX vi editor to create the file. Let's use the XENIX cat command to list it:

```
% cat hi.c←┘
/* a C program */

main()
    {
    int x;
    char name[80];

    printf("What is your name? ");
    scanf("%s", name);
    printf("What is your favorite number, %s? ", name);
    scanf("%d", &x);
    printf("Your favorite number is %d, %s.\n", x, name);
    }
```

This program asks for your name and your favorite number, then reports this information back to you. It uses the standard I/O functions printf and scanf.

During the development of this program, we compile it to run under XENIX with the command

```
% cc hi.c⏎
%lx⏎
```

which produces the file `a.out`. We run that with the command:

```
% a.out⏎
```

Once the program is working under XENIX, we compile the program for PC-DOS. We use the `-o` option to specify the file name `hi.com` with the `.com` (command) file extension for PC-DOS, and we use the `dos` option of the C compiler to request special `-dos` C libraries that connect to `dos` system calls and a special `dos` linker to create a command file with the proper `dos` format.

```
% cc -o hi.com -dos hi.c⏎
hi.c
```

Next we use the `doscp` command to move the resulting file `hi.com` to drive `b:` where we have placed a PC-DOS formatted diskette.

```
% doscp hi.com b:⏎
```

Now we can shut down XENIX, boot up PC-DOS, and try the new PC-DOS command `hi`:

```
A>b:hi◄┘
What is your name? Elizabeth◄┘
What is your favorite number, Elizabeth? 7◄┘
Your favorite number is 7, Elizabeth.
```

# Debugging

XENIX has a number of tools to help you understand programming errors. These include lint, a program to detect errors in C programs and adb, which allows you to examine a program in machine- and assembly code as it runs.

## Lint

Lint checks C language programs. It gives you details about possible errors in your program that the normal C compiler ignores. The C compiler was designed to run quickly, so its error checking was kept to a minimum. Thus, another program, namely lint, was developed to help programmers discover errors and otherwise clean up their programs.

Here is an example of a C program that has lots of bugs in it. We have used the nl utility to number the lines so that you can better read the error diagnostics from both the C compiler and lint. The ba option causes all lines to be numbered including "blank" lines.

```
% nl -ba marred.c◄┘
  1 /* example of a C program with errors for Lint to catch */
  2
  3 int x, y;
  4 char *str;
  5
  6 main()
  7    {
  8    initialize();
  9    process(3.1);
 10    closeup();
 11    }
 12
 13 initialize()
 14    {
 15    str = "Basic Method";
 16    x = 5.27;
 17    }
```

```
18
19 process(r)
20     int r;
21     {
22     double z;
23     while(1)
24         }
25         x -= z;
26         t =- z/2;
27         }
28     return(x + 0.1);
29     z += 1;
30     }
31
32 doit() /* This is never called. */
33     {
34     }
35
36 closeup()
37     {
38     printf("bye\n");
39     }
40
```

When we run the C compiler, we only get one error, namely an undeclared variable t on line 26.

```
% cc marred.c←┘
marred.c
marred.c(26) : error 65: "t" : undefined
```

However, when we run lint, we see lots of problems. In particular, lint suspects that on line 25, we have not initialized properly the variable z before using it. On line 26, it agrees with the C compiler that we have not declared the variable t, but also on that same line it notes that we have used the confusing notation: =-. This was abandoned because statements like

```
x=-3;
```

could be interpreted as either "x is assigned −3" or as "x is decremented by 3." Lint also detects that t has not been initialized and that it is never used. On line 30, it sees that the normal **return** (no argument) is not consistent with an earlier **return** (which returns the value of an expression).

```
% lint marred.c◄┘

marred.c
===============
(25)   warning: z may be used before set
(26)   t undefined
(26)   warning: old-fashioned assignment operator
(26)   warning: t may be used before set
(26)   warning: t set but not used in function process
(30)   warning: function process has return(e); and return;
warning: argument unused in function:
     (20)   r in process
warning: statement not reached
     (28)              (29)


==============
name used but not defined
   _JBLEN         llibc(54)
name defined but never used
     y              marred.c(3)
     doit           marred.c(33)
function argument ( number ) used inconsistently
     process( arg 1 )    marred.c(21) :: marred.c(9)
function returns value which is always ignored
     process        printf
```

Lint also finds on line 20 that we have never used the argument r in
the function process, and it finds that lines 28 and 29 are never executed.

As far as global variables and procedures are concerned, lint finds
that the variable y declared on line 3 and the function doit defined starting
on line 33 are never used.

Lint finds a problem on lines 21 (really 19-20) and 9 that the argument
to the function process is inconsistent as far as its data type (floating point
or integer). Finally, lint notes that values returned from the functions
process and printf are ignored.

Sometimes lint gets too paranoid or verbose about errors. Fortunately, there are ways to silence it, even selectively. This can be done by inserting comments like /* NOTREACHED */ before the potential problem.

Lint does not catch every kind of error. For example, you might accidentally load data into a string that has not been allocated the proper
amount of space. For this kind of error a "debugger," such as adb is often
helpful.

## Adb

Adb stands for *a debugger*. It allows you to run through your program on a
machine or assembly language level.

Suppose that you have written a C program that seems to be acting unpredictably, perhaps crashing the system. Here is an example:

```
% nl -ba thebug.c◄┘
 1 /* Example of C program for debugging */
 2
 3 char *str;
 4
 5 main()
 6 {
 7 initstr('Basic Method');
 8 }
 9
10 initstr(s)
11 char *s;
12 {
13 register int i;
14 register char c;
15 for(i = 0; (c = s[i]) != 0; i++) str[i]= c;
16 }
17
```

The program has one global variable: str a string pointer. The main program calls a subroutine that accepts a literal string **Basic Method** which we pass. The subroutine initstr then has a for loop that attempts to transfer the string to the global variable str. However, there is an error because str is not properly initialized. Let's see exactly what goes wrong.

Before running **adb** you should prepare an assembly language listing of the program. We obtained it by typing

```
cc -S thebug.c
```

which places the assembly language in a file called thebug.s:

```
;         Static Name Aliases
;
          TITLE    thebug
_TEXT     SEGMENT   BYTE PUBLIC "CODE"
_TEXT     ENDS
_DATA     SEGMENT   WORD PUBLIC "DATA"
_DATA     ENDS
CONST     SEGMENT   WORD PUBLIC "CONST"
CONST     ENDS
_BSS      SEGMENT   WORD PUBLIC "BSS"
_BSS      ENDS
```

```
DGROUP  GROUP   CONST,  _BSS, _DATA
        ASSUME  CS: _TEXT, DS: DGROUP, SS: DGROUP, ES: DGROUP
EXTRN   __chkstk:NEAR
_DATA   SEGMENT
EXTRN   _str:WORD
_DATA   ENDS
_DATA   SEGMENT
$SG11   DB 'Basic Method', 00H
        EVEN
;       .comm _str,02H
_DATA   ENDS
_TEXT       SEGMENT
; Line 6
        PUBLIC  _main
_main   PROC NEAR
        push    bp
        mov     bp,sp
        mov     ax,0
        call    __chkstk
        push    di
        push    si
; Line 7
        mov     ax,OFFSET DGROUP:$SG11
        push    ax
        call    _initstr
        add     sp,2
; Line 8
$EX9:
        pop     si
        pop     di
        mov     sp,bp
        pop     bp
        ret
_main   ENDP
;       s = 4
; Line 11
        PUBLIC  _initstr
_initstr        PROC NEAR
        push    bp
        mov     bp,sp
        mov     ax,4
        call    __chkstk
        push    di
        push    si
;       c = -2
;       register si = i
; Line 12
```

```
; Line 13
; Line 14
; Line 15
        mov     si,0
$F16:
        mov     bx,[bp+4] ;s
        mov     al,[bx][si]
        mov     [bp-2],al ;c
        cmp     al,0
        jne     $+5
        jmp     $FB18
        jmp     $F19
$FC17:
        inc     si
        jmp     $F16
$F19:
        mov     bx,_str
        mov     al,[bp-2] ;c
        mov     [bx][si],al
        jmp     $FC17
$FB18:
; Line 16
$EX13:
        pop     si
        pop     di
        mov     sp,bp
        pop     bp
        ret
_initstr        ENDP
_TEXT   ENDS
END
```

This is our road map. Now let's start adb:

```
% adb◂┘
*
```

Adb automatically reads in the file a.out and gives us the * prompt. Incidentally, if the file core (from a core dump) is present, it also reads that.

Let's look at various key points in this program. Start is at the very beginning of the code segment (see *8086/8088 16-Bit Microprocessor Primer* by Christopher L. Morgan and Mitchell Waite). We list the very first few instructions there. The syntax is the label start, followed by a ,4 to indicate the number of instructions (four) we wish to see, then a ? to indicate that we look in `a.out` rather than `core`, followed by i to indicate that we wish to see the output as instructions. Here is the result:

```
*  start,4?i

start:      jmp    near start0
__syscal:   jmp    near __stkgro+19.
__stkgro:   jmp    near __stkgro+16.
            jmp    near __stkgro+16.
```

`Main` is the name of the main program. We use the same format to list the first ten instructions there:

```
*  main,10?i
_main:   push   bp
         mov    bp,sp
         mov    ax,0.
         call   near __chkstk
         push   di
         push   si
         mov    ax,2130.
         push   ax
         call   near _initstr
         add    sp,2.
```

We see how our subroutine `initstr` is called. Apparently, a pointer to the literal string `Basic Method` is pushed on the stack before this function is called.

Let's set a breakpoint (stopping point) at `main` and another one at `initstr`. Do this by typing the name followed by a `:br`. In general, the colon (:) indicates program control commands.

```
*  main:br
*  initstr:br
```

Now that we've put on the "brakes," let's start it running. The command is `:r`.

```
* :r◄┘
a.out: running
breakpoint      _main: push bp
```

It stops at the first breakpoint main. To continue, we type :co:

```
* :co◄┘
a.out: running
breakpoint      _initstr: push bp
```

Now it stops at initstr. We use the ? command to display the first 25 instructions starting at the current address, which is now initstr. In this case, the current address is the default. The format is given by ia, which says to display absolute addresses in addition to instructions.

```
* ,25?ia◄┘
_initstr:     push     bp
_initstr+1.:  mov      bp,sp
_initstr+3.:  mov      ax,4.
_initstr+6.:  call     near __chkstk
_initstr+9.:  push     di
_initstr+10.: push     si
_initstr+11.: mov      si,0.
_initstr+14.: mov      bx,[bp+4.]
_initstr+17.: mov      al,[bx]+[si]
_initstr+19.: mov      [bp-2.],al
_initstr+22.: cmp      al,0.
_initstr+24.: jne      _initstr+29.
_initstr+26.: jmp      near _initstr+48.
_initstr+29.: jmp      near _initstr+36.
_initstr+32.: inc      si
_initstr+33.: jmp      near _initstr+14.
_initstr+36.: mov      bx,_str
_initstr+40.: mov      al,[bp-2.]
_initstr+43.: mov      [bx]+[si],al
_initstr+45.: jmp      near _initstr+32.
_initstr+48.: pop      si
_initstr+49.: pop      di
```

```
_initstr+50.:   mov     sp,bp
_initstr+52.:   pop     bp
_initstr+53.:   ret
_initstr+54.:
```

We now suspect that the problem is near initstr+43, which is a move instruction. Let's set a breakpoint there and continue execution to that place.

```
*  initstr+43:br◄┘
*  :co◄┘
a.out: running
breakpoint      _initstr+43.:   mov     [bx]+[si],al
```

Now let's see what is contained in the pointer registers bx and si that are used in our suspicious move instruction. The syntax is < followed by the name of the register, followed by an equal (=) sign to display its actual value:

```
*  <bx=◄┘
63.:0.
*  <si=◄┘
63.:0.
```

In both cases, the *offset* value (to the right of the colon) is zero. We now go back to str and to see what that is. It should be zero because it was loaded into bx.

We give the address str, a ? to indicate the a.out file, then an x to indicate hexadecimal notation.

```
*  str?x◄┘
_str:           0x0
```

The answer is zero. Now let's see what zero points to. We type 0? to find out.

```
* 0?↵
71.:0.:      0x7eeb
```

Something is there already. Let's single step past the suspicious instruction. The syntax is :s.

```
* :s↵
a.out: running
stopped at      _initstr+32.:   inc si
```

We find ourselves at `initstr` because of a jump. Let's look again at what's at zero:

```
* 0?↵
71.:0.:      0x7e42
```

Sure enough, the memory has changed, but where are we? Let's try `start`:

```
* start?↵
start:       0x7e42
```

It's the same stuff. If we display this in instruction format, we see that the code at `start` has been corrupted:

```
* start,4?i↵
start:       inc     dx
             jle     _etext+-2144.
             adc     bp,bx
             push    cs
```

Let's continue and see whether it gets more corrupted:

```
*  :co←┘
a.out: running
breakpoint        _initstr+43.:   mov    [bx]+[si],al
*  :co←┘
a.out: running
breakpoint        _initstr+43.:   mov    [bx]+[si],al
*  start?x←┘
start:            0x6142
*  start,4?i←┘
start:            inc    dx
                  popa
__syscal:    jmp    near __stkgro+19.
__stkgro:    jmp    near __stkgro+16.
```

Yes, it does. We have located the problem. The string is being transferred right over our program. If we had more text it would overwrite the
code that we are actually executing, perhaps causing a serious crash. Let's
quit adb with the command $q and go back to the drawing board.

```
*  $q←┘
```

## Automating Program Development

The make program helps control jobs that involve a number of different
source files and files that depend on them. This program expects to find a
file, normally called makefile, in your current directory. At least, that's
the default case. This file contains a list of *dependencies* and commands for
updating these files. Normally, this *updating* process involves compiling,
but any operating system commands could be used. To start the process,
the programmer types the command make.

Let's look at an example from Chapter 10 (without getting into any of
the concepts there). Suppose that we have four source files eng3.y, eng.l,
eng.h, and eng.c. The first is written in the yacc language, the second is
written in the lex language, and the last two are written in C.

To compile eng3.y, we type

```
yacc eng.y
```

and get the file `y.tab.c`, which is C source code. To compile `eng.l`, we type

```
lex eng.l
```

and get the file `lex.yy.c`, which is also C source code.

Because of `include` directives in `eng3.y`, the resulting C program file `y.tab.c` has include directives to include the files `lex.yy.c`, `eng.h`, and `eng.r`. Thus, compiling `y.tab.c` with the C compiler puts the entire program together. Figure 3-1 gives a diagram of these relationships.

**Figure 3-1**
**Dependency relations for eng**

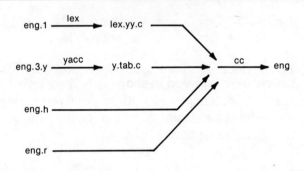

Here is the `makefile`:

```
# make file for eng

# A macro definition

ENG.Y=eng3.y

# The rules:

eng: lex.yy.c y.tab.c eng.h eng.r
     cc -o eng y.tab.c

lex.yy.c: eng.l
        lex eng.l

y.tab.c: $(ENG.Y)
        yacc $(ENG.Y)
```

The first line begins with a pound sign (**#**) and thus is a comment. Next comes a section for macro definitions. We have defined the macro `ENG.Y` to be equal to the file name `eng3.y`. We do this because `eng3.y` is just one of three possible `yacc` programs that we might want to use. Defining a macro allows us to make this selection by changing just one statement in our makefile.

`Makefile` contains three rules: one to make the file `eng` by compiling `y.tab.c`, a second to make the file `lex.yy.c`, using Lex on the file `eng.l`, and a third to make the file `y.tab.c`, using Yacc on the file defined by the macro `ENG.Y`.

Let's run this `make file`. The `lx` command demonstrates that we start with just the source files and the `make file` in a directory:

```
% lx◄┘
eng.h   eng.l   eng.r   eng1.y   eng2.y   eng3.y makefile
```

Let's use the n option to show what `make` actually does:

```
% make -n◄┘
        lex eng.l
        yacc eng3.y
        cc -o eng y.tab.c
```

We see that it invokes all three rules. Notice that the macro substitutes `eng3.y` for `ENG.Y`. Now, let's really run `make`.

```
% make◄┘
lex eng.l
yacc eng3.y
cc -o eng y.tab.c
y.tab.c
```

Now the directory contains more files:

```
% lx◄┘
eng    eng.h   eng.l   eng.r   eng.y   eng1.y eng2.y
eng3.y lex.yy.c makefile y.tab.c y.tab.o
```

Let's use the `touch` command to make the file `eng.r` newer than all the rest, then call make again. Only the C compiler is invoked because the other files are up to date.

```
% touch eng.r◀┘
% make◀┘
        cc -o eng y.tab.c
y.tab.c
```

If we touch eng3.y and type make again, both yacc and cc are invoked:

```
% touch eng3.y◀┘
% make◀┘
        yacc eng3.y
        cc -o eng y.tab.c
y.tab.c
```

If we type make again, we get a message saying that our files are up to date:

```
% make◀┘
'eng' is up to date.
```

# Summary

In this chapter, we have introduced and explored the basic tools that programmers use in the XENIX operating system. These include the vi screen editing program, the shell command language, the C compiler, the adb debugger, and the make program manager.

These tools provide a firm foundation for programmers to efficiently develop applications and systems programs. This chapter can be used as an example-driven reference for the basic tools needed to create programs discussed in the rest of the book.

# Questions and Answers

## Questions

1. Name XENIX's standard program development utilities.
2. How can you use the `vi` text editing program to move a block of text in a file?
3. What are script files and why are they useful?
4. How do you compile a C program under XENIX?
5. What is a debugger program?

## Answers

1. `Vi` is the standard screen editing program, `cc` is the C compiler, `lint` is the C program checker, `adb` is the debugger program, and `make` is the program maintainer.
2. There are several ways to move a block of text using `vi`. One way is to mark the end of the block by moving the cursor there and typing `ma`, then move the cursor to the beginning of the block and type `d'a` to delete it, and finally move the cursor right before the new position and type `p` to "put" it there.
3. Script files are text files that contain operating system (shell) commands. When these files are "run" the commands are interpreted and executed by one of the XENIX shell programs. Such scripts can contain complicated sequences of commands, such as are used in administering the system or developing programs and text documents. They can act as system utilities that tie together other system utilities.
4. If your C program is stored in a file `myfile.c`, type:

   ```
   % cc myfile.c⏎
   ```

   The result is stored in a file called `a.out`. The compiler has many options to handle various special circumstances.

5. A debugger program, such as `adb`, allows you to display memory and CPU registers in various formats and to run programs either a single step at a time or using breakpoints to halt at specified places in the program. It allows a programmer to see exactly what happens when a program executes.

*Tar - {txrac} [o - qvf bke lmn pu#F] [Tapefile] [Blocksize] [Tapesize] Fils.──*

*KEY*

*# Tar ↓*

| Key | Device | Block | Size | Tape |
|-----|--------|-------|------|------|
| 0 | /dev/rfd048d19 | 18 | 360 | No |
| 1 | | | | |
| 2 | | | | |
| 3 | | | | |
| 4 | | | | |
| 5 | | | | |
| 6 | /dev/rct0 | 20 | 5000 | YES |
| 7 | | | | |
| 8 | | | | |
| 9 | √ Tapfile | 1 | 0 | YES |

# 4

# Filters

■ What Is a Filter?
■ Redirection of I/O
■ Programming Filters
■ Summary
■ Questions and Answers

# Filters

Effective processing of text is an important central goal of XENIX. A program to process text is called a *filter*. This chapter explains what filters are and how they can be developed and used effectively in the XENIX operating system.

We explain the *standard input, output,* and *error streams.* We show how to use several existing filters and put them together to form larger programs. We also introduce a powerful programming tool called lex to create filters, and we develop a simple filter in the C programming language.

## What Is a Filter?

The idea of a filter is simple. It is a program that processes information from a single source and delivers that information to a single destination. In this chapter, we deal with filters that process character strings (see figure 4-1). An example is a sorting program, because it processes strings by arranging them in a specified order.

**Figure 4-1**
**The idea of a filter**

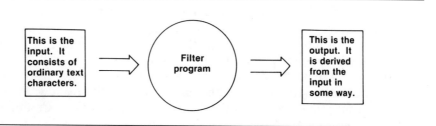

Putting it another way, for our point of view, a filter accepts textual input, then produces textual output that is derived from the input. In

XENIX, a filter is a program that accepts input from the standard input and sends its output to the standard output. The default source for standard input is the keyboard, and the default destination for the standard output is the screen.

As an example, the XENIX `sort` command is a filter. If we type the command line

```
% sort◄┘
```

in response to a shell prompt, the system waits for us to type some lines from the keyboard. Suppose we type

```
this◄┘
that◄┘
there◄┘
<control d>
```

the system prints these words after alphabetizing them:

```
that
there
this
```

## Some Simple Examples

The simplest example of a filter is a program that sends every character it receives without changing it (see figure 4-2). The `cat` command can act as such a filter. As we saw in Chapter 2, this command is not entirely useless even though it seems trivial at first.

Trivial things often play very important roles in building larger, more complex, structures. In this case, the `cat` filter allows us to copy text files from one place to another. In a following section, we build our own trivial filter using the C programming language.

A slightly more interesting example is a program that changes lowercase letters to uppercase (see figure 4-3). Of course, it should also pass numbers and punctuation marks through unchanged.

**Figure 4-2**
**A trivial filter**

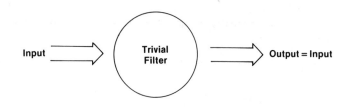

**Figure 4-3**
**Lower- and uppercase filter**

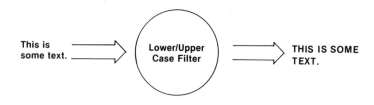

## What Are Filters Good For?

Many programming problems can be solved with the judicious use of filters. A classic example is a spelling checker. It can be constructed as a series of filters (see figure 4-4). We construct such a program in this chapter.

The first filter converts a document so that each word occupies a single line. This filter also removes all spaces, tabs, periods, commas, and other punctuation marks. A second filter sorts this list of words, and a third filter removes word repetitions. Finally, a system command is used to look for matches between the words in this list and the words in a dictionary file, reporting all mismatches. As we proceed through this chapter, we will see filters that perform many of these key steps, and we will put all the steps together to make such a program.

Filters can operate on either single characters or larger patterns such as words, and they can move these larger patterns around before they are output.

## Redirection of I/O

Because XENIX treats devices such as keyboards, screens, and printers as files, I/O redirection boils down to the ability to control the flow of a program's input and output to and from any specified file.

**Figure 4-4**
**A spelling checker**

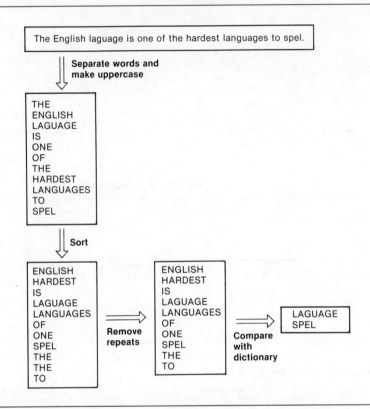

There are three standard *I/O streams*. They are called stdin, stdout, and stderr, which stand for *standard input, standard output,* and *standard error output.* The first handles standard input, the second handles standard output, and the third handles error messages separately from standard output. These "files" are automatically opened when your program starts and remain open until it finishes.

To a program, these streams act like files that are always open for reading (in the case of stdin) or writing (in the case of stdout and stderr). Stdin usually comes from the keyboard, but can be redirected to come from any specified source. Stdout usually goes to the screen, but can be redirected to go to any specified destination. The last one, stderr, is used to send error messages, usually to the screen.

The usefulness of filters stems from XENIX's inherent ability to redirect standard I/O, that is, obtain standard input from arbitrary sources and send standard output to arbitrary destinations. You might want the input to come from the keyboard or from a file, and you might want the output to go to the screen, a printer, or to the input of another filter (see figure 4-5).

**Figure 4-5**
**Redirection of I/O**

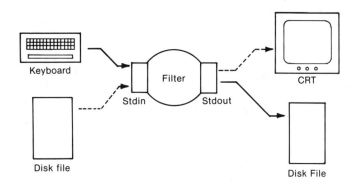

## Controlling Redirection

Let's start by learning how to specify redirection in a command line. In a following section, we see how to write programs that can use redirection.

Normally, without any special indications, a filter takes its input from the keyboard and sends its output to the screen. However, some simple additions to the command line allow you to specify the source of the input and the destination for the output.

PC-DOS users should be familiar with the most common cases. A < followed by a file name in the command line specifies the source for input and a > followed by a file name specifies the destination for output. For example the command line

```
% filter    <myfile   >yourfile◄┘
```

causes the program `filter` to take its input from `myfile` and send its output to `yourfile`. Also, a >> followed by a file name indicates that the output should be appended to the previous contents of the file. This avoids the problem of clobbering an existing file and is especially handy for system accounting in which data is accumulated over long periods of time.

The XENIX operating system handles these three redirection commands in the same way as PC-DOS. However, other variations are possible in XENIX. For example, in the C Shell, the addition of

```
>& myfile
```

to a command line diverts both the output and any error messages to the file `myfile`. For example, the command

```
% cc myprogram.c >&errors◀┘
```

sends all the diagnostic output from compiling `myprogram.c` to the file `errors`. Then later we can use the `more` command to examine `errors`:

```
% more errors◀┘
```

This can be very useful if we wish to execute jobs as background tasks (see Chapter 2). For example, placing an ampersand (**&**) at end of the command line

```
% cc myprogram.c >&errors &◀┘
```

runs the C compiler as a background task and collects all the output in the file `error`. Meanwhile, we can do something else without worrying about any of the output until we are ready for it.

Normally, diagnostic messages go to the screen, no matter where the standard output has been directed.

## Programming Standard I/O

The key to I/O redirection lies in the notion of "standard I/O." A C programmer can think of standard I/O as a collection of input and output routines that are called by any program that is to act as a filter. The programmer writes the program independently of where the input is coming from or where the output is going to, and uses these standard I/O functions.

Each of the standard I/O routines actually connects to a software "switch" hidden within the operating system that is activated by any redirection commands in the command line. For example, the statement

```
x = getchar();
```

in a C program normally takes a character from the keyboard as soon as one is ready and places it in the variable x. However, if <myfile appears in the command line, the system "turns the switch" so that standard input grabs a character from the file myfile, then puts it in x.

### Include Files and Standard C Libraries

XENIX's standard I/O routines are located in two places, the standard C library and the stdio.h include file. The standard C library is a machine language file located in the XENIX directory /lib. The C compiler knows where this is, so you don't have to know. The stdio.h file contains human readable C source code and is located in the XENIX directory /usr/include. Again, the C compiler knows where that is, so you don't have to. However, because it is human-readable you might want to find it and examine it. We won't discuss its contents here because it is proprietary and subject to change from system to system. The file extension .h is short for *header*. This extension is used because these files are customarily (but not necessarily) included at the head or top of C programs.

Many of the standard I/O routines are actually duplicated in these two places in slightly different form because of the space versus time trade-offs we discuss in the following text. However, you should compile your programs using both sources (as we describe in this section).

The XENIX manuals are written under the assumption that you are using both the C library and the stdio.h include file. Clearly, the designers of XENIX (and its UNIX ancestors) intended you to use both. It is to your advantage to use both, because you then have all the standard I/O features available to you. For example, the stdio.h file defines certain useful constants, such as the code for *end of file,* yet the stdio.h file depends on the standard C library to ultimately communicate with the system through a system call.

If you happen to be writing a C program that uses standard I/O, you must place the line

```
#include <stdio.h>
```

near the top of your C program, with the pound sign (#) in the leftmost column. In the example C program, you see this line.

To use the standard C library with any C program, compile the program in the normal way:

```
cc mycprogram.c
```

The compiler always automatically uses the standard C library, even when you specify other libraries. For example, the `-lm` option specifies the `math` library, which contains such things as the sine and cosine functions. Thus:

```
cc myprogram.c -lm
```

uses both the standard C library and the math library.

When there is a conflict between an include file and a C library, the include file wins. This is because the contents of any include file are combined with your program as it is compiled. In contrast, the C library is combined next during the linking process. The linking stage only knows about and tries to resolve subroutine references that still are unresolved after the compilation is complete.

Because include files are C source files, they are easy to maintain. This is true for both the include files that you write and for the ones that come with the system.

It is not a good idea to rely on a particular distribution of routines or other structures between the system's standard I/O include file and its standard C library. This is subject to change. The actions and behavior of these routines do not change. Thus, it is important to understand how these routines are used and how they are supposed to act. XENIX designers and implementers are very careful about maintaining consistency at this level. We discuss these behavior details in the next few subsections.

You can find a whole collection of such include files in the same directory as `stdio.h`. You can use such XENIX commands as `find` to find all public include files (with read permission all along the path) in your system. Just ask `find` to report all file names of the form `*.h`. Here is what such a command line would look like:

```
find / -name '*.h' -print
```

The first parameter, a slash (/), indicates that the search begins at the root of the directory system, the option -name followed by the `*.h` indicates that we are looking for file names of the form `*.h`, and the option -print indicates that the resulting path should be printed when such a name is found.

The string `*.h` is an example of a *regular expression*. A regular expression is a string pattern that is used as a template to match other strings. In this case, the `*` acts as a wild card that matches an arbitrary string of characters that begin a file name. The `.h` requires our search to find files whose name ends with a `.h`.

On a new system, most of the include files are in the directory `/usr/include`. This is called the standard include directory (see figure 4-6). A few more are in `/usr/include/sys`. For these you have to place a `sys/` in front of the file name to get down into the `sys` subdirectory of

/usr/include. As a system gets used, programmers develop their own include files, placing them in their own directories. When these files are included in a C program, the angle brackets are replaced by double quotes like this:

```
#include "myincludefile.h"
```

**Figure 4-6**
**The standard include directory**

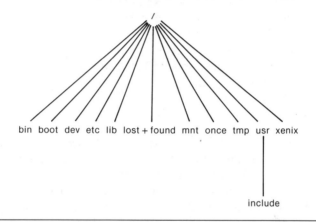

bin boot dev etc lib lost+found mnt once tmp usr xenix

include

## Standard I/O Streams

The standard I/O commands are special cases of more general file commands. Basically, file commands allow you to open, close, read from, and write to files, as well as determine and modify file parameters. In Chapter 7, we explore general files in much more detail. This chapter concentrates on standard I/O.

In general, when you open a file, you create an I/O *stream* that connects your program to that file. When you want to access that file, you pass its name as an argument to the appropriate file I/O function. Pascal programmers recognize streams as file variables.

More explicitly, a C program that opens a file with stream myfile must declare myfile with the statement

```
FILE *myfile;
```

and open the file with a statement such as

```
myfile = fopen("filename", r);
```

Then if you wish to use a file I/O function called getc to read a character from that file and put it into a character variable c, the following function call should appear within your program:

```
c = getc(myfile);
```

As we mentioned above, the three special standard I/O *streams are already open.* Thus you do not need to declare them or open them. You may simply use them by the names stdin, stdout, and stderr. The first handles standard input, the second handles standard output, and the third handles error messages separately from standard output.

Stdin, stdout, and stderr can be used as arguments in the general file system calls. However, we wish to use the special standard I/O functions that don't require a file (stream) reference as an argument but assume either stdin or stdout (whichever is appropriate). In the next couple of sections, we investigate these special functions and how they relate to functions that access arbitrary files.

## Standard Input

In versions of XENIX that we use, both the standard C library and the stdio.h include file contain the following input routines: getc, getchar, fgetc, getw, gets, fgets, scanf, and fscanf.

Getc is the most basic file function for reading characters from a file. The other input functions can be defined in terms of it. Its single argument is stream belonging to an open file. In this chapter, we deal only with standard I/O streams. These are predefined by the system and always open. As we mentioned before, in Chapter 7 we discuss how to set up streams that belong to arbitrary files.

The version of getc that is defined in the include file stdio.h is a macro. That is, each time you invoke it, an entire routine is inserted directly in your program. This scheme takes up more room than a normal function call, but it runs a bit faster, an important consideration if the routine is to be executed many thousands of times in a program.

Getc returns an integer that contains the ASCII code of the next character in the file. On some machines integers are 16 bits, but other machines use larger sized integers.

If getc develops an error or if you have reached the end of the file, getc returns a value of − 1. If you need to refer to this value to stop reading once you have reached the end of a file, you should use the constant identifier EOF instead of − 1. This makes the program more readable and portable. The assignment of − 1 to EOF is done in the stdio.h file.

Getchar is defined so that it acts just like getc(stdin). The name getchar is shorter to type and easier to understand than getc(stdin). It returns an integer that is the ASCII code of the next character from the standard input stream, and it also returns the values EOF upon error and end of file. Because the getchar function uses standard input, it tries without any special < indicator in the command line, to read a character from the keyboard, and it can be made to read from other files by placing a < file reference in the command line.

The copy of getchar in stdio.h is also a macro for speed of execution.

The fgetc function is equivalent to getc, but it is implemented as a C function. Each invocation of this becomes a *call* to a single block of code located elsewhere. Thus fgetc takes up less space in a program but runs slower.

It is interesting to note that there are also versions of getc and getchar in the standard C library that are implemented as C functions rather than as macros, but the include file versions take precedence.

Getw returns the next integer from a specified file. Considering that a file is just a series of bytes, it gets an integer worth of bytes. On the IBM XT this is two bytes. It is thus not character oriented and of little interest to us in this chapter.

Gets returns the address of a string that contains the next line of input from the standard input. C programmers say this is a pointer to the string. The gets function changes the newline characters at the end of the lines into a NULL (ASCII value zero). Fgets does the equivalent task for a specified file. It has three arguments, the first of which is a string where the data is placed, the second of which is an integer that specifies a maximum size for the string (including the zero), and the third is a stream belonging to an open file.

Scanf is a powerful routine for reading standard input according to a specified format. C programmers should be quite familiar with the way it works, but we provide a quick rundown here. It returns an integer that indicates how far it was able to get with its job. Scanf has a variable number of arguments. The first argument is a string that describes the *format* expected for the input, and the rest of the arguments are pointers to the various places to store the data. For example

```
scanf("%d%o%x%s", &x, &y, &z, yourstring);
```

reads from standard input, looking for a sequence of characters that represents an integer in decimal notation, an integer in octal notation, an integer in hexadecimal notation, then a string. It stores the integers in x, y, and z, respectively, and the string in yourstring. A full description of the various formats can be found in a XENIX manual or a book on the C language.

Fscanf is the general routine for reading input from a file according to a specified format. Its first argument specifies the file, and the rest are the same as for scanf.

## Standard Output

Standard output is much the same as standard input. Both the standard C library and the stdio.h include file contain the following input routines: putc, putchar, fputc, putw, puts, fputs, fprintf, and printf.

Again, putc is the most basic file function for writing characters to a file. The others can be defined in terms of it. It has two arguments: The first is an integer that contains the ASCII code of the character to be written, and the second is a stream that belongs to an open file.

The function putc returns an integer that is its first argument, namely the ASCII code of the character that was just written to the file.

Putchar(c) is defined to act like putc(c, stdout). That is, it writes the character in the integer variable c to the standard output. Because this function uses standard output, if there is no special > indicator in the command line, it writes the character to the screen.

Both putc and the putchar in the include file stdio.h are implemented as macros like the corresponding get routines. That is, each time you invoke one of them, an entire routine is inserted directly in your program.

Fputc is equivalent to putc, but it is implemented as a C function. That is, each invocation of this becomes a *call* to a single block of code located elsewhere. There are also versions of putc and putchar in the standard C library that are implemented as C functions rather than macros.

Putw sends an integer to a specified file. Because it is not character oriented, it is of little interest to us in this chapter.

Puts sends a specified string to the standard output. The string is the function's single argument. The string must be terminated by an ASCII zero (null) character. It returns the EOF value if there is an error. Fputs is the general file function to send a specified string to a specified file. It has two arguments. The first argument is the string to be sent and the second specifies the file to send it to.

Printf is a powerful routine for writing to the standard output according to a specified format. It corresponds to scanf, and like scanf should be quite familiar to C programmers.

Printf has a variable number of arguments. The first argument is a string that describes the format for the output, and the rest of the arguments are pointers to where the data is stored. For example

```
printf("Count = %d, address = %x, %s", x, addr, yourcomment);
```

prints Count = , the contents of x in decimal, the string ", address = ", then the contents of addr in hexadecimal, a comma, then the string stored in the variable yourcomment. A full description of the printf function and the various formats can be found in a XENIX manual or a book on the C language.

Fprintf is the general routine for writing formatted output to a specified file according to a specified format. Its first argument specifies the file, and the remaining arguments are the same as for printf.

## Buffer Control

I/O devices such as keyboards and disks often require temporary storage areas called *buffers*. Buffers are necessary because I/O generally comes and goes at rates of speed that the CPU cannot efficiently handle. Buffers store these characters in a fixed sized block while they are waiting to be processed or sent somewhere else.

In particular, a keyboard produces characters one by one in an irregular pattern at a rate much slower than the CPU could handle them. On the other hand, the disk system sends and receives fixed sized blocks of a thousand or so characters at speeds faster than the CPU might be able to handle them.

When keyboard input is buffered, each character you type is not immediately available to functions like getchar. Instead, you have to wait for a **return** at the end of a line of text before getchar returns any characters from that line. This is not appropriate for character-oriented applications such as editors, but it does have the advantage that a line of text can be modified with such actions as *delete character* (usually **backspace**) while the line is still being entered. The system automatically takes care of this editing, relieving your program of the responsibility.

Fortunately for applications that require it, there is also a way to make characters immediately available as soon as they are typed. You can use the setbuf routine to turn off buffering for the stdin stream when your program first starts up. In general, setbuf allows you to specify your own buffer for any open file. The first argument specifies the file, and the second argument is a pointer to the desired buffer. To turn off buffering for the file, make the buffer pointer in the second argument a null (zero) value.

### End of File Detection

The function feof can be used to determine when a file ends. It has a single parameter that is a file pointer. Feof returns an integer, which is zero as long as the file has not completely been read and nonzero when the end of the file has been reached. For standard input, the end of file condition is true after **return** or **enter** is pressed.

### Standard Error Stream

In addition to standard input and output streams, the stream stderr transmits errors to the user independently of where the standard output has been sent. It goes to the screen. From a command line in the C shell, it is possible to send the standard error stream to the same place as the standard output stream. From a command line in the Bourne shell, it is possible to send the standard error stream to any file.

## Programming Filters

Now let's look in detail at some filters. We start with a trivial example written in C, then we explore some filters provided with XENIX.

### Writing Filters in C

Our first example is a C program that just passes its input unchanged to its output. Such a program may seem completely useless. However, it can be used to copy files from one place to another. Later we see how filters that are already in the system do this and more.

Here is the C program:

```
/*    trivial filter program */

#include<stdio.h>

main()
  {
  int c;
  while ((c=getchar())!=EOF) putchar(c);
  }
```

Let's examine it in detail. The line

```
#include<stdio.h>
```

causes the standard I/O header file stdio.h to be included, providing all the features of standard I/O discussed previously. The angle brackets (< and > around the file name stdio.h indicate that the compiler should find this include file in the system's standard directory for include files. This happens to be /usr/include (see figure 4-6). If you enclose an include file name in double quotes rather than angle brackets, the compiler tries to find the file in your current working directory.

Our filter program essentially consists of a main function that is a while loop. This loop continues as long as the end of file character has not been received from the standard input. Each time through this loop, a single character is fetched from standard input and sent to standard output.

The int c; statement before the while loop declares the variable c to be an integer to match the output data type of the getchar function.

Let's look at the while statement in more detail. In the conditional part, the variable c is assigned the result returned from the function getchar and this is also compared to the constant EOF, which indicates the end of the file. The while loop continues as long as the function result and the constant EOF are not equal.

In the action part of the while statement, the integer ASCII code in c is sent to the standard output via the putchar function. The compiler automatically converts ASCII codes into their corresponding characters during the function call.

Assuming that we have entered this program in the system under the file name simple.c, we can compile it with the following command

```
cc simple.c
```

which produces a file called a.out.

Before we give a.out a better name, let's test it. We type:

```
% a.out◄┘
This is a test of our simple filter.◄┘
```

As soon as we press the final **return**, a second copy of the line of text "This is a test of our simple filter." appears just below the first. To end the session, type a **control d**.

The first copy of the text is produced by standard input as we type the individual characters. However, these characters are stored in a buffer until you press **return** at the end of the line. The second copy is produced by standard output once it gets the characters.

Let's rename the `a.out` file with the command:

```
mv a.out textcopy
```

With the aid of I/O redirection, we can use this command as its name suggests.

First let's use it to create a file. Try typing:

```
% textcopy >mytext◄┘
This is a line of text,◄┘
and this is a second line of text.◄┘
<control d>
```

Then the file `mytext` contains these two lines of text. Remember that each line of text ends with a **return,** and the entire text entry ends with a **control d.**

We can use our newly created `textcopy` command to list the file as well. For example, the command line

```
textcopy <mytext
```

prints the file `mytext` on the screen.

Finally, we can use this command to copy the contents of one file to another. For example, the command line

```
textcopy <mytext >yourtext
```

copies the contents of the file `mytext` to the file `yourtext`. You can, of course, use `textcopy` to verify this.

## Using Standard Filters

Most simple text processing tasks have already been developed for XENIX and are available to the ordinary user. The job that our `textcopy` does is no exception.

Let's look at some of the simple filters that come with XENIX. Some of the standard filters are: `tr`, `grep`, `egrep`, and `fgrep`. We see how these do what our `textcopy` program does and more. We also look at `sort`. These programs are typically written in C, but their source code is not included with the system.

**Using Tr—**`Tr` is a filter that transfers characters from the standard input to the standard output, substituting certain characters for others as specified in the command line. Its name is short for *translate* and it is, in effect, a character translation program. It converts text character by character according to a set of rules.

Without any parameters `tr` transfers characters directly without any substitutions. However, `tr` also can be "programmed" to perform a number of variations on the theme of character substitutions. For example, it can be programmed to perform the first stage of the spelling checker mentioned earlier, namely separating each word in the document and placing it on its own line of text.

Let's start with `tr` with no parameters. In this case, it sends characters from standard input straight through to standard output. Without any redirection, it prints each line you type on the keyboard to the screen--just like our `textcopy` program. Each character appears twice, once as it is being typed and again as the entire line is sent to standard output. For example, if you type

```
% tr◄┘
This is a line of text.◄┘
```

a second copy of the line

```
This is a line of text.
```

appears under the first. Like our own `textcopy` program, it can be used to create files, display files, and copy files.

You can see that with redirection, tr becomes a useful file utility. Most people use cat to perform these same functions. Although cat is not a true filter (because it normally accepts input from a file), it can be used as a filter if it is invoked with no parameters (excepting, of course, redirection commands).

Now let's look at how tr can be used in a nontrivial manner to do more than simply copy characters. Tr can accept any combination of three option flags, and it can accept zero, one, or two string parameters.

Without any option flags, the characters in the first string are replaced by the corresponding characters in the second string. For example, the command line

```
tr 'abcd' 'ABCD' <myfile
```

prints the file myfile on the screen, substituting uppercase equivalents only for the characters a, b, c, and d. Although not always necessary, it is a good idea to place single quotes around all strings in a command line. This prevents the shell from interpreting special characters such as *, [, or ] that we may want to pass without modification to tr.

Perhaps you wish to replace all lowercase characters with their uppercase equivalents. It would be awkward to type the entire alphabet twice, once in lowercase, then again in uppercase. Instead, you can use a range specifier.

Ranges of characters can be indicated with square brackets. For example, the command line

```
tr '[a-z]' '[A-Z]' <myfile >yourfile
```

translates all lowercase characters of myfile to uppercase and places the result in yourfile.

Finite or infinite repetitions of a character also can be indicated with square brackets ([]). For example, [X*6] stands for the string XXXXXX (that's six Xs). This is useful in the second string when a whole range of characters in the first string is to be replaced by a single character in the second string. The number following the * gives the repetition count. If it begins with a zero, it is in octal. Otherwise it uses decimal notation. If this number is missing or has a zero value, it is assumed to be infinite. For example, if you wanted to replace every character in the first string by an X, you would make the second string equal to [X*], which stands for

```
[XXXXXXXXXX...]
```

where the three dots represent an endless series of Xs. This means that all characters in the first string are converted to one of these Xs.

A special character, such as newline (which is normally triggered by pressing **return**) or tab, can be indicated with a backslash (\) followed by its ASCII code in octal. For example

```
tr ' ' '\011' <assmfile
```

replaces all spaces by the tab character (octal 011 = decimal ASCII code 9).

The −c option flag allows you to specify the set of characters *not* to convert. That is, the c stands for the *complement* of the given set of characters. For example

```
tr -c '[a-z][A-Z]' '[\012*]' <mytest
```

prints out the file mytest on the screen, replacing all nonalphabetical characters by the octal 012, which is decimal 10 ASCII or **control j**, the linefeed character. This is XENIX's newline character. The ∗ indicates infinite repetition of the linefeed character in the second string. This has the effect of putting each word on a new line, but things like multiple spaces cause lines to be double-spaced or worse.

Another option flag is -d. This causes all characters in the first string to be deleted from the output. For example

```
tr -d ' ' <mytest
```

prints the file mytest on the screen, deleting all spaces.

The third and final option is −s. This causes repeated substitute characters to be replaced by a single copy of that character. It can be used in combination with other options such as −c. For example

```
tr -cs '[a-z][A-Z]' '[\012*]' <mytest
```

prints the file on the screen, replacing all series of nonalphabetical characters by a single newline character. This has the effect of putting each word in the file on a separate line of the output. Recall that this is the first step of the spelling checker.

It would not be hard to write a C program that performs the actual character translation. Such a program would use a table stored in memory to look up a new ASCII code for each character. However, it would be much more difficult to write a C program that would set up this translation table according to specifications such as those used by tr. Thus, special cases of tr are easy to create, but its full power would take significant effort to match.

**Using Grep, Egrep, and Fgrep**—The grep family of programs provide a way to find matching patterns in lines of one or more files. They all can be used as filters. Generally, they print all lines that contain a specified pattern. For example the command line

```
% grep 'XENIX'◄┘
```

prints out lines of input that contain the word *XENIX*. The grep family is useful for doing such things as searching the password file for somebody's name or searching all the include files in /usr/include for a particular variable name.

The name grep stands for g/re/p, which means "globally match regular expression and print." The three different versions of grep vary in the type of pattern matching commands they accept and the type of string matching algorithms they use.

Egrep is a bit more powerful than grep both in commands and in the speed of the algorithm. However, egrep tends to take up more memory when executing.

Fgrep searches for fixed strings but runs fast and takes up little space.

In general, these commands have a number of options, including ignoring upper- and lowercase or reporting all lines not matched. After these options, they expect a string expression that describes the patterns to match. Finally, there is a list of files to search through. If no files are listed, standard input is used, making them filters. For example

```
grep -y 'report'
```

prints out all lines of input that contain the word *report* ignoring case.

In any case, the output of these grep programs goes to standard output, thus making these programs filters in this default case.

Let's start with fgrep because it has the simplest pattern matching commands, namely fixed strings. In following text, we investigate the more complicated cases possible with grep and egrep.

When fgrep is used with no parameters, it specifies no strings to match and operates on standard input. This means that it acts just like our trivial filter. That is, the command line

```
fgrep
```

produces the same results as textcopy, tr, or cat.

If we specify a string parameter for fgrep, we can use it to print only those lines that contain a copy of this string. For example

```
fgrep 'is' <mytext
```

prints out only those lines in myfile that contain the string is.

If you need to search for a list of strings, you can use the -f option to specify a file where the strings are located. In this case, fgrep would report whenever any of the strings matched. For example, if the file "matches" contained the following lines

```
is
the
```

the command

```
fgrep -f matches <mytext
```

would print out all the lines of mytext that contain *is* or *the*. If a line contains both strings, it is printed only once.

So far, we have only examined fixed strings. Now let's look at the string expressions that grep and egrep can handle. These are called *regular expressions*. Various varieties of regular expressions are used in editors and string matching programs throughout XENIX in such places.

Grep uses what is called *limited* regular expressions, and egrep uses a somewhat more powerful set called *full* regular expressions.

Regular expressions are defined according to a set of rules, starting with expressions for single character matches. These single character matching expressions then can be formed into matching expressions according to another set of rules.

Single character matching expressions can consist of any regular character (not including the characters [, ], ^, $, and \). These special characters can be used to indicate special kinds of matching situations.

A backslash ( \ ) is used to make an expression that matches a special character literally. Place the backslash in front of the special character. You can also match tabs, backspaces, and newlines with \t, \b, and \n respectively.

The square brackets ([ ]) enclose choices of characters. For example, [abc] stands for the choice of a, b, or c. Ranges can be indicated with a hyphen, even in combination with other choices. For example, [abc0-9] indicates the choice of a, b, c, or any digit.

An empty string inside square brackets is not allowed. In fact, a right square bracket immediately following a left square bracket is assumed to be one of the choices!

A caret (^) is used in two ways: 1) at the beginning of an entire string expression to indicate that the string expression is to match the beginning of the line, and 2) at the beginning of a string enclosed in square brackets to complement the set of choices given in the square brackets (to match all characters that are *not* in the string).

A dollar sign ($) is used at the end of a string expression to indicate that the string expression is to match the end of the line.

A period (.) is used to indicate a match of any one character sequence except newline.

Multicharacter regular expressions can be constructed from one character regular expressions in a number of ways that we describe next.

A one character regular expression is a special case of a regular expression.

A one character regular expression followed by an asterisk (*), is a regular expression that matches zero or more repetitions of the one character regular expression.

The special combinations \{ and \} are used to bracket ranges for matching repetitions of one character regular sequences. That is, if *m* and *n* are non-negative integers, then \{m\} indicates exactly m repetitions,

\{m,\} indicates at least m repetitions, \{m,n\} indicates at least m repetitions and at most n matches. These modifiers are placed after the one character regular expressions that they modify. For example X\{2,5\} indicates exactly 2, 3, 4, or 5 repetitions of the character *X*.

A sequence consisting of one or more regular expressions is itself a regular expression.

The special combinations \( and \) are used to bracket regular subexpressions that then can be referenced later with a special combination \n, where *n* is a single digit indicating one of as many as nine (possibly nested) subexpressions. For example, the expression abc\(1234\)de\1\1 expands to abc1234de12341234. It has one copy of 1234, some other characters, then two repetitions of it.

Finally, the caret (^) can begin a regular expression to indicate that matching must start at the beginning of the line, and a dollar sign ($) can end a regular expression to indicate that matching must happen all the way to the end of the line. For example, the expression ^This is the line$ must match the line This is the line exactly.

Combining all these special controls can lead to some pretty intricate and powerful string matching expressions. For example, the expression ^\([A-Za-z \.]*\)\1$ matches lines that contain exactly two repetitions of a string consisting of alphabetical characters, spaces, and periods.

We can use such expressions with grep. For example

```
grep '^\([A-Za-z \.]*\)\1$'
```

acts as a filter that sends all lines that match the above string expression.

Unfortunately, egrep does not work with the \(\) expressions, but it has other operators such as + (one or more repetitions of an expression).

**Sort**—Sort is another example of a filter supplied with XENIX. As its name implies, it takes its input (standard input if no files are specified), sorts it, and sends the result to standard output. It can also merge files if several files are listed as input.

The sort program has a number of option flags that control such things as the order of the sort, upper- and lowercase distinctions, and the character positions of the sorting key field within the line.

Here is an example:

```
% sort◄┘
here◄┘
is◄┘
a◄┘
list◄┘
of◄┘
words◄┘
in◄┘
```

```
lowercase◄┘
control d
```

produces the following output

```
a
here
in
is
list
lowercase
of
words
```

A more elaborate example would be

```
sort -t\; +1 -2 <shapes
```

where shapes contains the following

```
1;point
2;line
3;curve
4;circle
5;square
6;rectangle
```

would produce the list:

```
4;circle
3;curve
2;line
1;point
6;rectangle
5;square
```

In the command line, the −t option says that a semicolon (;) separates the fields. Notice that a backslash (\) precedes the semicolon, making sure that this semicolon is literally passed to sort. Otherwise, XENIX would think that the semicolon separated the command line into two separate commands.

Next, the +1 −2 specifies the key fields. Field numbers begin with zero. This combination says that to form the sorting key, use field number one (the second field) up to but not including field number two. Notice that the resulting list has this field in order, even though field zero is now out of order.

**Other Filters**—XENIX has other filter programs. The program sed (which stands for *stream editor*) is a programmable filter. The programs for sed are editing commands, much like ex mode commands of vi. Actually, they conform more to the line editing program ed.

An example is the command line:

```
% sed -e 's/integer/real/g' <test01 >test01.new◄┘
```

It causes the contents of the file test01 to be read, substituting all instances of integer with the word real, and placing the modified text in the file test01.new.

The -e option for sed specifies that an editing command follows on the command line. In this case, the editing command is the substitute command: 's/integer/real/g'. The initial s stands for *substitute*. It is followed by slashes (/) that delimit a regular string expression and a literal string. The regular expression (in this case, integer) matches the strings that are to be replaced, and the literal string (in this case real) specifies the string to replace them. The final g indicates that this process is to be done "globally," that is, for all nonoverlapping matching instances in the input.

If we don't specify a file for input, sed reads its input from the standard input. Here, we have redirected the input from the file test01 and output to the file test01.new.

The sed program accepts many other editing commands, but we do not discuss them here. With the -f option, these commands can even be specified in a separate file.

The program awk can also serve as a filter. The name awk is comprised of the initials *a, w,* and *k* of its developers: A. V. Aho, P. J. Weinberger, and B. W. Kernighan. Awk is useful for extracting and rearranging information from files that are organized in tabular form, such as the password file or a mailing list. It processes each line of a file according to specified rules that operate on the various fields in that line. Here is an example of its use. The command line

```
awk -F: '{print $1}' </etc/passwd
```

prints the login name for each account on the system.

For the awk command, the -F option specifies the field separator, which in this case is a colon (:). The quoted string indicates an action to take. In this case '{print $1}' specifies that the first field should be printed. For the password file, this is the login name.

The awk command has other options, including the -f option that specifies a file from which it reads instructions. Instructions to awk form a pro-

programming language with variables, arithmetic and relational operators, control structures, and built-in functions. With it, you can compose reports or build data tables that people and other programs can use.

## Putting Filters Together

Now that we have a variety of filters, let's show how to put them together to make larger programs. We present a spelling checker program, designed along the lines laid out in the beginning of this chapter.

The first step is to place each word on a separate line. To do this, use the `tr` command in the form:

```
tr -cs '[a-z][A-Z]' '[\012*]'
```

As we saw earlier, this replaces multiple occurrences of nonalphabetic characters by newlines.

The next step is to translate all lowercase letters to uppercase. This can also be done with the `tr` command:

```
tr '[a-z]' '[A-Z]'
```

Sorting comes next with the `sort` command

```
sort
```

Now we have to remove multiple occurrences of words. The system command `uniq` does this:

```
uniq
```

We can connect the commands with the pipeline symbol ¦, making the output for each command go to the input for the next command. We put what we have so far in a script file called `speller`. For more details on script files, see Chapter 3. We use the backslash (\) to continue the command line onto several lines. Here is our `speller` script:

```
#spelling checker - extracts words
tr -cs '[a-z][A-Z]' '[\012*]' ¦\
tr '[a-z]' '[A-Z]' ¦\
sort ¦\
uniq ¦\
```

This accepts text from the standard input and sends a sorted, capitalized list to the standard output. If `sptest` is a text file containing the text

```
This is a test of the spelling progrm. The output is reedy to
check against the distionary.
```

the command line

```
% speller <sptest◄┘
```

produces the list:

```
A
AGAINST
DISTIONARY
IS
OF
OUTPUT
PRGRAM
REEDY
SPELLING
TEST
THE
TO
```

It looks like we really do need a spelling checker!

The final step is to match the results against a dictionary. This can be done with the XENIX comm command that compares two files and prints the differences. Unfortunately, this is not a filter. We must direct the output of our speller to a file, then use comm to compare this file against the dictionary. We can use the −23 option of comm to show only the words in our list that do not match the dictionary. Here is how the complete job looks:

```
% speller <sptest >sptmp◄┘
% comm −23 sptemp mydictionary◄┘
DISTIONARY
PRGRAM
REEDY
```

This displays the misspelled words DISTIONARY, PRGRAM, and REEDY. We use a temporary file sptmp to hold the word list for comm.

### Writing Filters Using Tools Such as Lex

Now let's see how to write filter programs using lex. The name Lex stands for *Lexical Analyzer*. With lex, we specify the pattern matching that we wish, and lex generates the appropriate C program.

**A Quick Example**—Let's start with a program equivalent to our `textcopy` program. Here is the `lex` program:

```
%%
. ECHO;
```

We look at `lex` syntax in detail in following text, but let's preview this particular program now.

Each `lex` program has three parts: a definitions section, a rules section, and a user routines section. The `%%` separates the sections. In our case, the `%%` separates the first section (empty in this case) from the second part. This separator is always necessary.

If the third part (user routines) is empty (as it is in this case), no separator is needed after the second (rules) section.

Our program consists of a single rule:

```
. ECHO
```

This rule looks for arbitrary characters and prints them to the standard output stream.

The period (.) is a string matching expression that matches any character except newline, and ECHO is a C macro that prints whatever was found in the matching process. `ECHO` is defined in the `lex.yy.c`. We explain how this works in following text.

Suppose this is stored in a file called `trilex.l`. To turn it into a running program, you must first translate it into a C program via the command:

```
% lex trilex.l◄┘
```

The result is a C program stored in a file in `lex.yy.c`. To compile this, you should use the command:

```
% cc lex.yy.c -ll◄┘
```

Now you have an executable program called `a.out` that acts as a trivial filter. The `-ll` option causes the system (in particular, the linker) to search the Lex library for routines such as `main` to turn our code into a stand-alone program. Lex is often used in conjunction with yacc (discussed in Chapter 10) to produce a function that is part of a larger program.

You can test this program out, then rename it if you would like to keep it.

Now let's look at how lex programs work and develop some interesting examples.

**Lex Rules**—Let's start with a discussion of lex rules. Each lex rule has two parts: the first is a string matching expression and the second is a C action. The string matching expressions are similar to but even more elaborate than those available under the grep family.

The C action can be any valid C statement (or multiple C statements in curly brackets). Lex provides a number of variables that can be used in these action statements. Incidentally, lex can be used to create programs in certain other languages such as Ratfor. In that case, the action statements would be written in that language and the command line to "lex" the program would be a little different.

**Word Substitutions**—We now demonstrate some simple pattern substitutions that can be done rather nicely with lex. Our program replaces all occurrences of the string zero by the digit *0,* all occurrences of the string one by the digit *1,* and so on through the string nine. All other text is copied as is.

Here is the example:

```
%%
zero   printf("0");
one    printf("1");
two    printf("2");
three  printf("3");
four   printf("4");
five   printf("5");
six    printf("6");
seven  printf("7");
eight  printf("8");
nine   printf("9");
```

The string matching expressions are simple strings of ordinary characters, and the actions are simple formatted print statements to standard output.

This example, unfortunately, replaces occurrences of these strings in the middle of words as well as for whole words. It is possible to write a Lex program that would handle this situation in a reasonable way. The problem is in coming up with an appropriate definition.

**Inserting Material Before Each Line**—Now let's look at a program to insert a tab before each line:

```
%%
^. printf("\t%s", yytext);
```

As we discussed previously, an initial caret (^) in a string matching expression begins matching at the beginning of a line. The period (.) indicates any character except newline. Here we are looking for a beginning of a nonempty line.

In the action part, a string expression is printed that has a tab character followed by the string yytext, which is where the matching character is stored. You can use this string variable in your programs.

The line number is another variable that is available to the Lex programmer. It is stored as the variable yylineno. Here is an example Lex program to insert the line number, a colon, and a tab before each line:

```
%%
^.*\n printf("%d:\t%s", yylineno-1, yytext);
```

The pattern matching expression is ^.*\n. It matches an entire line, empty or nonempty. The initial caret (^) says that the match must begin at the beginning of a line. The period (.) stands for an arbitrary character that is not a newline character. The asterisk (*) says that this character may be repeated zero or more times. The newline \n indicates that the pattern includes the newline at the end of the line. If we used a dollar sign ($) in this spot, each line would be counted twice.

The action statement is a formatted print statement. It prints the expressions yylineno-1 and yytext according to the format %d:\t%s. Notice that the line number yylineno must be decremented by one because the line count increases after the newline character is found. In the format, %d indicates that the line number should be printed as an integer in decimal notation, the : is an actual colon, the \t indicates a tab, and the %s indicates that the second expression yytext should be printed as a string.

Lex has many other features that we have not even touched on, but this introduction should give you some idea of its power in making custom filters.

**How Lex Programs Work**—The C programs that lex creates for you are table driven with a relatively small amount of code. That is, most of the programming is controlled by tables of data associated with the program.

The main task is to match string expressions. When you "lex" your program, lex converts these expressions to a tree structure called a *transition diagram* that is stored in tables as part of the resulting C program. For example, figure 4-7 gives the transition diagram for the name-to-number filter given above.

Each leaf of this tree represents a successful search. The leaves are assigned numbers that drive a switch statement which houses the various C action statements given in your original lex program.

**Figure 4-7**
**A matching tree**

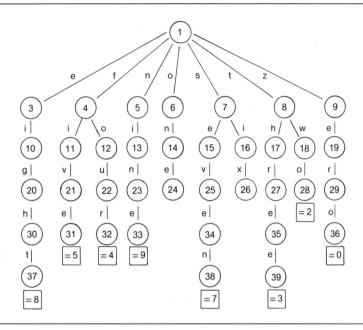

Because the resulting C programs are driven by data, much of the code is common to all programs produced by lex. Table-driven programs tend to work well once a moderate level of complexity has been reached. However, for a trivial case like our first lex program, it is definitely overkill.

# Summary

In this chapter we have discussed filters, the fundamental working programs in a XENIX system. These programs operate on standard input and send it out, transformed, to standard output. We discussed how filters can be used to solve programming problems; how to program them in C; how to use existing filters, such as tr, grep, and sort that come with the XENIX operating system; and how to use the lex program to quickly design your own custom filters.

In Chapter 10, we see how the lex program can be used in a different context to build C functions that recognize strings. The functions pass on numerical values called *tokens* depending on what strings they find. This is the first stage in constructing a language translation program.

# Questions and Answers

## Questions

1. What is a filter?
2. Why are filters useful in XENIX?
3. Can you write your own filter in XENIX?
4. Name several XENIX utilities that can be used as filters.
5. Write a Lex program to change double-spaced text into single-spaced text.

## Answers

1. A filter is a program that takes input from a single source and sends it to a single destination. In XENIX the source should be the standard input and the destination should be the standard output.

2. Filters are useful in XENIX because they allow a large class of complicated jobs to be broken into a series of small, simple steps that can be performed by general purpose utilities. Using pipelines or ordinary files with I/O redirection, output from one step can be easily sent to the input of the next step or conveniently stored for future processing.

3. Yes, you can write filter programs in a language such as C. Such programs use standard I/O functions from the standard C library to handle their input and output. You can also use Lex to write filter programs.

4. Some XENIX utilities that can act as filters are: `tr`, `sort`, `grep`, `egrep`, `fgrep`, `sed`, and `awk`.

5. Here is a Lex program to change double-spaced text into single-spaced text:

```
%%
"\n\n" {printf("\n");}
```

# 5

# System Variables

- The Environment
- Shell Variables
- Using Shell Variables in Scripts
- Summary
- Questions and Answers

# System Variables

This chapter explains *shell* and *environmental* variables and *parameter* passing. XENIX handles all of these as *string variables*. Using string variables for these has the advantage over using numerical variables, in that many different types of information, including both numerical and string, can be stored and handled in a uniform manner. Conversions between string and numerical types can be performed by the system and the user as needed.

Shell and environmental variables are used to set up an environment that controls how your commands are interpreted. This applies to both existing system programs and programs that you write. In this chapter, we explore these variables in detail, and see how to use them and pass them along from process to process in the system.

## The Environment

Let's begin with environmental variables. Each *process* has its own *environment*. The environment is a list of string variables that is passed along with any command parameters. A process then can access these variables via addresses passed to it as arguments for its main program.

The environmental variables contain useful information about the user to whom that particular process belongs. They specify such things as the user's home directory, path for searching for commands, and starting shell.

When a user logs on, the system spawns a process that runs the user's *shell*. This shell process is the user's primary process, the one from which all other of the user's processes descend. The environment attached to this process is the user's primary environment.

The system sets up the starting environment for the shell process. This includes the user's home directory HOME, the initial path to the user's commands PATH, the current terminal type TERM, a speed variable HZ (hertz) that gives the number of times per second that the system timer interrupts the CPU, the time zone TZ, and the initial shell SHELL.

Right after a shell starts up, it executes some scripts that may redefine these string variables and set others. These additional variables may include `MAIL` and `TERMCAP`. `MAIL` specifies a path to a file that contains incoming mail, and `TERMCAP` is a copy of the `termcap` entry (see Chapter 6). These scripts can be modified by the user or system manager to customize the user's operating "environment."

When a new process is launched, it normally "inherits" its environment from the original process. We study this phenomenon in subsequent text.

Certain programs, such as the shell, mail, and editor programs, use environmental variables to determine how to act. For example, programs in Chapter 6 that involve terminal I/O use, `TERM` and `TERMCAP`. We present a program later in this chapter that uses `PATH` to find commands in the directory system.

### Structure of an Environment

Environment consists of an array of pointers to strings. The last pointer is null, which signifies the end of the list.

Each string consists of a name, followed by an equal sign (=) and a value. The entire string is terminated by a zero byte. Thus, the *name* of the variable is packed into the string together with its *value*, separated by the equal sign.

Our next example demonstrates this structure and shows how it relates to parameter passing. In this short "warm up" exercise, we do not need to pass any arguments to this command. In a subsequent C program we will.

### Example C Program to Display Environment

Let's look at a C program that displays its environment. When you invoke this program as a command, it displays the addresses and contents of its environment variables. You should be aware that these addresses are relative to the value of the data segment pointer (the DS register for the 8086 or 8088 CPU), which is generally different for each process running in the machine.

```
@65258: HOME=/usr/morgan
@65275: PATH=:/usr/morgan/bin:/bin:/usr/bin
@65311: TERM=unknown
@65324: HZ=20
@65330: TZ=PST8PDT
@65341: SHELL=/bin/csh
@65356: TERMCAP=au¦a1000:co#80:li#23:am:bs:cm=\E=%+\040%+\040:
ho=\E\040\040:ce=\E\001\021:cd=\E\001\022:cl=^L:so=\E\004\025
0\024a:se=\E\004\025a\0240:us=\E\002\024J:ue=\E\002\0240
```

Here is a listing of the `showenv` command::

```
/* program to show environment */
main(argc, argv, envp)
    int argc;
    char *argv[]
    char *envp[];
    {
    int i=0;
    char *ptr;
    while (ptr=envp[i++])
printf("@%u: %s\n", ptr, ptr);
    }
```

The main program has two arguments to help pass parameters from the command line and a third to pass the environment. The first argument `argc` is an integer that specifies how many parameters were given, the second argument `argv` is an array of strings that are the actual parameters given in the command line, and the third parameter `envp` points to an array that holds the environment variables. This is how our process inherits its environment.

Notice that the arguments `argc`, `argv`, and `envp` are declared right after `main` is declared, but before its initial curly bracket. You can see that `argc` is an integer, and that `argv` and `envp` are pointers that point to a list of pointers which point to characters. This is what the combination of an asterisk (`*`) and `[]` mean literally. This combination is the standard mechanism used by C to handle arrays of strings. Other languages use pointers, but they often hide many of these details from the programmer. For example, normally a string array in BASIC, such as A$(5), is stored internally as an array of character counts and pointers to where the characters of the strings are actually stored.

Within the main program, an integer `i` and a string `ptr` are declared as local variables. This makes them only accessible to `main`.

The main program consists of a `while` loop that grabs a pointer from `envp`, advances to the next pointer, and prints its value as an unsigned integer (its address) and as a string (the characters that it points to). The `while` loop continues as long as the pointer is not null. Recall that a null pointer signifies the end of the list.

## Example System Commands

Fortunately, you really don't need to write a C program to examine your environment. The `env` command (without any parameters) does this for you, providing a display much like the one from our `showenv` command, but without the address information. Here is a typical output from `env`.

```
HOME=/usr/morgan
PATH=:/usr/morgan/bin:/bin:/usr/bin
TERM=a1000
HZ=20
TZ=PST8PDT
SHELL=/bin/csh
TERMCAP=au¦a1000:co#80:li#23:am:bs:cm=\E=%+\040%+\040:
ho=\E=\040\040:ce=\E\001\021:cd=\E\001\022:cl=^L:so=\E
\004\0250\024⌐:se=\E\004\025⌐\0240:us=\E\002\024J:ue=\
E\002\0240
```

### Inheriting Environments

We have seen how our showenv program inherits an environment. In general, when the user runs a command from the shell (other than built-in shell commands), the shell spawns a new process to handle that command which inherits the environment of the shell (see figure 5-1).

**Figure 5-1**
**Inheriting environments**

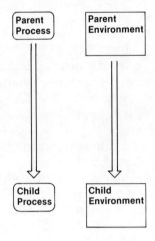

If this process spawns still another process, it normally passes the environment along, although you can modify the environment as it is passed along. It is quite possible for this to continue for some time. In fact, a shell can launch another shell, and so on.

You might notice that there are no C functions or non-shell commands to permanently change the environment. This is because each process can only change its own environment or the environment of the command that it is launching. Like genetic mutations, any changes to a particular command's environment can only be inherited "forward" and never "backward" to the parent shell.

## The Env Command

The `env` command can be used to assist with passing modified environments forward. For example:

```
% env "TEMP=HI THERE" showenv◄┘
```

executes our program `showenv` with an added environment variable `TEMP` that is equal to `HI THERE`. Notice that quotes are needed because of the space character in our string.

When this command line is executed, it displays the current shell environment plus the new environment variable `TEMP=HI THERE`. If you then type

```
% env◄┘
```

or

```
% showenv◄┘
```

you see the current shell environment, but without `TEMP=HI THERE` because the environment is inherited "forward" but never "backward."

The `env` command can also be used to start up a new copy of a shell with a specially modified environment. For example

```
% env TERM=unknown TERMCAP= csh◄┘
```

invokes a copy of the csh shell with an unknown terminal and a blank
**TERMCAP** descriptor. Notice that no quotes are needed around the string
variables because there are no spaces and other special characters in these
strings.

When you run commands, such as vi and more, from this copy of the
shell, you get different results than at other times. For example, vi assumes
that your terminal does not allow cursor motion on the screen and more
does not try to display its highlighted --More-- message at the bottom of
the screen. However, if you exit from this shell (by pressing control d or
typing the exit command), and return to the shell from which env was invoked, vi and more behave as they did previously.

### The Run Program

Various forms of the exec function can help the C programmer achieve results similar to those obtained from the env command. We illustrate this
with our next example, a C program called run. It works much like the env
command when it launches another command. Our run command executes
a specified program with a modified inherited environment.

The run program expects a list of arguments. The first ones specify
new or modified environmental variables that are to be added or replaced.
These are distinguished by the presence of equal signs (=). The remaining
arguments form the name of a command file and its arguments.

When run executes, it first displays the new environment that it is creating, numbering, and displaying each variable as it is processed. Next, run
displays the new set of arguments, starting with the name of the new command. Finally, it displays messages as it searches directories for the specified command file. It always searches the current directory first, then the
directories specified in the user's **PATH** variable. When it finds the file containing the command, it executes that command.

Let's try the following command line to illustrate how run works:

```
% run A=B TERM=unknown env showenv◄┘
```

First, comes the run command. Then the environmental variables A=B
and TERM=unknown, followed by the command env with an argument
showenv.

The output looks something like this:

```
Environment:
0: HOME=/usr/morgan
1: PATH=:/usr/morgan/bin:/bin:/usr/bin
2: TERM=a1000
3: HZ=20
4: TZ=PST8PDT
5: SHELL=/bin/csh
6: TERMCAP=au¦a1000:co#80:li#23:am:bs:cm=\E=%+\040%+\040:
ho=\E\040\040:ce=\E\001\021:cd=\E\001\022:cl=^L:so=\E\00
4\025O\024a:se=\E\004\025a\0240:us=\E\002\024J:ue=\E\002\
0240
7: A=B
2: TERM=unknown

Arguments:
env
showenv

Paths: :/usr/morgan/bin:/bin:/usr/bin
Name: env

Searching for env
Searching for /usr/morgan/bin/env
Searching for /bin/env
a65258: HOME=/usr/morgan
a65275: PATH=:/usr/morgan/bin:/bin:/usr/bin
a65311: TERM=unknown
a65324: HZ=20
a65330: TZ=PST8PDT
a65341: SHELL=/bin/csh
a65356: TERMCAP=au¦a1000:co#80:li#23:am:bs:cm=\E=%+\040%+\040:
ho=\E\040\040:ce=\E\001\021:cd=\E\001\022:cl=^L:so=\E\004\025
O\024a:se=\E\004\025a\0240:us=\E\002\024J:ue=\E\002\0240
a65529: A=B
```

Let's go through this output slowly. You might notice that this output
is much more verbose than usual for XENIX commands because our version of run is designed to educate rather than be used as a normal command. With a bit of editing surgery, it could be made suitable for ordinary
use, but in that form it would duplicate the env command.

First, you see the modified environment being created. Variables such
as HOME, PATH, and TERM are read from the old environment. Then the new
variable A=B is added to the end of the list and the modification for TERM is
processed, replacing the old value. When the list is displayed later, everything is properly arranged.

Next, you see the two new arguments: env and showenv. The first is the new command and the second is its "first" argument, a command that eventually is executed by env.

Next, you see the PATH variable:

```
:/usr/morgan/bin:/bin:/usr/bin
```

the command name env, and a series of statements showing which particular paths are being searched.

Finally, you see the env showenv command being executed. It displays the output of showenv showing the new environment, including the new value of TERM and the new variable A=B.

Here is the program:

```
/* execute a program with a modified environment */

#define MAXENVC 100
char *getenv(), *strtok(), *strcat();

int envc;
char *envp[MAXENVC];

main(oldargc, oldargv, oldenvp)
    int oldargc;
    char *oldargv[];
    char *oldenvp[];
    {
    int i, argc;
    char **argv, paths[100], *dir;

    if (oldargc < 2) { printf("Too few arguments.\n"); exit(1);};

    printf("\nEnvironment:\n");

    /* insert old environment into new environment */
    for(i=0; (oldenvp[i] != 0) && envc<MAXENVC; i++)
        insertenv(oldenvp[i]);

    /* insert new variables from arg list into environment */
    for(i=1; (i<oldargc) && envc<MAXENVC; i++)
        if(!insertenv(oldargv[i])) break;

    /* set up new arg list */
    printf("\nArguments:\n");
    argc = oldargc - i;
    argv = &oldargv[i];
    for(i=0; i<argc; i++) printf("%s\n", argv[i]);
```

```
    /* find the new command's paths and name */
    strcpy(paths, getenv("PATH"));
    printf("\nPaths: %s\n", paths);
    printf("Name:  %s\n\n", argv[0]);

    /* search and execute new command */
    exec(0, argv);
    if(dir=strtok(paths,":")) exec(dir, argv);
    while(dir=strtok(0,":")) exec(dir, argv);
    }

/* insert variable into environment */
/* replace item if match, append if no match */
int insertenv(var)
    char *var;
    {
    int match = 0;
    int j;
    char ename1[1000], ename2[1000];

    strcpy(ename1,var);
    strtok(ename1,"=");
    if(!strtok(0,"=")) return 0;

    for(j=0; j < envc; j++)
       {
       strcpy(ename2,envp[j]);
       strtok(ename2,"=");
       if(strcmp(ename1, ename2) == 0)
          {
          printf("%d: %s\n", j, envp[j] = var);
          match = 1;
          }
       }
    if(!match)
       {
       printf("%d: %s\n", envc, envp[envc] = var);
       envc++;
       }
    return 1;
    }

/* search path and launch command */
exec(dir, argv)
    char *dir, *argv[];
    {
    char command[40];
```

```
if (!dir) sprintf(command, "%s", argv[0]);
else      sprintf(command, "%s/%s", dir, argv[0]);

printf("Searching for %s\n", command);
execve(command, argv, envp);
}
```

Let's go through the code for this program. It uses three external string functions `getenv`, `strtok`, and `strcat`. The first gets a single variable from the environment, and the others help with the computation of the path for the commands.

The integer `envc` is used to count the environmental variables, and the string array `envp` is used to store pointers to the new environmental variables. The `envp` is declared to have space for 100 string pointers, which should be enough to handle most environments.

**The Main Program**—The main program has three arguments: an integer `oldagc`, and two string arrays, `oldagv` and `oldenvp`. These access the original parameters and environment.

Several local variables are declared. The integer `i` is a general purpose indexing variable. The variables `argc` and `argv` form the arguments of the new command. We pass them to the new program through the system's `execve` function.

Two string variables `paths` and `dir` are also declared. They assist in computing paths to search for the command file.

The first statement of the main program makes sure that there are enough arguments. There must be at least two, one for the `run` command itself and one for the command it executes. If there are less than two, it aborts the program with an error message.

The next section of the program builds the new environment. First we insert the old environment into the new environment. A `for` loop indexes through the old environment, calling our `insertenv` routine to place each old variable into the new environment. In the following text, we study this routine. We have only allocated `MAXENVC` number of "slots" for variables in our new environment, thus we restrict the index i from going beyond this limit with the condition `envc<MAXENVC`. We also want to make sure that we stop at the end of the list of old variables, hence we also have the termination condition `oldenvp[i] != 0`.

Next we insert the new variables into the environment. We use a `for` loop that indexes, starting with i=1 to grab the first variable from the command line. The termination condition is similar to the one for the previous `for` loop, except that here we check to see whether i is less than the count `oldargc`. Each time through the loop we call `insertenv` to place the new variable in the environment. If this function returns false, indicating no equal sign (=), we "break" out of the `for` loop.

The next section of the main program computes and prints the arguments of the new command. The value of the index i immediately after the last for loop points to the name of the new command. Thus the expression oldargc – i becomes the new argument count argc, and the statement:

```
argv = &oldargv[i];
```

causes the pointer argv to point to the new command in the list of command arguments. Here the ampersand (&) computes a pointer to the ith argument. Thus the array argv of string pointers is a subset of the original array oldarg. One advantage of this approach is that we don't need additional storage for argv.

We then execute a for loop to print all of these arguments.

Next, we compute the paths to find the new command. We call strcpy to copy the PATH variable to our own local variable paths. We must copy this string because we will be inserting zeros into it as we pick out the individual directory paths in it. We use the getenv function to get PATH from the old environment. We print this value, then we print the command name as found in argv[0].

We begin by searching for the command in the current directory by calling our own routine exec. Its first parameter has a value of zero, which indicates that no directory is to prefix the command name. Its second parameter is argv. This contains the name of the command as its zeroth entry.

We call strtok to find the directory names in our paths variable. This routine extracts substrings (tokens) from a string given as the first parameter. The substrings are assumed to be separated by a character given by the second parameter. In this case, colons separate the directory paths within the PATH variable. Thus our second parameter is a colon (:). Later we use this same "token" routine to get the name of an environmental variable from its string definition.

We call strtok once, naming the string explicitly as its first parameter. This gets the first substring. Then we call it repeatedly with a value of zero to get subsequent substrings. A while loop controls the repeated applications of this routine. The while loop continues until strtok returns a value of zero. Each time that we get a possible directory pathname, we call our exec routine to search for and execute the command within that directory. If the command's name is found, the exec routine executes the command and never returns back to our run program. Otherwise it returns, ready to try the next path. If no path is successful, the run command returns to the shell.

**The Insertenv Routine**—The routine insertenv is defined next. It has one argument, a string pointer var that specifies the variable to be inserted into the new environment.

The routine has several local variables: match is an integer to help look for matches between the new variable and variables already placed in the environment, j is an integer used for indexing through the new environment, and ename1 and ename2 are strings for temporary storage of the environmental variables as we compare their names. Notice that ename1 and ename are each allocated 1000 bytes of storage to handle such large variables as TERMCAP definitions. (This is studied in the next chapter.)

The insertenv routine first calls strcpy to copy the new variable string var into ename 1 and calls strtok to find the *name* of this environmental variable within its defining string. In this case the string separator character is an equal sign (=). We can strtok again with a zero pointer to look for the right side of the equal sign. If the right-hand side doesn't exit, strtok returns with a zero (null) value, and we return from our routine with a value of zero. Thus we continue only if var is of the correct form.

Next a for loop runs through the current new environment. For each variable in the new environment, we call strcpy to copy it into ename2 and strtok to extract the variable name (the left side of the equal sign). The strtok routine replaces the equal sign with a zero, terminating the substring that consists of the name. We then call strcmp to compare the two names, ename1 and ename2. If the names are equal, we replace the current string with the new string and set the variable match to 1.

If we complete the entire for loop without finding a match, we place the new variable at the end of the environment, incrementing the count variable envc. We then return with a value of 1, indicating a successful placement of the new variable.

**The Exec Routine**—Next comes the exec routine. This prepares a call to the system's execve routine. It has two parameters: dir is a pathname and argv is a list of arguments. This routine has one local variable command, which is a string that contains the path to the command.

If dir is zero, we form the command name from just its name (as contained in argv[0]), otherwise we form the command name from the directory path in dir as well as the name in argv[0]. In either case we call sprintf to place the path in the string "command."

Finally, we call execve to attempt to execute the command. The execve command is just one version of the system's execute commands. See the XENIX Development System Reference Guide for more details. In this form, there are three parameters: a path to a command, a pointer to a list of arguments, and a pointer to a list of environmental variables. This last parameter is our new environment.

## Shell Variables

Each shell can have a set of variables distinct from its environment. These variables are stored as program variables within the shell. They may include copies of the environmental variables, plus others such as ignoreeof and noclobber, that affect the way the shell behaves. The first prevents the C shell from exiting when **control d** is entered, and the second prevents the shell from overwriting an existing file without special override commands. You can also create and use your own shell variables as string variables in shell scripts.

Shells have commands to examine and modify their variables and ways to move values from the shell variables to the environment. These commands vary from shell to shell. For example, under the Bourne shell, a shell variable may be defined with a simple assignment statement such as:

```
$TERM=a1000◄┘
```

(Notice the dollar sign ($) prompt that is used by the Bourne shell).

Under the C shell, the set command must be used like this:

```
% set TERM=a1000◄┘
```

In both shells, the set command with no parameters lists the shell variables.

For some shells, certain shell variables are copied automatically to the environment when they are changed. For example, under the C shell, a modification to term changes TERM.

## Using Shell Variables in Scripts

Shell variables can be used as program variables for shell scripts. Following is an example of a script for the C shell that searches the system's password file for a given set of login names. The names are read from a separate file that is specified by the user.

The example also illustrates some of the control structures available in the C shell and both file and interactive input to shell scripts.

Let's look at how this program runs. If the file loglist contains the following

```
root
bob
morgan
chris
Morgan
uucp
```

the output of our script program might look like

```
Checking login names in file: loglist◄┘
Searching for root in password file:
root:7wO4yuSbC/t3U:0:0:The Super User:/:/bin/sh
"root" found.

Searching for bob in password file:
"bob" not found.

Searching for morgan in password file:
morgan:j9JijX7ztTR1E:203:51:morgan's csh
account:/usr/morgan:/bin/csh
"morgan" found.

Searching for chris in password file:
"chris" not found.

Searching for Morgan in password file:
"Morgan" not found.

Searching for uucp in password file:
uucp::4:4:Account for uucp
program:/usr/spool/uucp:/usr/lib/uucp/uucico
"uucp" found.
```

The script first prompts the user for the name of the file containing the login names. Here we typed loglist. Then for each name in that file, it issues a message saying that it is searching for that name. If it finds the name, it prints out its entry from the password file. It then reports whether or not the name was found.

In a real situation, the loglist file might be a class list with the last and first names of 30 students, and the script might try to assign unique login names to each student, perhaps using each first name and some of each last name as needed. It might also go ahead and set up the account once a unique name has been found.

Here is the listing for our script:

```
# example script for C shell

echo "Checking login names in file: \c"
set lfile = `line`
set list = `cat $lfile`

foreach logname ($list)
   echo "\nSearching for $logname in password file:"
   grep "^${logname}:" /etc/passwd
```

```
        if($status) then
            echo "\""${logname}\" not found."
        else
            echo "\""${logname}\" found."
        endif
    end
```

The script begins with a comment line, a good idea in any programming environment. The first line uses the built-in echo command to print a prompt asking for the name of the file containing the names. The prompt is enclosed in double quotes to make the trailing \c work. This suppresses the usual ''newline'' character at the end of the echo, leaving the cursor at the end of this line.

The next line sets a variable lfile, reading its value from the output of the line command. This command is enclosed in backward quotes to cause its output to be used as part of the command line. The line command reads a line (terminated by a ''newline'') from the console.

Next we use set again to define the shell variable list as equal to the contents of the specified file. Here we enclose cat $lfile in backward quotes so that the output of cat applied to this file is used as part of the command line for the set command. Here the dollar sign ($) causes the lfile variable to be evaluated. Without the dollar sign ($), the word lfile would have been used literally in the cat command.

A foreach loop comes next. It uses the variable logname as a kind of indexing variable, setting it to each name in list in turn.

Within the loop, the echo command explains that we are searching for this particular name in the password file, and the grep command searches for it in /etc/passwd. Notice that the search pattern ^${logname}: is a bit complicated. The initial caret (^) character tells grep to look for the name only at the beginning of lines. The dollar sign ($) introduces the shell variable and the curly brackets separate it from the colon that follows it. The colon is needed to match the colon separating the login name from the next field of this entry in the password file. This ensures a match with complete login names. Otherwise, grep might be satisfied by matching just the first few letters of a name.

After grep, an if then else construction prints a message reporting the success of the match. Here the variable status contains the true/false result from grep. This result becomes the argument of the if. Notice the backslashes in front of the quotes to allow the quotes to be printed on the screen rather than being interpreted immediately.

The if then else is terminated with an endif and the foreach is terminated with an end. Notice that we have used indentation to make our script more readable.

## Summary

In this chapter we have studied environmental and shell variables. These variables are stored as strings within the computer's memory.

Environmental variables are attached to particular processes and are inherited along with command arguments from a process to its children.

Shell variables belong to a particular shell. They can be used as program variables in shell scripts and to control the way the shell itself behaves.

Our examples include C programs, simple system commands, and shell scripts that use and display these variables.

## Questions and Answers

### Questions

1. What is the difference between environmental variables and shell variables?

2. Is PATH a shell variable or an environmental variable? Why?

3. How can you find out the values of your shell and environmental variables?

4. Where are the shell and environmental variables stored?

5. What kind of programs can use these variables?

6. What kind of information is normally stored in these variables? Give three examples.

### Answers

1. Environmental variables are associated with each process and are inherited from process to process, whereas shell variables are associated with a particular copy of a shell program.

2. No. PATH is an environmental variable. Environmental variables customarily are written with all uppercase letters. Also, PATH can be used by any process (not just shell processes) to help launch another process. There is also a shell variable called path that contains the same information.

3. The env command can be used to display your environmental variables, and the set command can be used to display your shell variables. The echo command can be used to display individual environmental and shell variables.

4. Environmental variables for each process are stored in memory with the arguments of the command that launched the process. Shell variables are stored within a shell program.

5. Scripts and the shell itself use shell variables. Environmental variables can be passed to and used by any program. (This includes shell programs.)

6. Environmental variables store system and user information such as the path to the user's home directory, the paths to search for commands, the user's terminal type, and paths where mail is stored. Shell variables store some of the same information, plus information about how the shell is to behave and variables used by shell scripts.

# 6

# XENIX Screen and Keyboard: Curses and Termcap

- Screen Routines
- String I/O
- Terminal Capabilities
- Summary
- Questions and Answers

# XENIX Screen and Keyboard: Curses and Termcap

Providing an easy-to-use "human interface" for users is an increasingly important requirement for operating systems. Such a connection between machine and the humans that use it plays an important role in the overall productivity of the system.

This chapter describes screen and keyboard I/O. We study packages of terminal I/O routines called *curses* and *termcap*. These routines allow intelligent terminals to use such visually oriented programs as the vi editing program and the visual shell.

The curses and termcap programs were developed at the University of California, Berkeley, to support their vi screen editor. This editor relies on these routines for all of its screen editing capabilities. It just won't function as a screen editor if you tell the system that you have a "dumb" terminal. Instead, it remains in the line editor ex mode.

An accompanying public data file called termcap contains descriptions of almost every type of terminal that you might connect to a XENIX system. This makes it easy to attach new terminals. No new programs need be written. Only a new termcap data entry must be created. This can save hours of programming time, especially in large organizations where many types of terminals are required.

Because curses and termcap are implemented as function calls to system library routines, they make it convenient for any XENIX utility to fully use the screen and keyboard capabilities common to most modern computer terminals and workstations. These include the ability to clear and write text to selected portions of the screen, to scroll, to insert and delete lines, and to use special keys such as **home** and the arrow keys.

To better explain these facilities, we present three example programs: a program called turtle, which allows you to "drive" the cursor around the screen; a program called dialog, which allows a user to enter a mailing address by filling in blanks on the screen using simple editing commands; and a program called showterm, which shows the vital statistics about your terminal.

## Screen Routines

We start with some curses screen routines. They comprise one of several system libraries available to a C programmer. Other system libraries include the standard C library, which we have used in previous chapters; the termcap library, which supports curses; the standard math library, which contains such functions as sine and cosine; the lex library to support lex; and the yacc library to support yacc. These libraries are located within the directory /lib. The C compiler knows where they are and which ones to use when you provide on the command line the right hints to compile your program. For example, the −lm option invokes the standard math library and the −lcurses option invokes the curses library.

The functions in the curses library allow us to move a cursor around a screen.

### The Turtle Program

Let's introduce an example C program called turtle that demonstrates the most basic capabilities of curses. This program allows the user to "drive" around the screen using the the **h, j, k,** and **l** keys, just as you can with vi. See figure 6-1 for a sample screen.

**Figure 6-1**
**Output of turtle program**

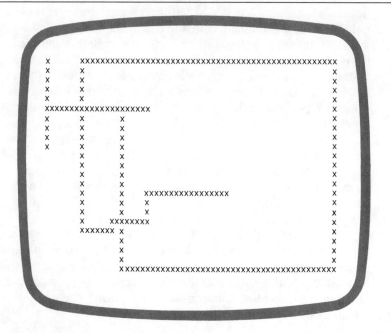

When this program starts, it clears the screen and displays an *x* in the upper left corner of the screen. To move down, press **j**; to move up, press **k**; to move right, press **l**; and to move left press **h**. As you move the cursor, a trail of *x* characters is printed on the screen.

The program "assumes" that you have an intelligent terminal, that is, one that can respond to cursor commands, and it "assumes" that the screen has at least 80 columns and 20 rows. Later in the chapter we will see how a program can read the `termcap` file to find these things out itself and take needed defensive action if such assumptions are not true.

Our program uses the `curses` header file and the associated library file `curses`, which in turn uses functions in the library file `termcap`. Accordingly, our program has the following include statement:

```
#include <curses.h>
```

and can be compiled as follows:

```
cc turtle.c -lcurses -ltermcap
```

Here is the program:

```
/* C program to move cursor around the screen */

#include <curses.h>
#define EOT 4

/* (x, y) is position on screen */
int x=1, y=1;

main()
    {
    char ch;

    /* set up screen and terminal I/O */
    initscr();
    crmode();
    noecho();
    nonl();

    /*clear screen and mark first position */
    clear();
    markit();

    /* main loop for moving around screen */
    while((ch=getch())!=EOT)
       switch(ch)
          {
```

```
            case 'h': if(x > 1) x--; markit(); break;
            case 'j': if(y < 20) y++; markit(); break;
            case 'k': if(y > 1) y--; markit(); break;
            case 'l': if(x < 78) x++; markit(); break;
            case 12: x=1; y=1; clear(); markit();
            }

     /* restore screen and terminal I/O */
     endwin();
   }

   /* routine to move cursor and mark it with an x */
   markit()
   {
      move(y, x);
      addch('x');
      addch('\b');
      refresh();
   }
```

Let's examine this program carefully because it demonstrates many of the most basic features of the curses and termcap packages. By studying it you can learn some of the basic ways the vi works. Perhaps you want to use this as a basis for your own screen editor.

The include directive causes the header file curses.h to be included in your program. The define statement defines a global constant EOT to have a value of 4 (the ASCII code for **control d**).

Two global variables x and y are declared to be integers and are both initialized to a value of 1. These hold the cursor position during the program.

The main part of the program declares one variable ch of type char. This variable is used to hold a character from the keyboard.

**Initialization**—The first few commands in the main program initialize the variables needed by the cursor routines and set up the keyboard I/O for interactive editing.

The initscr routine initializes the curses library. You must call this routine before you use any of these routines. It performs such duties as allocate and initialize a copy of a screen in memory, called the *standard* screen. All curses commands first write to this screen, and the results are later copied to the terminal as needed.

Having a copy of the screen in memory is very handy. It allows you to interrupt your programs that use curses, then return to them later with the screen exactly as you left it. The same kind of thing happens when you switch from one console user screen to another with the **alt** function-key combinations of SCO's version of XENIX. In this case, each console user has a separate copy of the screen in memory. When you switch console users, the next screen image is rapidly sent to the console screen. This process can happen so quickly because the actual physical screen is memory mapped. That is, the image that appears at each character position on the screen is stored as a code in the memory of the computer. Thus, changing screens merely involves moving blocks of data around in memory.

In the C program, the three `curses` function calls `crmode`, `noecho`, and `nonl` affect `stty` settings for communication to and from your terminal.

The `crmode` routine causes each character to be processed as soon as it is ready. Specifically, a newline character doesn't need to be present before each individual character is processed. As a result, this routine also turns off the usual editing for lines of keyboard input, such as deleting characters and killing lines.

The `noecho` routine suppresses the echoing for characters. Four different kinds of echoing actually are turned off by this routine: ordinary character echoing, backspacing while deleting characters, echoing newline characters, and echoing a newline on killing a line.

The `nonl` routine causes an ASCII 10 (the newline character) to be treated just like any other character. The normal situation is for this character to be "mapped" to a carriage return (ASCII 13), then a linefeed (ASCII 10—the "official" newline). Normally during input the **return** or **enter** (ASCII 13) key also is "mapped" to newline (ASCII 10). If this feature is on, some of our cursor commands get mauled on certain terminals.

In addition, there is a routine called `raw`, which is of no help to us in this program. In fact, using it would cause our program to "hang," and it would not even respond to the interrupt key. This routine completely ignores all of the special character mapping, including our cursor commands.

Each of these terminal mode setting routines has an opposite that reverses its effect.

From the shell, the `stty` command displays and allows you to set many terminal characteristics. It turns out that the `curses` routines affect various groups of terminal characteristics controlled by `stty`. For example, the `echo` and `noecho` routines control the `echo`, `echoe`, `echonl`, and `echok` terminal characteristics under `stty`'s control.

If you press the interrupt key (usually **delete** or ASCII 127), you return to the shell with your terminal in a rather terrible state: no echoing and no special handling of newline.

**Clearing the Screen**—The next routine, `clear`, clears the standard screen. However, the standard screen is merely a copy of the screen in memory. This is not enough to clear the terminal screen itself. We need to call a `curses` routine called `refresh` before the information is transferred from the standard screen to the actual screen. `Refresh` is called in our own routine `markit`, which is called next.

Our `markit` routine moves the cursor to row y and column x and places an *x* there. It also backspaces, returning the cursor to row y, column x. This routine follows the main program.

**The Main Loop**—The main loop comes next. It consists of a `while` loop that fetches a character using the `curses` routine `getch` and continues as long as this character is not EOT (ASCII 4). Inside the `while` loop a `switch` statement selects among five different actions depending on which character was fetched. In the first four cases (the cursor keys [**h, j, k,** or **l**]), it checks for a bounds limit for the cursor position. Then if the cursor is in bounds, it adjusts the x, y position accordingly and calls `markit` to update the actual screen. Finally, if the character is an ASCII 12 (formfeed), it clears the standard screen, resets x and y to 1, and calls `markit` to transfer this information to the actual screen.

**Closing Up**—After the `while` loop completes, the `curses` routine `endwin` is called to return the screen output and keyboard to the state they were in before the program was run. The main program then ends.

**Marking the Character Position**—Let's take a look at our `markit` routine. It first calls the `curses` routine `move` to move the cursor to position x, y. The arguments for this function are two integer variables: first the row position, then the column position. Recall that x and y are global variables, defined before the main program, thus the `markit` routine can refer to them freely.

Then the routine calls `addch` to place an *x* at the cursor position and calls `addch` a second time to backspace the cursor, returning it to position x, y. The `addch` routine has a single argument that is a character. Note that backspace is denoted by the escape sequence $\setminus b$.

Lastly, the `curses` routine `refresh` is called. It has no arguments. As we said earlier, its function is to refresh the terminal screen.

If we wanted to move the cursor around without marking its position, we would eliminate the two calls to `addch`. However, then there would be no "trail" of *x* characters.

# String I/O

Our next program illustrates some more `curses` routines, including ones to display strings arbitrarily placed on the screen. These routines form the basis for visually oriented interaction between users and computers, an increasingly more important part of modern computing environments.

## The Dialog Program

The example program called `dialog` helps a user enter a mailing address. It displays labels for the various parts of the address, including the first name, last name, street, city, state, and zip code. The user can type each part in a blank area following the label for that part (see figure 6-2).

In this program, pressing **return** moves the cursor to the next item. Pressing **return** while on the last item moves the cursor to the first item.

**Figure 6-2**
**Screen layout for** dialog **program**

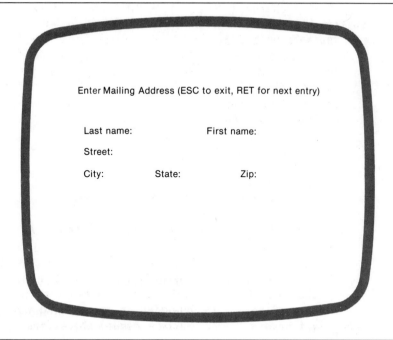

Enter Mailing Address (ESC to exit, RET for next entry)

Last name:          First name:

Street:

City:          State:          Zip:

Pressing **escape** ends the session. In our case, ending the session ends the program. However, this would normally be part of a larger program that allows the user to enter and modify an entire mailing list. In that case, an **escape** might move to the next mailing address or, perhaps, return to some command mode.

The program is compiled as follows:

```
cc dialog.c -lcurses -ltermcap
```

Now let's examine the program:

```
/* dialog to enter a mailing address */

/* The user fills in the blanks on the screen, pressing
   return key to go to the next part of the address and
   escape key to finish. Backspace key erases individual
   characters and control-u keystroke deletes an entire
   item.
*/

#include <curses.h>
```

```
/* maxi is number of items in address */
#define maxi ((sizeof(dList))/(sizeof(struct dItem)))

/* (x, y) is position on screen */
int x=1, y=1;

/* the title for the screen */
struct dTitle
   {
   int y, x;   /* position of title */
   char *str;  /* title string */
   }
title =
 { 1, 3, "Enter mailing address\
 (use ESC to exit and RET for next item)"};

/* a mailing address is an array of dItems */
struct dItem
   {
   int yl, xl;    /* position of label */
   char *strl;    /* pointer to the label string */
   int ye, xe;    /* position of edit string */
   int maxe;      /* maximum number characters in edit string */
   int cnte;      /* character count in edit string */
   char stre[41]; /* the edit string */
   }
dList[]=
   {
    /* yl, xl, strl,            ye, xe, maxe, cnte, stre */
      { 3,  5, "Last name:",    3, 16,  15,   0, "" },
      { 3, 33, "First name:",   3, 45,  15,   0, "" },
      { 5,  5, "Street:",       5, 13,  40,   0, "" },
      { 7,  5, "City:",         7, 11,  12,   0, "" },
      { 7, 25, "State:",        7, 32,  12,   0, "" },
      { 7, 46, "Zip:",          7, 51,   5,   0, "" }
   };

main()
   {
   char ch;
   int i, j;
   int done=FALSE;

   /* set up screen and terminal I/O */
   initscr(); crmode(); noecho(); nonl();

   /* clear screen and display title and item labels */
```

```
clear();
mvaddstr(title.y, title.x, title.str);
for(i = 0; i < maxi; i++)
    mvaddstr(dList[i].yl, dList[i].xl, dList[i].strl);
refresh();

i=0;
move(dList[i].ye, dList[i].xe);
refresh();

while (!done)
    {
    switch(ch=getch())
        {
        case 27: /* escape key to exit */
            done = TRUE;
            break;

        case '\r': /* return key to select next item */
            if(++i==maxi) i=0;
            move(dList[i].ye, dList[i].xe +dList[i].cnte);
            break;

        case '\b': /* backspace deletes a character */
            if (dList[i].cnte > 0)
                {
                addstr("\b \b");
                dList[i].cnte--;
                (dList[i].stre)[dList[i].cnte] = 0;
                }
            break;

        case 21: /* control u deletes the item */
            for(j=0; dList[i].cnte > 0; j++)
                {
                addstr("\b \b");
                dList[i].cnte--;
                (dList[i].stre)[dList[i].cnte] = 0;
                }
            break;

        default: /* handle regular characters */
            if(dList[i].cnte < dList[i].maxe && ch >= 32)
                {
                (dList[i].stre)[dList[i].cnte] = ch;
                dList[i].cnte++;
                addch(ch);
```

```
            }
         break;
      }
   refresh();
   }
/* display the final values in the list */
nl();
move(dList[maxi-1].ye +2, dList[maxi-1].xe);
printw("\n\n");
for( i=0; i<maxi; i++) printw("%d:\t%s\n", i, dList[i].stre);
printw("\n\n");
refresh();

endwin();
}
```

**Initialization**—As in the previous program, we include the header file curses.h and declare global variables x and y that hold the position of the cursor on the screen.

We also define a macro maxi that is the number of items in an address. It is defined using a #define directive. The name *maxi* is replaced when you run the program by the string given in the define statement before that portion of the program is compiled. In this case, we define maxi as:

```
((sizeof(dList))/(sizeof(struct dItem)))
```

This definition is the total size of the mailing list dList divided by the length of any of its entries. Such a definition allows us to add items to dList without having to update maxi each time.

**The Data Structures**—In this program, we have two C structures: the first dTitle holds information for a title that is displayed along the top of the screen, and the second dList holds information about the mailing address itself. These are variables declared outside of any function, thus they are static external variables. This means that they are global to all procedures and remain in memory throughout the execution of the program.

The dTitle structure contains the line and column positions for the location of the beginning of the title on the screen and a string containing the text of the title.

The dList structure is an array of dItem, where each dItem is a structure that specifies one mailing address. Within dItem are the individual parts of the mailing address, such as the first name, last name, city, or state. In each case, there is a label, such as City:, and an edit string where the actual data (for example, the name of the city) is stored. In particular, the structure dItem has the following members: two integers containing the line and column positions for the beginning of the label, a pointer to a string containing the text of the label, two more integers for the line and column for the beginning of an edit string, the maximum size of the edit string, the current size of the edit string, and a pointer to the edit string.

Both structures are initialized as part of their declaration. You should study the values given within the program.

For each item, the current size is set to 0 and the text string is empty. Notice that the string pointers for the label string and the edit string are defined differently. In the first case, the string pointer for the label is defined via:

```
char *strl
```

This allots space within the dItem structure for a pointer and allows the actual contents of the string (which is stored elsewhere) to be any length. The length is then determined by the initialization section of the definition for dList. For example, because the label string City: has five characters, the label string pointer strl for the city item points to an area of memory containing six bytes of storage (one extra to hold a zero to terminate the string).

In contrast, the pointer for the edit strings is defined via:

```
char stre[41]
```

This provides a pointer (within the dItem structure) to an area of memory containing exactly 41 character positions (bytes) for the edit string. Notice that we need one more than the maximum length of any of the edit strings. This is because of the trailing zero byte that is required as a string terminator. If we used the same type of definition as for the label, we might have to specify a string of 41 zeros. As it is, we waste some space because only one item, namely the street address, can allow as many as forty characters. The others occupy only the first 5, 12, or 15 bytes of the allocated space.

**The Main Program**—In the main program, several more variables are declared: a character variable ch to hold characters as they are being processed, an integer i used as an index to dList, an integer j used to index through the edit string, and an integer done used to control the termination of the program. These are "automatic" variables; that is, they are created and initialized each time the function is called.

In this case main would be called only once, but if this function is renamed and used as a part of a larger program, these variables would be properly initialized each time the function is called. In particular, the variable done needs to be initialized to FALSE (zero) each time.

The first actions of the main program are to set up the screen and terminal I/O. Here initscr initializes the curses variables, and crmode, noecho, and nonl configure the terminal I/O for single character input with no echo and no special mapping for newline.

We call clear (to clear the screen) and mvaddstr a number of times to place the title and all the labels on the screen. A `for` loop runs through all the labels stored in `dList`. Notice that `mvaddstr` allows us to specify both the position and content of the string. After we place all this information on the standard screen, we call `refresh` to cause the information to appear on the actual screen.

Before we begin the main loop, we reinitialize `i` to a value of zero to indicate the first item of the mailing address, and we call `move` to place the cursor at the beginning of the edit string for the first item. We call `refresh` to display this cursor update.

The main loop is a `while` loop that executes as long as `done` is false. Recall that `done` is initialed to FALSE at the beginning of `main` each time it is called. The `while` loop contains a `switch` statement and a call to `refresh`. The argument for the `switch` is the expression `ch=getch()` that fetches the next character from the standard input and sends it to the `switch`. The ability to do two actions at once like this is one feature that makes C so powerful. It can, however, make C harder to read than other languages.

The first case of the `switch` statement is if the character is **escape**. Here, we set `done` equal to TRUE to end the main loop.

The next case is if the character is **return**. This is used to select the next item. To accomplish this, we increment `i`, setting it equal to 0 if it becomes equal to `maxi`. This allows the user to cycle through all items of the address. After `i` is updated, we use the `move` function to move the cursor to the end of the `i`th edit string.

Next is the case for **backspace**. This is used to delete characters from the current edit string. If the character count (as given by `dList[i].cnte`) is greater than zero, we issue a **backspace**, a **space**, then another **backspace**. We also place a zero in the corresponding character position of the edit string, thus shortening the string. Notice that we use two hyphens (--) to decrement the count variable before we use it as an index in the statement that zeros the character position.

The last regular case is for a **control u**. This is used to "kill" an entire edit string for an item. Here we use a `for` loop to delete all characters in the edit string in the same way that individual characters are deleted with the **backspace**.

The last case under the `switch` is the `default`. This is used to handle regular characters that are to be entered into the edit string. Here, we test to see whether the edit string has reached its maximum length and whether the character is within the normal character set (ASCII code at least 32). If so, we move the character into the edit string and call `addch` to display the character on the screen. Notice that the `++` increment happens after we load the character into the edit string. In this way, we always point to the next available character position in the string.

At the end of the program, we display the list to confirm that the information was properly stored in the edit strings. We use a `for` containing a `printw` function to display the edit string in formatted form. Here, we display the item's number, a colon, a tab, then the string, followed by a newline. After a couple of newlines and a refresh, the program ends.

# Terminal Capabilities

Now that we have seen how terminal I/O routines can be used, let's go deeper into how they work. In this section we explore the `termcap` file and its associated routines.

The name *termcap* is short for *terminal capabilities*. This file contains entries for each type of terminal that can be connected to the system. Each entry describes how a particular type of terminal behaves for such programs as the screen editor `vi` and the visual shell `vsh`. In particular, these entries store terminal characteristics such as the number of rows and columns on the screen, the command sequences for moving the cursor, and the command sequences for clearing selected parts of the screen.

Because many different kinds of terminals exist, this file can be fairly large, perhaps 100K for a really complete set of terminals. Many general types of terminals have several entries, each describing a different variant. For example, an IBM PC might have different entries for each type of display. At the time of this writing, the IBM PC does have different entries, but they all do the same thing.

The `termcap` file is located in the `etc` directory, thus its full pathname is `/etc/termcap`. Just type the command

```
more /etc/termcap
```

to view the file. It is a public file, so any user may read it and use the information contained within it.

If you wish to develop or use your own special private `termcap` entries, you can set them up. You merely set the environment variable `TERMCAP` equal to either the path name of the `termcap` file of your choice or a string containing your termcap entry. Each shell has a slightly different way of doing this. For example, under the C-shell, you might type

```
setenv TERMCAP /usr/myaccount/mytermcap
```

if your `termcap` file is called `mytermcap` and is located in `myaccount` in the directory `usr`.

## Sample Termcap Entry

Let's look at a sample `termcap` entry to see how information is encoded there. Later we provide a program that displays this information in a more readable form.

Our sample `termcap` entry describes a simple terminal emulation program that is run on a graphics workstation connected to our XENIX system. This program turns a microcomputer workstation into an intelligent terminal that responds to a few control sequences to do such things as move the cursor and change the attributes of displayed text. We choose this example for a number of reasons—it's simple, it's ours, and it illustrates a wide range of terminal capabilities.

Here is what the entry looks like:

```
au¦a1000¦Graphics Terminal Emulator:\
  :co#80:li#23:\
  :am:bs:\
  :cm=\E=%+ %+ :\
  :ho=\E  :\
  :ce=\E\001\021:cd=\E\001\022:cl=^L:\
  :so=\E\004\0250\024@:se=\E\004\025@\0240:\
  :us=\E\002\024J:ue=\E\002\0240:
```

Let's go through each "capability" of this entry. Notice that although it is just one long string, it has several lines and lots of "white space" for readability. To indicate continuation, each line, except the last, ends in a backslash ( \ ).

The first line gives identification codes for this particular terminal. These identifiers are separated by the vertical bar (¦) character. The first identifier, au, is a two-letter designator required for historical reasons. That is, it was used by an older version (UNIX version 6) of the operating system, but is no longer used directly. It now acts as a place marker. The second identifier, a1000, is the official name that the users and the system use to refer to this terminal type. The third identifier is a longer name that acts like a comment and describes the terminal in English. We have called this terminal emulator a1000 because it uses the A-1000 graphics subsystem by Graphics Development Laboratories for its text display screen. (Incidentally, this emulator program also has a graphics mode that allows us to run full color graphics programs on the XENIX system with the display handled by the A-1000.)

The rest of the entry consists of capabilities. Each capability has a two-letter designator. There are three types of capabilities: Boolean, numerical, and string. They can be listed in any order. We shall describe each type as we proceed through our particular entry.

The second line of our termcap entry gives the number of columns and lines of characters on the terminal screen. In this case, we have 80 columns and 23 lines. Both of these quantities are numerical capabilities. Numerical capabilities are specified by giving the two-letter designator of the capability (for example, co for number of columns and li for number of lines) followed by a #, then the decimal representation of its value. For example co#80 says that the screen has 80 columns.

The third line contains some Boolean capabilities. These "flags" act like logical variables that specify whether a certain feature is present or absent. Here, am specifies that the terminal has *automatic margins,* and bs specifies that the terminal uses the normal backspace character (ASCII 8). Automatic margins means that the terminal automatically wraps around to the next line and scrolls if necessary when text goes beyond the end of any line. Boolean capabilities are indicated by merely listing the two-letter identifier.

The next line contains a string capability cm that specifies how to move the cursor around the screen. This is perhaps the most complex capability. It requires that two integers secretly be sent to the terminal. By secretly, we mean that these integers do not actually appear on the screen, but rather are used to control it. A number of different formats can be used for encoding this information.

The cm string capability uses format specifiers much like the ones used by the printf function in C. However, they are extended to take care of special cases that are normally programmed in C. In our case, the cm string is given by:

```
"cm=\E=%+ %+ "
```

The \E stands for the escape character (ASCII 27). This is sent first. Most terminal control sequences begin with an escape.

Next is an equal sign (=). This is sent literally to the terminal after the escape. After the equal sign is a byte described by the format specifier %+. This means that the sent character has an ASCII code consisting of the desired integer plus the ASCII code for a space (ASCII 32). In this case, we are sending the row (the line number, counting from 0 from the top of the screen). A second %+ says that the column is to be sent in the same way. If the row and column are to be sent in the reverse order, a %r is placed in the string before either format specifier.

In designing our terminal emulation program, we choose the above representation because it is very compact and does not conflict with other control sequences. Other formats for cm use decimal expansions for the row and column. These use such things as %d that are closer to the formats available in C. These are less compact because more characters must be sent to expand a number into its decimal representation.

You might wonder why 32 was added to the row and column values. Adding this "bias" causes the transmitted byte values to fall between 32 and 111, thus allowing the terminal or terminal emulator to avoid "dangerous" values between 0 and 31. Some of these values such as 0 and 10 are intercepted by the XENIX system and either absorbed or mapped to different codes. A value of 0 is especially bad because it is used as a string terminator (signaling the end of a string) and as a pad character (sent but ignored later to cause timing delays). A value of 10 is also bad because it is the ASCII code for newline. This is often expanded by XENIX to a carriage return-linefeed sequence (ASCII 13, then 10).

The next line specifies the control character for "homing" the cursor. Here we use a special case of the cm specifier that we just described. The string \E means "Move the cursor to column 0 and row 0,", which is exactly what is meant by "home." The vi editor uses this control sequence directly when it brings the cursor to the home position after displaying the file information on the bottom of the screen.

The next line of our termcap entry gives three commands to clear portions of the screen. The first ce clears to the end of the line, the second cd clears to the end of the display, and the third cl clears the entire screen. The first two ce=\E\001\021 and cd=\E\001\022 cause special codes (octal 021 and octal 022, respectively) to be sent to the A-1000 display system.

Here we use an interesting trick to get the code to the A-1000. Immediately after the escape (designated by a \E) is an "escape count" that specifies how many additional characters are in the escape sequence. This allows us to send a specified number of characters directly to the A-1000 without the usual interpretations performed by the terminal emulation program.

In both cases, we have just one additional character, thus a \001 follows the escape designator. For ce (clear to end of line), the additional character's code is octal 021, and for cd (clear to end of display), the code is octal 022. It is relatively easy to design a terminal emulation program so that whenever it detects an escape, it picks up the count, then sends that many subsequent characters directly to the display subsystem.

The cl (clear the whole screen) capability is handled differently. Here, a single control character ^L (formfeed) is sent. We could have used cl=\E= \E\001\022, which combines "home" and "clear to end of display," but that would have been much longer, and it is useful for other applications to have the terminal emulator respond directly to formfeed.

On the next line are the codes for standout mode. In this mode, characters are displayed in high contrast to their normal appearance. Most terminals implement this mode as reverse video. Here, the capability so=\E\004\0250\024@ causes the terminal to start standout mode and the capability se=\E\004\025@\0240 causes the terminal to end standout mode.

Let's look more closely. In both cases we generate escape sequences that are four additional characters long, thus each begins with an escape \E followed by an escape count of four \004. Next, the A-1000 code 025 (octal) controls the background color of the characters subsequently displayed. For so (start standout), an O (ASCII 4F hexadecimal) is sent. Only the four lowest bits (0F hex) are used by the A-1000. This selects color 15 (0F in hexadecimal), which is normally bright white. Next the A-1000 code 024 (octal) controls the foreground color of the characters subsequently displayed. Here we send an at sign (@, ASCII 40 hex), which is stripped by the A-1000 to make color 0—normally black. The se (end standout) capability just reverses the above actions. You can see that we went to considerable trouble to avoid sending codes in the range 0 through 15, which as we noted above cause problems with XENIX.

The last line specifies how underscore mode is to be actuated. Here, the capability us=\E\002\024J starts the underscoring of all subsequent characters and the capability ue=\E\002\0240 ends it. You should be able to see that us changes the foreground color of characters to color number 10 and ue changes the foreground color back to color number 15.

## The Showterm Program

Let's look at an example program that displays this information and more in a readable format. This program also illustrates how to use the system's termcap library routines, which read the termcap file and its entries for you.

We call the program showterm. Once it is compiled and given this name, you can run it. You should see a display something like this:

```
Your terminal is called a1000 and has 23 lines and 80 columns,
automatic margins, and the usual backspace. Some of its
capabilities are:

        cursor backward         bc:
        cursor forward          nd:
        cursor up               up:
        cursor down             do:
        cursor home             ho: 14
        insert character        ic:
        delete character        dc:
        insert line             al:
        delete line             dl:
        clear to end of display cd: 27 1 19
        clear to end of line    ce: 27 1 17
        clear whole screen      cl: 12
        start standout mode     so: 27 4 21 79 20 64
        end standout mode       se: 27 4 21 64 20 79
        start underscore mode   us: 27 2 20 74
        end underscore mode     ue: 27 2 20 79
        cursor key left         kl:
        cursor key right        kr:
        cursor key up           ku:
        cursor key down         kd:

Used 48 bytes to store capabilities.

Absolute cursor motion (cm) examples:
col  0, row 0: 27 61 32 32
col  0, row 1: 27 61 33 32
col  0, row 2: 27 61 34 32
col  0, row 3: 27 61 35 32
col 10, row 0: 27 61 32 42
```

```
col 10, row 1: 27 61 33 42
col 10, row 2: 27 61 34 42
col 10, row 3: 27 61 35 42
col 20, row 0: 27 61 32 52
col 20, row 1: 27 61 33 52
col 20, row 2: 27 61 34 52
col 20, row 3: 27 61 35 52
col 30, row 0: 27 61 32 62
col 30, row 1: 27 61 33 62
col 30, row 2: 27 61 34 62
col 30, row 3: 27 61 35 62
```

You might want to pipe this through more as follows:

```
% showterm ¦ more◄┘
```

This allows you to examine the output one screenful at a time. Notice that the --More-- at the bottom of the screen appears in "standout" mode.

Notice that many of these capabilities are blank; that is, they are not implemented. You only need to implement the ones that we have in order to make vi, more, and our dialog and turtle programs work properly.

The showterm program requires the standard C library and the termcap library, but not the curses library, hence it is compiled as follows:

```
% cc showterm.c -ltermcap◄┘
```

Now let's examine the program.

```
/* show terminal capabilities */

#include <stdio.h>
#include <sgtty.h>

    char terminfo[1024];    /* terminal information */
    char PC;                /* pad character */
    char *UP;               /* up character sequence */
```

```
    int bs;                 /* usual backspace? */
    char *BC;               /* backspace sequence */
    short ospeed = B2400;   /* baud rate */


    static char twork[100];
    int outc();


    static char *cmptr;


main()
   {
   char *p, *tname;
   int i, lastcap, col, row;
   char *tgetstr(), *tgoto(), *getenv();


   static struct
   {
   char *id;
   char *label;
   char *loc;
   }
   cap[] =
   {
      {"bc", "cursor backward          bc: ", },
      {"nd", "cursor forward           nd: ", },
      {"up", "cursor up                up: ", },
      {"do", "cursor down              do: ", },
      {"ho", "cursor home              ho: ", },
      {"ic", "insert character         ic: ", },
      {"dc", "delete character         dc: ", },
      {"al", "insert line              al: ", },
      {"dl", "delete line              dl: ", },
      {"cd", "clear to end of display cd: ", },
      {"ce", "clear to end of line     ce: ", },
      {"cl", "clear whole screen       cl: ", },
      {"so", "start standout mode      so: ", },
      {"se", "end standout mode        se: ", },
      {"us", "start underscore mode    us: ", },
      {"ue", "end underscore mode      ue: ", },
      {"kl", "cursor key left          kl: ", },
      {"kr", "cursor key right         kr: ", },
      {"ku", "cursor key up            ku: ", },
      {"kd", "cursor key down          kd: ", }
   };
   lastcap = 20;
```

```
tname = getenv("TERM");
printf("\fYour terminal is called %s ", tname);

switch (tgetent(terminfo, tname))
   {
   case -1: printf("\nCannot open termcap file.\n");
            exit(1);
            break;
   case  0: printf(", but is not in termcap file.\n");
            exit(1);
            break;
   }
printf("and has %d lines and %d columns,\n",
       tgetnum("li"), tgetnum("co"));

if (tgetflag("am")) printf("automatic margins, ");
else               printf("no automatic margins, ");

if (bs=tgetflag("bs")) printf("and the usual backspace. ");
else    printf("and does not have the usual backspace. ");

/* load and display selected capability strings */

printf("Some of its\ncapabilities are:\n\n");

p = twork;
for (i=0; i<lastcap; i++)
   {
   cap[i].loc = tgetstr(cap[i].id,&p);
   printf(" %s", cap[i].label);
   tputs(cap[i].loc, 1, outc);
   printf("\n");
   }

/* display examples of absolute cursor motion */

if (bs) BC = "\b"; else BC = cap[0].loc;
UP = cap[2].loc;

cmptr = tgetstr("cm",&p);
printf("\nUsed %d bytes to store capabilities.\n", p - twork);

printf("\nAbsolute cursor motion (cm) examples:\n");
for (col=0; col<40; col+=10)
   for (row=0; row<4; row++)
      {
      printf("col %2d, row %2d: ", col, row);
```

```
        tputs(tgoto(cmptr, col, row), 1, outc);
        printf("\n");
        }
    }
/* character output routine used by tputs */

outc(c)
    char c;
    {
    printf("%d ", c);
    }
```

The program includes two header files: stdio.h and sgetty. The first is needed because we use the standard I/O printf routine, and the second is used when we specify the baud rate of the terminal.

There are a number of external variables: terminfo is an array of 1024 characters that holds your termcap entry. PC is the "pad" character used to help create timing delays. UP is a string that points to the control sequence for moving the cursor up one line of text, bs is an integer that holds the bs Boolean capability, BC is a string that holds the backspace control sequence, and ospeed is of type short (a byte in many current implementations of C) and holds a code for the baud rate.

Twork is a static array of characters that holds the string capabilities in the form in which they are to be sent (except for cm, which needs further processing before it is ready to be sent). Outc is a function that sends individual characters to the terminal. We define our own "diagnostic" outc function at the end of the program. It must be declared here because it is passed as a parameter in some of the termcap routines. Finally, cmptr is a pointer to where the cm capability is stored in twork.

The main program has a number of "local" variables. P is a general string pointer, used to help load capabilities from their termcap format to twork where they are stored in a more compact form. Tname is a string pointer for the terminal's name. The integers i, lastcap, col, and row are used in our program in ways that we shall soon describe. The functions tgetstr, tgoto, and getenv are external string functions and thus must be declared to be used. Tgetstr and tgoto belong to the termcap library, and getenv belongs to the regular C library.

Next, we build a static structure array cap that houses in a compact, orderly, and readable form all the information that we need for each string capability. It is an array of structures, each containing a string pointer id that points to the two-letter designator for the capability, a string pointer to label that points to a longer description of the capability, and a string pointer loc that points to where the compact form of the capability command is to be stored in the local work string buffer twork. After building this structure, we set lastcap equal to the number of string capabilities currently in cap. To add more capabilities to cap, we simply type in more lines into its initialization section, and increase the value assigned to lastcap accordingly.

Now the work begins. We use getenv to obtain the name of the terminal as it is stored in the environment variable TERM. This name is stored in the string tname. Our first printf statement announces this name to the user. Next we call tgetent to load the corresponding termcap entry into the string buffer terminfo. This buffer must be at least 1024 characters long to accommodate the largest possible termcap entry.

We use the result from tgetenv to determine whether the load operation was successful. A switch statement prints out two possible errors: Cannot open termcap file and does not have entry in termcap file. In either case, we call exit. If all goes well, we proceed with the program.

Our next printf statement displays the number of rows and columns on your terminal screen. We call tgetnum to get these numerical capabilities for printf.

Next we check the Boolean capabilities am and bs. We use tgetflag to fetch their values from the termcap entry. We feed these values into if else statements, which print messages to the user about these capabilities.

The string capabilities are displayed next. Here, a for loop indexes (with the variable i) through our cap structure, loading each capability into the work area twork, getting a pointer cap[i].loc to it, printing out the label description, and calling tputs to send it to the terminal. The local string pointer p increments through twork as we load each string capability.

In our case we have arranged it so that tputs prints diagnostic information only. In fact, each ''character'' is sent to our own outc function that displays the decimal expansion of that character. In real life, the character would be sent directly to the screen.

The final set of displays that our program produces show sample cursor motion sequences. Before we can do this, we must properly initialize the strings BC and UP and make cmptr point to the cm capability string in twork (loading it there as we do). We also print a message indicating how much storage we have used in twork. This is the final value of p minus the base address of twork. In C we can merely subtract these pointers and print the result as an integer.

The cursor motion examples are printed using a double for loop, indexing through the rows and columns (integer variables row and col). At the heart of this double for loop, we call tgoto to evaluate the cm command string for specific rows and columns, then call tputs to send the result to the terminal. We use a printf statement to label each sample output.

The program concludes with the outc routine to send characters to the screen. Here we use a printf statement to convert the character to the decimal expansion of its ASCII code.

# Summary

In this chapter we have discussed terminal I/O. We presented three C programs that illustrate important aspects about how terminal I/O works.

First we showed how to use the `curses` system library function to control terminal I/O. We saw that a programmer can write code that fully uses the screen editing capabilities of modern terminals and yet is independent of the particular terminal that is connected to the system.

Finally, we showed how a program can use `termcap` routines to determine exactly what terminal capabilities are available on the currently connected terminal.

# Questions and Answers

## Questions

1. What are some terminal capabilities?
2. How does the system know your terminal's capabilities?
3. What kinds of programs use terminal capabilities?
4. Give a C statement that moves the cursor to the second line, third column on the terminal screen.
5. On the SCO version of XENIX, the user can rapidly flip among several console screens. How it is possible for cursor control to work on several programs running at once, each on a different console screen?
6. Why is it necessary to call the `crmode` routine in certain interactive programs?

## Answers

1. The capabilities of accepting commands to 1) move the cursor to any position on the screen, 2) clear the screen, and 3) selectively erase portions of the screen.
2. The environmental variable `TERM` tells which type of terminal you are using, and the environmental variable `TERMCAP` can store the actual capabilities. These variables can be set automatically by the `.login` script during login, and they can be set or changed later by the user. The file `/etc/termcap` contains the capabilities of almost any terminal that you might wish to connect to the system.
3. Screen editor programs, interactive programs that allow the user to move around a terminal screen, and programs that highlight portions of the screen use terminal capabilities.

4. The C statement

   ```
   move(1, 2);
   ```

   moves the cursor to line 1, column 2. Note that the numbering for lines and columns begins with 0. Also note that the `curses` commands require a call to `refresh` before you see the results.

5. Each program writes its screen output to a copy of the screen that resides in regular memory. When the user flips to the screen that belongs to the program, the copy of the screen in regular memory is quickly loaded to the actual screen memory.

6. The `crmode` routine causes each character to be interpreted immediately rather than waiting until a newline is pressed. This is important for interactive programs that use single character commands.

# 7

# Files and Directories

- Files, Directories, and File Systems
- Physical and Logical Organization of Files
- Paths, Trees, and Directories
- Exploring the Super Block
- I-Nodes
- Modifying File Attributes
- Fundamental File Reading and Writing Routines
- Summary
- Questions and Answers

# Files and Directories

Because keyboards, disk drives, terminal screens, commands, directories, and even memory appear as files in the XENIX system, understanding XENIX file systems is crucial to understanding the entire system.

This chapter shows how to write programs that examine and modify the way files are stored and managed, including file permissions and ownership. We also discuss and demonstrate how to read from and write to files at the lowest levels of file I/O.

We discuss file security. In particular, we discuss how file ownership and read/write/execute permissions provide a three-level system to help protect data and programs from unauthorized access and modification.

In this chapter you can find example programs to display the contents of a directory, display file attributes, and display and interactively modify current user and group identification numbers and permissions. There is also a short program to illustrate the most basic file system calls.

## Files, Directories, and File Systems

Like most other operating systems, XENIX organizes the information that it manages in files which are stored on a medium such as a floppy or hard disk (see figure 7-1). A file can be thought of as a logically organized block of data that can be accessed by a name, or more precisely a *path*.

### Accessing Files

A file normally resides in a kind of dormant status on the storage device. To get information to or from a file, it must be opened. When you are finished with a file, especially if you have written to it, you should close it to return it to its dormant status. This last step flushes any last bytes from memory to storage and updates any parameters, such as its new size. In this chapter, we see how this is done in XENIX. We explore high- and low-level routines that do this.

**Figure 7-1
A file**

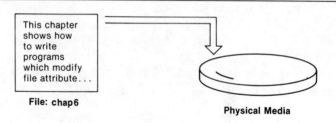

**File: chap6**

**Physical Media**

## File Systems

In XENIX and many other systems, files are located within a tree structure of directories called a file system. A file system is stored on a device such as a hard disk. Several file systems can be "grafted" together to form a larger tree system of directories (see figure 7-2).

**Figure 7-2
Grafting file systems**

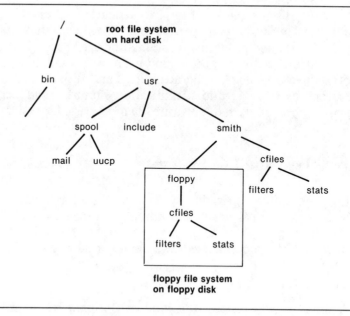

## Physical and Logical Organization of Files

The way files are organized can be understood from two major points of view: *physical* and *logical*. By physical organization, we mean how and where the individual bytes of the file are stored on the storage media. For example, physically, XENIX files are normally stored on a hard disk in *blocks*. They can, however, be stored on sectors of floppy disks or on tape. By logical *organization,* we mean how the user, programmer, or higher levels of the system gain access to files. This is normally via their names or paths.

The physical organization of files is controlled at lower levels of the system and should not be of great concern to an applications programmer or even to a systems manager. Physical organization becomes important only when things go wrong, for example, failures in the storage media. However, in this chapter, we discuss the physical organization to help provide a better understanding of files.

The logical organization of files is of much more concern to users, programmers, and managers of a XENIX system. In this chapter we mostly approach XENIX files through their logical organization.

## Paths, Trees, and Directories

If you have worked with PC-DOS or MS-DOS, you should be familiar with tree-structured directories. In fact, some of the commands to navigate the tree are almost identical in DOS and XENIX. For example, in both systems cd is used to change the currently selected directory. There are, however, some differences. For example, in PC-DOS, cd with no parameter prints the current directory without changing directories, but in XENIX it changes the current directory, making it the user's "home" directory.

XENIX, like PC-DOS, has a root directory at the top of the tree (see figure 7-3). The root is distinguished by the fact that it is contained in no other directories.

**Figure 7-3**
**The root**

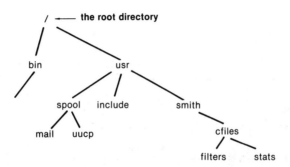

As we have indicated, each file in the system can be located by a path. A path consists of a list of names separated by slashes (/). The names in the list specify a downward journey through the tree structure (see figure 7-4). This downward journey is performed automatically by the operating system when you specify a path to many of the file management routines.

**Figure 7-4**
**A path through the tree**

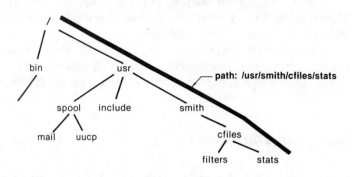

Notice that the name separator slash (/) used in XENIX is different than the backslash (\) used by PC- and MS-DOS. In XENIX the root directory is symbolically indicated by a /, and the same symbol is used to separate names in a path.

A path that begins with a / starts at the root. A path that does not begin with a / starts at the user's current directory. For example, the path /usr/include/stdio.h indicates the file stdio.h contained in the directory include, which is contained in the directory usr, which is contained in the root directory. In contrast, if the current directory is /usr/myname, the path chap7/dl.c indicates the file dl.c that is contained in the directory chap7 that is contained in the directory myname that is contained in the directory usr, which is in the root.

## Structure of Directory Files

Enough generalities—let's look at what makes this system work.

Each directory, including the root directory, is itself a file containing a list of the names of the files directly under it in the tree.

The organization of a XENIX directory file is very simple: It is an array of structures that are pairs consisting of a 16-bit integer called an i-node number and a 14-byte string containing a file name. The i-node number specifies a particular 64-byte entity called an i-node where the physical information about how the file is stored is kept. Each different file in the system, including each different directory, requires a separate i-node. We look at the contents of i-nodes in more detail in following text.

You can view a directory as a part of a relational data base for the operating system. It is a table that relates a set of file names with i-nodes. Each file name/i-node pair is called a *link* because it links the logical structure file system (nodes of a tree structure) with information about its physical storage (blocks on a disk).

By knowing the name of each directory and all the links that it contains, you (and the operating system) can reconstruct the tree structure of the directory system. If you examine the resulting structure carefully, you see that some links have the same i-node number. For example, the l, lc, lf, lr, ls, and the lx commands in the /bin directory have the same i-node number. This means that these commands share a common storage. That is, they share the same *node*.

It is interesting to note that the code for a family of commands with the same i-node can determine which command was invoked to call it by looking at the zeroth parameter from the command line. Thus, different command names can be used to generate different options of basically the same command. Once a file is placed in the system under one name, the ln command can be used to create other links to it.

## Directory Display Program

Let's look at a C program called dl that displays the contents of a directory. The program can read the directory, just like other programs can read other files. As an extra bonus, in addition to demonstrating the structure of directory files, this program also illustrates how to read files and pass parameters from the command line.

By examining the program and its output, we can see explicitly how directories are organized. To run it, type its name, dl, with a single parameter that is a path to a directory. The output displays the links, one per line with an i-node number followed by a file name. Here is the output:

```
691 .
632 ..
684 test
696 diraa
```

From this output, we see that the file . that indicates the present directory has i-node number 691, the file .. that indicates the directory directly above has i-node number 632, the file test has i-node number 684, and the file diraa has i-node number 696.

Here is the program:

```
/* directory dump */

#include<stdio.h>
```

```
main(argc, argv)
int argc;
char *argv[];
{
FILE *input;
int inode, i, done=0;
char name[14];
if (argc < 2) { printf("Too few arguments.\n"); exit(1);}
if((input = fopen(argv[1], "r")) != NULL)
    {
    while (!done)
        {
        inode = getw(input);
        for (i=0; i < 14; i++) name[i] = getc(input);
        if(!(done=feof(input))) printf("%5d %s\n", inode, name);
        }
    fclose(input);
    }
else printf("Cannot open directory file.\n");
}
```

To compile the program, type:

```
cc dl.c
```

It requires no special libraries other than the standard C library.

Let's examine this program in detail.

Because we use standard I/O functions `getw`, `getc`, `feof`, and `printf`, we include the header file `stdio.h`.

The main program has two arguments to help pass parameters from the command line. The first argument `argc` is an integer that specifies how many parameters were given, and the second argument `argv` is an array of strings that are the actual parameters given in the command line. Notice that the arguments `argc` and `argv` are declared right after `main` is declared but before its initial curly bracket.

The main program begins with the declaration of local parameters for main. The file pointer `input` is used as a parameter to specify the file that we are reading from. The integer `inode` is used to hold the i-node numbers. The integer `i` is used to index through the characters of the file names in the directory. The integer `done` is used to control the program flow. It is initialized to 0, which means FALSE because initially we are not *done*.

The first action in `main` is to make sure that there are at least two parameters: the zeroth parameter, which is the name of the program, and the first parameter, which should be a path to the desired directory. If there are less than two parameters, we print an error message and exit the program.

Next, we attempt to open the specified directory file with the `fopen` function. This prepares the file for reading by loading the appropriate file management data into memory. The first argument of fopen is argv[1] that points to the first parameter in the command line. The second parameter of fopen is a string r, indicating that the file is being opened for reading. Fopen returns a pointer which we assign to the file pointer input.

If the file is successfully opened, the returned pointer is nonzero and can be used to access the file. In that case we enter a while to read the file and display its contents.

The while loop continues as long as done is false. In it, we first get an integer that we store in inode. This should be the i-node number. Next, we use a for loop to read the bytes of a file's name from the directory, placing them in the string name. We call feof to check whether we have gone beyond the end of the directory file. If not, we print a line of text that contains the i-node number (5 digits and a space), and the file name. Each time through, the while loop prints a line of information about one file in the directory.

After the directory has been read, we call fclose to close it. Notice that the calls getw and getc, used to read from the directory file, and the fclose function all have a single argument that is our file pointer input. Thus, one of the roles of the fopen function is to return this file pointer for use by all the rest of the file functions we wish to use.

If fopen was unsuccessful, we print an error message: Cannot open directory file.

This program displays precisely what is contained in a directory file. There are regular commands that display this information. For example, the ls command with the i and a options

```
ls -ia
```

produces a listing much like our dl program. Here is the output of ls -ia:

```
ls -ia dira
  691 .
  632 ..
  696 diraa
  684 test
```

Notice that the output of the ls is sorted, whereas the output of our program is not. Also, note that our program produces strange results if it is applied to a file that is not a directory. Thus, our dl program is not appropriate as a regular system command.

## Physical Layout of a File System

Physically, a file system occupies a number of blocks on a disk or similar media (see figure 7-5). On a hard disk for an IBM XT, each block contains 1024 bytes. In subsequent discussion we assume this block size.

**Figure 7-5**
**A file system occupies blocks of storage**

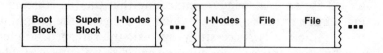

The first block is not used directly by the file system itself but is available to be used for such things as a boot program to start up the system.

Next comes a block, called the *super block,* that contains information about how the file system itself is organized. It specifies such things as how many blocks are dedicated to the file systems, what blocks are free, and how large the blocks are.

After the super block comes a number of blocks that contain i-nodes. Since i-nodes are 64 bytes long and each block contains 1024 bytes, each block contains 16 i-nodes. Because the i-node numbers are 16-bit integers, there can be at most 65,536 of them. However, only about 2,000 are allocated on an IBM XT or an IBM PC with a 10-megabyte hard disk.

After the i-node blocks come the blocks containing the actual file data.

## Exploring the Super Block

Let's look at the super block in more detail. It contains information, such as the number of blocks devoted to i-nodes and the total number of blocks in the entire file system. It also contains lists and counts of free blocks and i-nodes. The exact format for this information is described in the header file /usr/include/sys/filsys.h.

If you have the proper permissions (just become the superuser), you may examine the file systems directly to see these numbers. Each file system actually appears as a file that is normally located in the directory /dev. A list of the files representing the currently operational file systems is contained in the public file /etc/mnttab. The format of this file is described in the include file /usr/include/sys/mnttab.h. You can then use a tool such as od (octal dump) to dump the contents of /etc/mnttab and the files listed in it.

Here is an od dump of /etc/mnttab:

```
% od -oc /etc/mnttab◄┘
0000000 067562 072157 000000 000000 000000 000000 000000 027400
          r   o   o   t \0      \0      \0      \0      \0      \0      \
0000020 000000 000000 000000 000000 000000 000000 000000 000000
```

```
        \0      \0      \0      \0      \0      \0      \0      \0      \0
  ★
  0000220 000000 055423 017262
          \0      \0       023  [ 262 036
  0000226
```

We use the `oc` option of `od` to display the contents in both octal and character format. The first 15 bytes gives the file name `root` where the file system appears as a file in the directory `/dev`. The next 15 give the pathname `/` where it is logically attached to the whole directory system.

If we use the `-l` (long) option of the `ls` command to look at the ownership and permissions for this file, we see:

```
% ls -l /dev/root◄┘
brw-------  1 sysinfo  sysinfo   1, 40 Oct 21 1985 /dev/root
```

This file belongs to `sysinfo`, one of the system accounts. Let's use the `su` command to switch to this user, then use `od` with the `-d` (decimal number format) to view this file. Of course, these numbers (and perhaps addresses) are different on your system. Notice that we need the password for `sysinfo`. This password is usually determined when the system is installed.

```
% su sysinfo◄┘
Password:  (We give the password for "sysinfo" here)
$ od -d /dev/root◄┘
0000000 28086 28086 28086 28086 28086 28086 28086 28086
★
0002000 00141 08837 00000 00006 06182 00000 05800 00000
0002020 06573 00000 06639 00000 06546 00000 06438 00000
0002040 06642 00000 06651 00000 06629 00000 06652 00000
```

We hit the interrupt key (usually **del**) to stop the dump. Otherwise it would go on for millions of bytes. The addresses beginning at 2000 belong to the super block. According to the include file `filsys.h`, the first word (two bytes) contains the number of blocks used for the i-node list (141 in this dump), the second and third words contain the total number of blocks in the file system (8837 here), and the fourth word contains the number of i-nodes in the list of free i-nodes (100 here). Next comes the list of free i-nodes. As we just saw, there are 100 of these in our system. Each one takes four bytes. This list does not contain all free i-nodes, just the first few

(100 in this case). The system can use this list to quickly allocate storage for new files as they are created.

Continuing past this list and the list of free blocks, let's look at the area near the end of the super block.

```
0003140  00826  00000  00000  24545  07858  02205  00000  01293
0003160  00001  00068  00000  00000  00000  00000  00000  00000
0003200  00000  00000  00000  00000  00000  00000  00000  00000
```

At address 3152 is the number of free blocks (2205 here) and at address 3156 is the number of free i-nodes (1293).

## The Df Command

Fortunately, there are more convenient ways that even ordinary users can use to get the useful information about a file system. For example, the df command with the -t option given like this

```
df -t
```

produces an output something like this:

```
% df -t↵
/ (/dev/root ):     4410 blocks     1293 i-nodes
              (   17674 total blocks,   282 for i-nodes)
```

Here, there is just one file system. It is attached at /, the root, and it can be directly accessed as the file /dev/root. The output says that currently there are 4410 free (unused) blocks out of a total of 17674 blocks. It also says that there are 1293 free i-nodes and 282 blocks reserved for i-nodes.

Unfortunately, the term *block* in this printout means something different than the physical 1024 byte blocks discussed previously. Here, a block contains 512 bytes. As a result we must divide the numbers of blocks given in the printout by two to give the actual numbers of physical blocks. Thus, 2205 physical blocks are free out of 8837, 141 blocks are reserved for i-nodes. Actually, two of these i-node blocks are used for the other purposes, namely the boot block and the super block. With 16 i-nodes per physical block and a net 139 blocks for i-nodes, there is room for a total 2224 i-nodes.

## The Fsck Command

The fsck command also gives some of this information, but it is measured in 512-byte logical blocks. Fsck is normally used during bootup to check the file system out after a crash or other kind of abnormal shutdown, but you can run it under the sysinfo account. In that case, it only checks the file system and doesn't try to fix any problems.

It might print out the following:

```
$ fsck◄┘

/dev/root
** Phase 1 - Check Blocks and Sizes
** Phase 2 - Check Pathnames
** Phase 3 - Check Connectivity
** Phase 4 - Check Reference Counts
** Phase 5 - Check Free List
931 files 12982 blocks 4410 free
```

This was printed just after the previous output screen, and, in fact, it is reporting under the same conditions as the preceding screen. You can see that there are still 4410 logical (512 byte) blocks free. We also see that 12982 logical blocks have been used for files. Adding the number of free blocks (4410 logical = 2205 physical) with the number of blocks used (12982) gives 17392. Adding the number of logical blocks used for boot (2 logical = 1 physical), super block (2 logical = 1 physical), and i-nodes (278 logical = 139 physical), gives 17674, which are the total logical blocks allocated to the file system as listed on the screen reproduced previously. Thus we can account for every block in the file system. This is one of the jobs of fsck.

As far as the i-nodes are concerned, 931 already are used for files. Adding the number free (1293) gives 2224, the same total that we calculated above.

## Example C Program: Ustat

You can obtain also the number of free blocks and i-nodes in a C program by calling the ustat function. This function requires that you give the *device number* of the file system. We discuss how to obtain this number and what it means in the next section.

Following is the output of our C program, which is called ustat, named after its principal system function:

```
% ustat 296◄┘
Device number: 296
 Number of free blocks: 2205
 Number of free inodes: 1293
```

Here, the device number of the file system is 296. Again, the number of free blocks is 2205 physical blocks and the number of free i-nodes is 1293.

To compile the program, type:

```
cc -o ustat ustat.c
```

No special libraries are needed.

To use the program, type its name, followed by a list of device numbers that belong to file systems.

Here is a listing of the C program `ustat`:

```
/* file system statistics */

#include <sys/types.h>
#include <ustat.h>
main (argc, argv)
    int argc;
    char *argv[];
    {
    struct ustat thebuf;
    int dev, i;

    if (argc < 2) { printf("Too few arguments.\n"); exit(1);}
    for (i=1; i < argc; i++)
        {
        dev = atoi(argv[i]);
        printf("Device number: %d\n", dev);

        if (!ustat(dev,&thebuf))
            {
            printf(" Number of free blocks: %ld\n", thebuf.f_tfree);
            printf(" Number of free inodes: %d\n", thebuf.f_tinode);
            }
        else printf("Cannot get statistics on device %d\n", dev);
        }
    }
```

Examining the program in detail, we see that it includes two "header" files: `sys/types.h` (actually `/usr/include/sys/types.h`) and `ustat.h` (actually `/usr/include/ustat.h`). The first contains definitions of various types used in the data structure returned by `ustat` that is described in the second.

The main program has the two parameter passing arguments `argc` (the count) and `argv` (the array of strings). This program can accept a whole list of device numbers of file systems. Thus `argc` can be large.

The local variables for `main` are declared next. `Thebuf` is defined as a structure of type `ustat`, which is defined in the include file `ustat.h`. `Dev` is an integer that holds the device number, and `i` is an integer that indexes through the list of device numbers given by the user.

As before, we make sure that there are at least two arguments: the name of the program and the first device number. If not, we print an error message and return back to the shell.

Then we execute a `for` loop that goes through the entire list of device numbers specified in the command line. For each one we call `atoi` to convert from the string representation of the number to its internal binary integer representation, storing this in the integer variable `dev`. We print this number for verification, and we use it to call `ustat`.

The call to `ustat` is inside an `if` statement. Its arguments are `dev` and `&thebuf`. We have already explained the first argument. The second is a pointer (using &) to `thebuf` where the results of `ustat` are stored after the call. `Ustat` returns an integer that tells whether the call was successful. A zero value means success. By placing a logical not operator `!` before the name `ustat`, we cause the conclusion part of the `if` to be executed if all goes well.

With a successful call to `ustat`, we call `printf` to print the number of free blocks and the number of free i-nodes. These now are stored in the structure members `f_tfree` and `f_tinode` of `thebuf`. These members correspond to members of the structure for the super block. `Ustat` transfers these values from the super block of the specified file system.

If the call to `ustat` is unsuccessful, we print an error message to that effect.

# I-Nodes

Now let's examine i-nodes in detail. As we mentioned above, these are stored in the blocks immediately after the super block and before the actual files. They are data structures that act as gateways to the physical storage of the files.

### Example Program: Stat

The system's `stat` function provides a C programmer with access to much of the information contained in an i-node. We will look at a C program called `stat` that calls this function and displays the information it provides.

To use the program, type its name followed by a list of paths. Wildcards can be used to automatically generate such lists.

Here is a typical output of our `stat` program:

```
$ stat /◄┘
Path: /
File mode          st_mode:  40755
Inode number       st_ino:   2
Device ID          st_dev:   296
```

```
Special device ID    st_rdev:  397
Number of links      st_nlink: 11
User ID              st_uid:   3 (bin)
Group ID             st_gid:   3 (bin)
Size in bytes        st_size:  240
Last access          st_atime: Sun Apr 27 00:05:47 1986
Last modification    st_mtime: Mon Oct 21 23:29:48 1985
Last status change   st_ctime: Mon Oct 21 23:29:48 1985
```

This shows the data for just one path, namely /, which is the root of the entire directory system and hence the root of our file system. The first line of output confirms the path.

Before we describe each of these quantities in detail, let's look at the program to see how they are obtained.

```
/* file statistics */
#include <sys/types.h>
#include <sys/stat.h>
#include <pwd.h>
#include <grp.h>
#include <time.h>

struct passwd *getpwuid();
struct group  *getgrgid();

main (argc, argv)
   int argc;
   char *argv[];
   {
   struct stat thebuf;
   char *path;
   int i;

   if (argc < 2) { printf("Too few arguments.\n"); exit(1);}
   for (i=1; i < argc; i++)
      {
      path = argv[i];
      printf("Path: %s\n", path);

      if (!stat(path,&thebuf))
         {
         printf("File mode         st_mode:  %o\n",
               thebuf.st_mode);
         printf("Inode number      st_ino:   %d\n",
               thebuf.st_ino);
         printf("Device ID         st_dev:   %d\n",
               thebuf.st_dev);
```

```
        printf("Special device ID  st_rdev:  %d\n",
               thebuf.st_rdev);
        printf("Number of links    st_nlink: %d\n",
               thebuf.st_nlink);
        printf("User ID            st_uid:   %d",
               thebuf.st_uid);
        printf(" (%s)\n",
               getpwuid(thebuf.st_uid)->pw_name);
        printf("Group ID           st_gid:   %d",
               thebuf.st_gid);
        printf(" (%s)\n",
               getgrgid(thebuf.st_gid)->gr_name);
        printf("Size in bytes      st_size:  %ld\n",
               thebuf.st_size);
        printf("Last access        st_atime: %s",
               ctime(&thebuf.st_atime));
        printf("Last modification  st_mtime:  %s",
               ctime(&thebuf.st_mtime));
        printf("Last status change st_ctime: %s",
               ctime(&thebuf.st_ctime));
        printf("\n");
        }
        else printf("Cannot get statistics on %s\n", path);
        }
    }
```

The program is compiled as follows:

```
cc stat.c
```

That is, it requires no special C libraries.

The program has a large number of include files. Types.h defines certain basic data types used by the system. Stat.h defines the members of the stat structure returned by the stat function. Pwd.h provides definitions used to access information about user ID contained in the password file (/etc/passwd). Grp.h contains definitions needed to access information about group IDs contained in the group file (/etc/group). Time.h helps us use the date and time data.

Next, we declare two external functions getpwuid, which returns a pointer to a structure of type passwd, and getgrgid, which returns a pointer to a structure of type group. The structure passwd contains the information from an entry in the password file and the structure group contains the information from an entry in the group file.

The main program has two arguments argc and argv that are used to pass parameters from the command line as we have done in previous programs. Argc and argv also are declared as before.

The main program has a number of local variables. Thebuf is a structure of type `stat`. Notice that we actually declare `thebuf` and not a pointer to it. This ensures that space is allocated for this structure. It is the programmer's responsibility to maintain space for the data returned from `stat`. `Path` is a string pointer to a copy of the pathname. `I` is an integer that indexes through a list of paths.

The program first checks to make sure that there are enough arguments (at least two, one for the command name and one for at least one pathname). If there are too few arguments, we print an error message and exit the program.

Next a `for` loop, indexed by `i`, runs through the list of pathnames invoked by the command line. Here, wildcards and other such expansions can be used in the command line to cause a long list of pathnames to appear in `argv`.

Each pathname is fetched from `argv[i]` and printed. The `path` and a pointer to `thebuf` are passed to the `stat` function. If `stat` was successful, it returns a zero value, otherwise it returns a −1. We test this value in an `if` statement, printing out the values of the various members of the `stat` structure if `stat` is successful, and if not, printing out an error message.

We also call `getpsuid` and `getgrgid` to access the *password* and *group* files to convert the ID numbers into *user* and *group* names.

### Exploring File Attributes

Now let's return to the output from our `stat` program, using it to motivate discussion of various quantities stored in an i-node.

**File Modes**—The second line of output from our `stat` program gives the file mode. This contains permission bits to control access to the file. It is displayed in octal because most of the bits come in groups of three. Let's examine these bits, starting from the left.

**File Types**—The upper four bits, bits 15 through 12, form the file type. There are four main types of files, then some more elusive types. Table 7-1 shows the types.

Type 10 is used for ordinary files. These include text files and files that contain programs, such as `ls`, `cat`, or `vi`. Type 04 is used for directories. Type 02 is used for files that represent character-oriented devices, such as terminals. Type 06 is used for block-oriented devices, such as disks or file systems.

The remaining four listed are harder to find. For example, type 01 is used for currently active `pipes`. These are temporary files created to hold output when commands are pipelined together. For example, for the pipeline

```
ls -l ¦ more
```

a temporary file is created to hold the output of the `ls` command while it is being displayed by `more`.

**Table 7-1**
**Codes for file types**

| Octal Code | Binary Code | Type |
|:---:|:---:|:---|
| 10 | 1000 | ordinary files |
| 04 | 0100 | directories |
| 02 | 0010 | special: character |
| 06 | 0110 | special: block |
| 07 | 0111 | special: multiplexed block |
| 03 | 0011 | special: multiplexed character |
| 05 | 0101 | special: name |
| 01 | 0001 | special: pipe |

Pipes are so elusive that they don't appear in the directory system. However, you can find currently open pipes by looking down the MODE column in the output of pstat. The pipes are associated with the i-nodes with mode 10000 (octal), which has the pattern 0001 for its upper four bits.

Types 03 and 07 refer to files that are shared by several processes.

**Special Permissions**—The next two bits, 11 and 10, of the mode word help regulate some special security situations, allowing or preventing processes to take on higher privileges than normally allowed for the user. These bits only work for files that contain directly executable programs. They have no effect for shell scripts.

As we discussed in Chapters 2 and 5, when a program is run, a process is "spawned" to manage it. This process has a number of identification numbers associated with it. These include: the real user ID, the effective user ID, the real group ID, and the effective group ID. These IDs are checked against the IDs and permissions of any file that the process tries to access.

Bit 11 is described as the *set user ID on execution* bit, and bit 10 is described as the *set group ID on execution* bit. If bit 11 has a value of 0, the process that is being spawned takes on an effective user ID equal to the user's ID. If bit 11 has a value of 1, the process takes on its effective user ID equal to the user ID of the owner of program file. In either case, the real user ID of the process is set equal to the ID of the user. Thus the "real" user ID is always available.

Most commands have bit 11 equal to 0, thus, they take on the same effective user ID as the real user ID and are treated with the same level of privilege as the user who executes them. Some commands, such as su, mv, passwd, and newgrp have this bit equal to 1. They need extra privileges to get their work done, so they can act like the owner of some very critical files, such as the password and group files.

Bit 10 is similar to bit 11, but it controls the group ID instead of the user ID. This gives a more subtle way of getting extra privileges.

Here is a C program that displays the real user ID, the effective user ID, real group ID, and the effective group ID. All of these quantities are returned by various system functions as you can see from this program.

```
/* get user and group IDs */

main()
    {
    printf("Real user ID number:        %d\n", getuid());
    printf("Effective user ID number:   %d\n", geteuid());
    printf("Real group ID number:       %d\n", getgid());
    printf("Effective group ID number: %d\n", getegid());
    printf("Process group ID number:    %d\n", getpgrp());
    }
```

Try compiling this program

```
cc getid.c
```

renaming it `getid`, then setting bits 11 and 10 with the command:

```
chmod u+s,g+s getid
```

Now run the command from some other user and some other group and see what happens. Suppose that the file was created by user number 203, whose current group ID number is 51, and that the command is called by user number 204, whose group ID number is 52. Then the output looks like:

```
Real user ID number:      204
Effective user ID number: 203
Real group ID number:     52
Effective group ID number: 53
```

**The Sticky Bit**—Bit 9 is called the sticky bit because it controls how hard the system holds onto the file after users are finished with it. When this bit has a value of 1, the program is retained in *swap* (memory or temporary disk storage) even if all users have finished with it. This speeds up the next use of it. The sticky bit can only be set by the super user using the `t` permission designation in the `chmod` command. Popular programs such as `vi`, `cc`, and `ls` have this bit set.

**User, Group, and Other Permissions**—The last nine bits, in bit positions 8 through 0, control permissions (see figure 7-6). They come in sets of three.

Bits 8, 7, and 6 control permissions for the file's owner. Bits 5, 4, and 3 control permissions for the file's group. Bits 2, 1, and 0 control permission for all others.

**Figure 7-6**
**Permission bits**

| bit 8 | bit 7 | bit 6 | bit 5 | bit 4 | bit 3 | bit 2 | bit 1 | bit 0 |
|---|---|---|---|---|---|---|---|---|
| read by owner | write by owner | execute by owner | read by group | write by group | execute by group | read by others | write by others | execute by others |

Within each set, the first bit controls *reading,* the second bit controls *writing,* and the third controls *execution.* Thus, bit 8 controls reading by the owner, bit 7 controls writing by the owner, bit 6 controls execution by the owner, bit 5 controls reading by a member of the file's group, and so on. These permissions use the *effective* user and group so that the set user and group bits work as "advertised."

As mentioned before, the chmod commands allow the owner and the super user to change these permissions. The C function chmod lets C programs run by the owner or by the super user do the same.

## Other Fields of the I-Node

Let's look at some of the other members of the i-node structure reported by stat.

**Device Numbers**—There are two device ID numbers stored in the i-node. The first device ID number indicates the particular device on which the file is stored. That is, this device number indicates membership. In our case, all our files belong to device number 296.

A second device ID, called the special device ID, is used for files that represent devices (special block or character types of files). In our case, the file system is represented by file /dev/root that has special device number 296. That is, it is the physical *owner* of all our files.

Device ID numbers are 16-bit integers whose upper byte is called the major device number and whose lower byte is called the minor device number. The major number indicates a particular physical *device driver* (see Chapters 2 and 9) to control a class of devices, such as hard disks, floppy disks, or memory. The minor device number indicates a particular use or function. The minor device numbers are passed to the device drivers so that they may select a particular function to perform.

In our case, the major special device number of /dev/root is 1 (because 296 is 1*256+40). This is also the major special device number of the files

/dev/hd0, /dev/hd00, /dev/hd02, and /dev/swap, all of which represent the hard disk in some way and are handled by the hard disk device driver.

Normally devices are stored in the directory dev. To check out the various device numbers, type:

    l /dev

This is equivalent to the -l option of the ls command.

**Number of Links**—Each i-node keeps track of the number of links that reference it (including . and .. names). For example, if the directory dira contains the files diraa and test, where diraa is a directory and test is an ordinary file, the i-node for dira has three links: one because it belongs to a directory itself, a second because of its . reference to itself, and a third because of a .. reference in the diraa file.

**User and Group IDs**—Each i-node contains identification for the file's owner and the file's group. These numbers, together with the permission bits and a process's effective user and group IDs, help determine who can access the file. For example, if a process has its user number equal to the user number in the i-node, and the permission bit for writing by the owner is equal to 1, the process can write to the file (or erase it).

The name of the owner can be found in the file /etc/passwd and the name of the group (if there is a name) can be found in the file /etc/group. Our program stat demonstrates how a C program can access these files to find these names. The files can be read by anyone but only written to by the super user because of the way that their permission bits are set.

**Size**—The size of the file is also stored in the i-node. It is stored as a 32-bit integer, thus limiting the size to a mere 4,294,967,296 bytes.

**Times**—There are *three* times stored in an i-node: the time of last access, the time of last modification, and the time of last status change.

The time of last access is set by the system calls creat, mknod, pipe, utime, and read. These commands either create the file, "touch" it (update its status), or read from it.

The time of last modification is set by the system calls creat, mknod, pipe, utime, and write. These commands either create the file, "touch" it, or write to it.

The time of last status change is set by the system calls chmod, chown, creat, link, mknod, pipe, utime, and write. These commands either create the file, "touch" it, write to it, or change its attributes.

Table 7-2 summarizes all of this.

## Modifying File Attributes

The last program in this chapter demonstrates how to modify a file using a *dialog*. The program called vm (for view and modify) displays the ownership

**Table 7-2**
**Updating times**

| Function | Last Access | Last Modification | Last Status Change |
|----------|:-----------:|:-----------------:|:------------------:|
| creat | x | x | x |
| mknod | x | x | x |
| pipe | x | x | x |
| utime | x | x | x |
| read | x | | |
| write | | x | x |
| chmod | | | x |
| chown | | | x |
| link | | | x |

and permissions of a specified file and allows a user to edit each item (see figure 7-7).

**Figure 7-7**
**Output of the vm program**

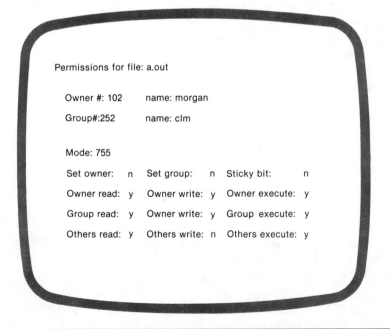

```
Permissions for file: a.out

    Owner #: 102      name: morgan
    Group#:252        name: clm


Mode: 755

Set owner:   n   Set group:    n   Sticky bit:        n
Owner read:  y   Owner write:  y   Owner execute:   y
Group read:  y   Owner write:  y   Group execute:   y
Others read: y   Others write: n   Others execute:  y
```

While the program is running, you can move the cursor from one file attribute to the next by pressing **control z**. **Control a** backs up one item, **return** enters the new value of an item (staying at the same item), **backspace** backs up one character while editing, and **escape** exits the program. When you exit, the current values are printed on the screen and you are asked whether you want them saved. Pressing **y** or **Y** updates the file's attributes with the new values. Pressing any other key causes the program to exit without saving this information.

Some of the items are linked together. For example, the owner's name is derived from the owner's ID number using the system's password file /etc/passwd. Thus, when the ID number is changed, the program automatically updates the name. Conversely, whenever you change the name, the program automatically tries to update the ID number. However, many possible ID numbers do not correspond to any user names. In this case, the name is made blank, but the ID number is left as entered.

The group ID and name are similarly linked using the system group file /etc/group.

The permission bits (displayed individually as y or n values) are linked to the file mode number (displayed here in octal). When you change a permission bit (pressing **return**, **control a**, or **control z** to register the new value), the mode changes. When you change the mode, the permission bits also change accordingly.

Here is the program:

```
/* view and modify permissions of a file */

#include <curses.h>
#include <sys/types.h>
#include <sys/stat.h>
#include <pwd.h>
#include <grp.h>

struct passwd *getpwuid(), *getpwnam();
struct group  *getgrgid(), *getgrnam();

/* the title for the screen */
struct dTitle
   {
   int y, x;       /* position of title */
   char str[255]; /* title string */
   }
title[] =
   {
   /*  y,  x, str */
     { 1,  3, " "},
     { 2,  3, "Cntl A = prev item, Cntl Z = next item,\
 RET = enter item, ESC = finish"}
```

```
      };
#define lasttitle ((sizeof(title))/(sizeof(struct dTitle)))


/* structure of the screen */
struct dItem
    {
    int yl, xl;    /* position of label */
    char *strl;    /* pointer to the label string */
    int ye, xe;    /* position of edit string */
    int maxe;      /* maximum number characters in edit string */
    int cnte;      /* character count in edit string */
    char stre[41]; /* pointer to edit string */
    }
dList[]=
    {
    /* yl, xl, strl,               ye, xe, maxe, cnte, stre */
      { 5,  5, "Owner #:",          5, 14,  5,    0, },
      { 5, 22, "name:",             5, 28, 12,    0, },
      { 7,  5, "Group #:",          7, 14,  5,    0, },
      { 7, 22, "name:",             7, 28, 12,    0, },
      {11,  5, "Mode:",            11, 11,  4,    0, },
      {13,  5, "Set owner:",       13, 19,  1,    0, },
      {13, 22, "Set group:",       13, 36,  1,    0, },
      {13, 39, "Sticky bit:",      13, 55,  1,    0, },
      {15,  5, "Owner read:",      15, 19,  1,    0, },
      {15, 22, "Owner write:",     15, 36,  1,    0, },
      {15, 39, "Owner execute:",   15, 55,  1,    0, },
      {17,  5, "Group read:",      17, 19,  1,    0, },
      {17, 22, "Group write:",     17, 36,  1,    0, },
      {17, 39, "Group execute:",   17, 55,  1,    0, },
      {19,  5, "Others read:",     19, 19,  1,    0, },
      {19, 22, "Others write:",    19, 36,  1,    0, },
      {19, 39, "Others execute:",  19, 55,  1,    0, }
    };
#define lastitem ((sizeof(dList))/(sizeof(struct dItem)))


  main(argc, argv)
    int argc;
    char *argv[];
    {
    struct stat thebuf;
    char *path;
    char ch;
    int i, j;
    int newedit=TRUE, done=FALSE;
    int flags;
```

```
if (argc < 2) { printf("Too few arguments.\n");  exit(1);}
path = argv[1];

if (stat(path,&thebuf))
   {printf("Cannot get statistics on %s\n", path); exit(1);}

/* set up screen and terminal I/O */
initscr(); crmode(); noecho(); nonl();

/* clear screen and display title and item labels */
clear();

sprintf(title[0].str,"Permissions for file: %s", path);
for(i=0; i < lasttitle; i++)
   mvaddstr(title[i].y, title[i].x, title[i].str);

sprintf(dList[0].stre,"%d", thebuf.st_uid);
sprintf(dList[2].stre,"%d", thebuf.st_gid);
sprintf(dList[4].stre,"%4o", thebuf.st_mode & 07777);

for(i = 0; i < lastitem; i++)
   {
   mvaddstr(dList[i].yl, dList[i].xl, dList[i].strl);
   insert(i);
   }

update(0);
update(2);
update(4);

moveto(i=0);
refresh();

while (!done)
   {
   switch(ch=getch())
      {
      case 27: /* escape key to exit */
         done = TRUE;
         break;

      case '\r': /* return key to select next item */
         if(!newedit) update(i);
         newedit = TRUE;
         break;

      case 1: /* control a goes backward one item */
```

```
            if(!newedit) update(i);
            newedit = TRUE;
            i--;
            if(i==-1) i=lastitem-1;
            moveto(i);
            break;

    case 26: /* control z goes forward one item */
            if(!newedit) update(i);
            newedit = TRUE;
            i++;
            if(i==lastitem) i=0;
            moveto(i);
            break;

    case 21: /* control u deletes the item */
            delete(i);
            update(i);
            newedit = TRUE;
            break;

    case '\b': /* backspace deletes a character */
            if ((dList[i].cnte > 0) && !newedit)
                {
                addstr("\b \b");
                dList[i].cnte--;
                dList[i].stre[dList[i].cnte] = 0;
                }
            break;

    default: /* handle regular characters */
            if (ch >= 32)
                {
                if (newedit) delete(i);
                newedit = FALSE;
                if(dList[i].cnte < dList[i].maxe)
                    {
                    dList[i].stre[dList[i].cnte] = ch;
                    dList[i].cnte++;
                    addch(ch);
                    }
                }
            break;
    }
refresh();
}
```

```
        /* display the final values in the list */
        nl();
        clear();
        move(1,0);
        printw("Path:  %s\n", path);
        printw("Owner: %s\t(%s)\n", dList[0].stre, dList[1].stre);
        printw("Group: %s\t(%s)\n", dList[2].stre, dList[3].stre);
        printw("Mode:  %s\n", dList[4].stre);
        printw("\n\n");
        printw("Save changes (y/n)? ");
        refresh();

        ch = getch();
        printw("%c\n\n",ch);
        refresh();
        if((ch=='y') || (ch=='Y'))
            {
            sscanf(dList[4].stre,"%o", &flags);
            chmod(path, flags);
            chown(path, atoi(dList[0].stre), atoi(dList[2].stre));
            }
        endwin();
}

update(i)
    int i;
    {
    int j, flags;
    struct passwd *pwptr;
    struct group  *grptr;

    switch(i)
        {
        case 0: /* i==0 */
            j = atoi(dList[0].stre);
            delete(0);
            sprintf(dList[0].stre,"%d",j);
            insert(0);
            delete(1);
            setpwent();
            if((pwptr = getpwuid(j)) != NULL)
                sprintf(dList[1].stre,"%s", pwptr->pw_name);
            else sprintf(dList[1].stre, " ");
            insert(1);
            break;
        case 1: /* i==1 */
            setpwent();
```

```
        if((pwptr = getpwnam(dList[1].stre)) != NULL)
            {
            delete(0);
            sprintf(dList[0].stre,"%d", pwptr->pw_uid);
            insert(0);
            }
        else
            {
            delete(1);
            sprintf(dList[1].stre, " ");
            insert(1);
            }
        break;
    case 2: /*  i==2 */
        j = atoi(dList[2].stre);
        delete(2);
        sprintf(dList[2].stre,"%d",j);
        insert(2);

        delete(3);
        setgrent();
        if((grptr = getgrgid(j)) != NULL)
            sprintf(dList[3].stre, "%s", grptr->gr_name);
        else sprintf(dList[3].stre, " ");
        insert(3);
        break;
    case 3: /*  i==3 */
        setgrent();
        if((grptr = getgrnam(dList[3].stre)) != NULL)
            {
            delete(2);
            sprintf(dList[2].stre,"%d", grptr->gr_gid);
            insert(2);
            }
        else
            {
            delete(3);
            sprintf(dList[3].stre, " ");
            insert(3);
            }
        break;
    case 4: /*  i==4 */
        flags = 0;
        sscanf(dList[4].stre,"%o", &flags);
        delete(4);
        sprintf(dList[4].stre,"%4o", flags);
        insert(4);
```

```
                for(j=0; j<12; j++)
                    {
                    if ((1<<j) & flags) sprintf(dList[16-j].stre, "y");
                    else            sprintf(dList[16-j].stre, "n");
                    insert(16-j);
                    }
                break;

        case 5:
        case 6:
        case 7:
        case 8:
        case 9:
        case 10:
        case 11:
        case 12:
        case 13:
        case 14:
        case 15:
        case 16:
            switch(dList[i].stre[0])
                {
                case('y'): break;
                case('1'):
                case('Y'): dList[i].stre[0] = 'y'; break;
                default:   dList[i].stre[0] = 'n'; break;
                }
            insert(i);

            flags = 0;
            for(j=0; j<12; j++)
                flags |= (((dList[16-j].stre[0] == 'y') & 1) << j);
            delete(4);
            sprintf(dList[4].stre,"%4o", flags);
            insert(4);
            break;
        }
    moveto(i);
    }

delete(i)
    int i;
    {
    int j;
    moveto(i);
    for(j=0; j < dList[i].cnte; j++)
        {
```

```
            addstr(" ");
            dList[i].stre[j] = 0;
            }
        dList[i].cnte = 0;
        moveto(i);
        }

    insert(i)
        int i;
        {
        mvaddstr(dList[i].ye, dList[i].xe, dList[i].stre);
        dList[i].cnte = strlen(dList[i].stre);
        }

    moveto(i)
        int i;
        {
        move(dList[i].ye, dList[i].xe);
        }
```

Now let's examine this program in detail.

It uses five include files: curses.h because we wish to move the cursor around the screen, sys/types.h and sys/stat.h because we need file statistics, pwd.h because we are looking things up in the password file, and grp.h because we are using the group file.

Four external string functions, getpwuid, getpwnam, getgrgid, and getgrname, are declared. The first two are used to search the password file, and the second two are used to search the group file.

There are two global structures, title and dList that we declare and initialize. Title contains a couple of lines of titles for the screen. The first line is initially blank and is filled in later with the name of the file. At the end of title, lasttitle is a macro that specifies the number of title entries.

The second structure dList contains a list of the items that are displayed on the screen. Every item has a label and an edit string, each with x and y coordinates to designate placement on the screen. In this list are the owner's ID, the owner's name, the group ID, the group name, the file mode, and twelve permission bits. At the end of dList, the macro lastitem specifies the number of entries in dList.

The main program has the usual two arguments to help pass arguments from the command line. In this case, we pass the pathname of the file that we wish to change.

There are a number of local variables in the main program. Thebuf is a buffer of type stat for holding information about the file returned from the stat function. Path is a string that holds the pathname, ch is used to hold single characters, i is an integer variable used as an index to title and dList, and j is an integer used as a temporary variable in several different ways.

Newedit is an integer that helps with the editing of items. It is true (nonzero) if an item is being edited, but not yet entered or reconciled with the password file, group file, or other items. It is initialized to a value of TRUE.

Done is an integer that helps with program control. It is initially set to FALSE, and it is set to TRUE when the program should terminate.

Flags is a temporary variable used to hold the file mode during computation.

The program begins by checking to see whether there are too few arguments in the command line or whether it cannot find the file. In either case, it issues the appropriate error message and exits.

Next, we initialize the screen and keyboard I/O for the curses routines, turning off echoing and the usual mapping of carriage return and linefeed. We also clear the screen.

We use the sprintf (formatted print to a string) function to load a message about the pathname into the title, then we use the curses routine mvaddstr to place the titles on the screen.

We next use sprintf to load the owner ID number, the group ID number, and the file mode from the stat buffer into the edit strings of dList for display on the screen. A for loop displays the data in dList on the screen. We then call a routine update three times to fill in the owner name, group name, and permission bits. The update routine appears near the end of the program. It is used mainly to adjust certain items when other related items are modified.

Next we initialize some variables for our main loop, setting i equal to 0 to edit the first item and calling our own moveto function to move the cursor to that item. We call refresh to update the display screen before entering the main loop.

The main loop is handled by a while statement that contains switch to select and perform an action and a refresh to show the results on the display.

The switch statement fetches a character from the keyboard and selects the appropriate action based on the value of that character.

For **escape** (ASCII 27), done is set equal to TRUE to terminate the program. This first terminates the while loop, then gives the user a chance to save the new values before the program terminates.

For **return** (\r) we "close" the editing of the currently selected item. Here, we call update if newedit is FALSE, then set newedit to TRUE.

For **control a** (ASCII 1), we call update in the same way that we do for a **return** and we increment i, setting it to zero if it becomes equal to the number of items. This ensures that we cycle through all of the items.

For **control z** (ASCII 26), we close editing as before and decrement i, setting it equal to one less than the number of items if it becomes equal to −1. This ensures that we cycle through all items when we go in backward order.

For **control u** (ASCII 21), we call our delete routine to delete the item, then call update to adjust the other values accordingly. We also set newedit to TRUE.

For **backspace** (\b) we check to see whether there are any characters to delete and that we are currently editing an item. If so, we send the string consisting of: **backspace, space, backspace**, and we make the last character in the edit string equal to zero. This terminates the string at the correct place. We use j as a temporary variable to store the position of the last character in the string, which we compute from the length of the string.

All other characters are handled as the default case. Here we check to see whether the character is a control character. If it is not, we proceed. If newedit is true, we delete the item first before inserting the character. We add the character only if the edit string is not too long (less than the maximum count for that item). If all conditions are met, we place the character onto the screen and in the next character position.

After the while loop, we call clear to clear the screen; move to line 1, column 0 of the screen; and call printw to display the values on the screen. We then ask users if they want to save the values. If so, we call chmod to set the permission bits and chown to set the owner's and group's IDs. Notice that we use the formatted scan function sscanf to convert the octal string representation of the file permissions to an integer.

The main program concludes with a call to endwin.

The update routine is next. It has one argument, an integer i that specifies the current item we have been editing. Within the function, j is an integer that points to character positions, flags is used to temporarily hold the permission bits, pwptr points to entries from the password file, and grptr points to group entries in the group file.

The routine consists of a switch statement to cover the different cases of i, the item number. That is, each item requires a different procedure for updating.

For items 0 and 2, we must translate numbers into names, looking them up in the password or group file respectively. First we establish the current value of the respective ID number. This is to rid ourselves of any inappropriate input typed by the user. Then we update the name in the next item.

To establish the ID number, we first call the atoi (ASCII to integer) function to grab the value from the edit string. This function returns the integer value represented by the string. However, if the string cannot be interpreted as an integer, it returns a zero value. We call our delete function to remove the item from the edit string and from the screen, call sprintf to put a newly reformatted copy of the number in the edit string, then call insert to display it on the screen.

To update the name, we delete it, then call get...id to search the password or group file. This returns a pointer, which is NULL if the search was unsuccessful. If we find a valid name, we call sprintf to place it in the edit string. If not, we put an empty string there. Finally, we call insert to place it on the screen.

Items 1 and 3 work the other way. That is, we are given newly edited names and we wish to look up the corresponding number. Here, an if statement fetches and checks the results of a search through the password or group file. If the search is successful, we update the number. If not, we blank the unsuccessful name.

Item 4 is the file mode. It is similar to items 0 and 2. However, the number is in octal, so we must use the sscanf function to convert from octal ASCII to internal integer format. We then update the permission bits with a for loop. We use sprintf to place y or n in the edit string and insert to display the result on the screen.

Items 5 and greater are the permission bits. We use a switch statement to clean up the edit string, making it either y or n. Three choices, Y, y, and 1 become y. All others become n. We then recompute the file mode (bits 0 through 11). A for loop checks each permission bit edit string looking for a y to indicate that the corresponding bit should be set. The result is accumulated into a temporary variable called flags. We delete the old value, load the new value, and display it on the screen.

The last step in the update routine is to call moveto to move the cursor to the beginning of the currently selected item.

The delete function is much like a repeated character delete. It has a single integer parameter that is the item number. We use essentially the same code as the case of backspace in the main loop. Notice that we delete in a backward fashion. This means that the cursor is in the proper place when we finish.

The insert function uses the mvaddstr function of curses to place the edit string for an item in the proper place on the screen. It has a single integer parameter, which is the item number.

The moveto function uses the move function of curses to place the cursor at the beginning of the edit string for an item. It has a single integer parameter, which is the item number.

# Fundamental File Reading and Writing Routines

Now that we have explored the structure of the file and directory system, let's look at some fundamental system calls for reading from and writing to files.

We have already used some higher level routines, such as fopen, getc, and fclose, which are part of the standard I/O package. We now briefly discuss the five basic system functions that these are built on. If you need more details, consult the XENIX manuals.

## The Creat Function

The creat function creates a new file or makes an existing file ready for writing by first deleting its current contents. It expects two parameters, a string that is a pathname and an integer which contains the lower nine bits of the file mode word. If successful, it returns an integer called the file descriptor. If unsuccessful, it returns a value of −1.

## The Open Function

The open function opens a file for reading or writing. It expects two or three parameters. The first is a string that contains the pathname, the second is an integer containing information about how the file is to behave, and the third is optional and is an integer containing permission bits. If successful, it returns an integer called the file descriptor. If not, it returns −1.

## The Lseek Function

The lseek function moves the current position (called the read/write pointer) within an open file. It expects three parameters: an integer containing a valid file descriptor, such as one returned from creat or open, a long integer that helps specify the desired byte position within the file, and an integer whence that also helps specify the position. If the last parameter is 0, the current position is set to the value contained in the second parameter. If the last parameter is 1, the current position is incremented by the second parameter. If the last parameter is 2, the current position is set equal to the size of the file plus the second parameter. If the function is successful, it returns the newly set value of the current position. If unsuccessful, it returns a value of −1.

## The Read Function

The read function reads a specified number of bytes from an open file. It expects three parameters: an integer containing a valid file descriptor, a character pointer to buffer where the bytes are stored once they are read, and an unsigned integer that specifies how many bytes to read. If successful, it returns the actual number of characters read. This number may be less than the number of bytes requested if fewer characters are available. This happens for regular files stored on the disk and for files that are really I/O channels. If unsuccessful the function returns a value of −1. If the end of the file is reached, a value of 0 is returned.

## The Write Function

The write function writes a specified number of bytes to an open file. It expects three parameters: an integer containing a valid file descriptor, a character pointer to buffer where the bytes are stored that are to be written to the file, and an unsigned integer that specifies how many bytes to write. If successful, it returns the actual number of characters written. If not enough room is available on the disk, this number may be less than the number of bytes requested. If unsuccessful in writing any bytes, the function returns a value of −1.

## Example Program: Save

Here is a short example of a program that opens a file, writes to it, then closes it. To simplify matters, the characters that it writes come from standard input.

To use this program, type its name followed by the name of the file in which you want to save the text.

```
/* save a file from standard input */
#include<stdio.h>
main(argc, argv)
    int argc;
    char *argv[];
    {
    int fid, ch;


    if (argc < 2) {printf("Too few arguments\n"); exit(1);}


    if((fid = creat(argv[1], 0777)) != -1)
        {
        while((ch= getchar()) != EOF) write(fid, &ch, 1);
        close(fid);
        }
    else printf("Cannot create the file %s\n", argv[1]);
    }
```

The program is compiled without explicitly mentioning any C libraries.

We see that the program passes arguments in the usual way from the command line using argc and argv parameters.

The program has two integer variables, fid contains the file descriptor and ch holds the characters as they are being transferred from standard input to the file.

After checking that there are a least two arguments (one that is the command itself), the program calls creat to try to create the specified file. Here, we pass the file permissions as an octal 0777, which indicates that all permissions are to be granted. However, any bits in a system variable called umask are cleared.

If creat is successful, we enter a while loop, reading characters from standard input with the getchar function and calling write to send them to the specified file. The loop continues until we reach the end of the input file (**control d** for keyboard input).

The write function uses a single character buffer ch, thus, its second parameter is the pointer &ch to ch and its third parameter is 1, which represents the length of the buffer.

After the while loop, we call close to close the file. Its single parameter is the file descriptor.

This concludes our discussion of save.c. There are several other low level file routines including dup and fcntl that we won't go into here.

# Summary

In this chapter we have explored files, their attributes, and how they are organized in file systems. We have seen how directories help organize files in a hierarchical manner. We have seen that the directories themselves are files in the file system that contain links to i-nodes where file attributes and information about files are stored.

We have seen example programs that display the contents of directories and i-nodes, and a program to interactively modify file permissions and ownership.

We have also discussed five fundamental file routines from which many of the others are built. With these you can read and write to files in a reasonably direct manner.

# Questions and Answers

## Questions

1. Can everything in XENIX be represented by a file?
2. How do the rules for forming pathnames differ between XENIX, UNIX, and PC-DOS?
3. What information is stored in a directory file in XENIX? Where is the rest of the information stored for the files in a directory?
4. How are file permissions stored?
5. Name five fundamental XENIX system calls for file I/O.

## Answers

1. No, not everything in XENIX can be represented by a file, but ordinary files; directories; peripheral devices, such as keyboards, screens, terminals, printers, communication networks; and even internal devices, such as memory, can be represented by files. An example of something that is not represented by a file is a process.
2. XENIX and UNIX use the same rules for forming pathnames. PC-DOS uses backslashes ( \ ) instead of ordinary slashes ( / ) to separate the individual directory names in a pathname.
3. A directory file contains a list of names (file or directory) with their i-node number. The rest of the information about these files and subdirectories is stored in the corresponding i-nodes. I-nodes are stored near the beginning of the physical storage for a file system.

4. The read, write, and execute permissions for a file's owner, group, and all others are stored as bits in a 16-bit computer word within the file's i-node.

5. Five fundamental XENIX file I/O system calls are: `open`, `close`, `read`, `write`, and `lseek`.

# 8

# Process Control

- Processes
- The Fork Function
- A First Warmup Example
- Using Semaphores
- Example Program
- Signals
- Example Program
- Pipes
- Example Program
- Summary
- Questions and Answers

# Process Control

XENIX is essentially a multitasking system for a single user. It divides its work into manageable packages called *processes*. Each process runs its own program and is allowed to compete with all the other processes for the computer's CPU, memory, and other resources.

This chapter discusses how XENIX manages its processes through a master control table, and how it allows them to give birth, wait for each other, exchange data, and die. A number of example programs written in the C programming language illustrate these concepts.

## Processes

As we have seen, work is accomplished in the XENIX system by processes. Whenever a program is to be run, a process is created to manage the execution of that program.

In Chapter 2, we studied the output of the ps command that displays information about the various processes currently in the system. Let's take a closer look at some different output from this command. The −el option displays a "long" (detailed) listing:

```
% ps -el◀┘
 F S UID PID PPID  C PRI NI ADDR SZ WCHAN TTY TIME CMD
 3 S   0   0    0  0   0 20 2a40  2 47472  ? 0:01 swapper
 0 S   0   1    0  0  30 20   98 15 65566  ? 0:02 init
 0 S 201  33    1  0  30 20   ef 23 65646 co 0:17 csh
 0 S 202  34    1  0  30 20  137 23 65726 02 0:17 csh
 1 S   0  18    1  0  40 20 3900 12 37252  ? 0:02 update
 0 S  14  25    1  0  26 20   aa 26 150650 ? 0:02 lpsched
 1 S   0  29    1  0  26 20 4500 26 151214 ? 0:02 cron
 0 S  10  35    1  0  30 20   dc 17 66226 03 0:10 sh
```

```
1 S 201  36   1   0  30 20 5980 23  66306 04 0:18 csh
1 S 201  37   1   0  30 20 4f80 23  66366 2a 0:17 csh
0 S 201  46  33   0  29 20  1e0 58  47546 co 0:02 ls
0 S 202  47  34   0  28 20  21a 44  47636 02 0:08 vi
1 S  10  49  35   0  29 20 6ac0 13  47756 03 0:01 od
1 R 201  51  36  17  58 20 3c00  6        04 4:09 yes
1 R 201  57  37  16  58 20 31c0 26        2a 0:13 ps
```

This gives a view of the system's *process control table,* which it uses to keep track of all its processes.

The first column, F, contains the process flags. This is a number that gives the status of processes. Various bits of this number indicate such things as the process' presence in memory. For the first process (running swapper as indicated by the last column), a value of three (bits 0 and 1 on) indicates that the process is in main memory and is a system (kernel) process. For the second, third, and fourth processes, a value of 0 indicates that the process is not currently in main memory. That is, it is currently "swapped out." For the fifth process (and others), a value of 1 indicates that it is currently in memory, definitely a prerequisite for it to run.

The second column, S, gives the process state. This is a letter designating whether the process is running (R), sleeping (S), waiting (W), stopped (T), or terminated (Z). Most of these processes are sleeping (an S), but the last two, yes and ps, are running (R).

The third column, UID, gives the user identification number. User number 0 denotes the root, the super user. The root owns several of the system's processes, including swapper, init, update, and cron. User number 10 denotes the account sysinfo. It is running a shell csh and the od command (octal dump). User number 201 is running several shells (csh) and the ps command.

The fourth column, PID, gives the process identification number.

The fifth column, PPID, gives the identification number of the process's *parent.* In Chapter 2, we used these numbers to trace the ancestry of some processes, making a family tree.

The sixth column, C, gives the CPU utilization. This is the percent of usage that the process is making of the CPU.

The seventh column, PRI, gives the priority. Priority is used by the kernel to help schedule processes in an equitable fashion. A lower priority number means better treatment and a higher number means worse treatment. Generally, whenever a process is getting use of the CPU, its priority is increased, so it is given worse treatment next. This prevents any process from "hogging" the CPU.

The eighth column, NI, gives the "niceness" for the process. This is a number used in computation of the priority. It can be increased by the user with the nice command. For example

```
nice +10 ps -el
```

causes the ps command to be run with a nice number augmented by 10, which results in a higher priority number. This gives worse service to our command and is "nice" to everyone else. Only the super user can decrease the niceness. In this display all processes have niceness 20, the default.

The ninth column, ADDR, gives the location of the process in memory, if it is in memory, or on the disk, if it is swapped out.

The tenth column, SZ, gives the size of the process in blocks.

The eleventh column, WCHAN, is used to control *sleeping* and *waking up*. In Chapter 9, we see how this works.

The twelfth column, TTY, identifies the terminal that the process is using. Several of the system's process commands, including swapper, init, update, and cron are not attached to any terminal and thus have a ? in this column. The console is denoted by co. This is running a shell and the ls command. The other console screens are denoted by 02, 03, and 04. These are all in use. The serial line 2a is also being used to run this particular ps command.

The thirteenth column, TIME, shows the execution time for each process in minutes and seconds.

The last column, CMD, displays the command that the process is executing.

## The Fork Function

The primary method for creating new processes is the fork function. It truly acts like a fork in the road of execution, causing a process to split into two with each half heading down a separate side of the fork.

The two processes are identical, except for the functional result returned from the fork function. For the *child* process, the fork function returns an integer value of zero, and for the parent, it returns the process identification number of the child. Otherwise they have the same code to execute. Of course, they can behave radically differently based upon this one value.

## A First Warmup Example

Here is a short warmup program that illustrates how the fork function works. When you run this program, it prints two lines on the screen. One line reads: I am the parent., and the other reads: I am the child. These lines may occur in either order because they are generated by two separate processes running independently of each other.

```
main()
 {
 if(fork()==0) printf("I am the parent.\n");
 else          printf("I am the child.\n");
 }
```

Let's look the program listing. There is only a main program consisting of an `if` statement. The condition for the `if` executes the `fork` function. A zero result from `fork` indicates the parent, and so the message `I am the parent.` is printed. A nonzero result indicates the child, and so the message `I am the child.` is printed.

## Using Semaphores

Let's explore how processes can be synchronized as they demand exclusive access to resources such as the terminal.

We will look at an example program called `sem` that uses a synchronizing technique called a `semaphore`. In XENIX, a `semaphore` is a special type of file that always has zero length. We will see how it acts as a "flagman" controlling traffic on a one-way stretch of road, causing some processes to wait while others proceed. This is valuable when several processes share something (a resource) like a terminal, file, or printer that requires exclusive access for proper performance of the system. In our example we will see why access to the user's terminal needs to be protected in this way.

Several system operations are associated with semaphores. They include `creatsem` to create semaphore files, `waitsem` to wait for exclusive access to a semaphore, and `sigsem` to signal when a process wants to relinquish a semaphore. There are other operations as well, but these are all we need.

You can think of a semaphore as a ticket, granting a process exclusive access to a section of code in your program. You place a `waitsem` at the beginning of the section of code and the `sigsem` at the end. Such a section of code is called a *critical section*. Within its boundaries you can place statements that require exclusive access to a particular resource.

Several rules must be carefully followed.

1. Critical sections must not overlap.
2. Critical sections must not contain loop structures.
3. All statements that access the shared resource must fall within a critical section bounded by the semaphore operations.

Rule number three is particularly important. The proper protection of shared resources depends on having each process observe this rule. If process A sets up a critical section correctly, but process B does not, process A gets *no* protection.

## Example Program

Let's see how our `sem` program creates a `semaphore`, then uses it to control a parent and child process resulting from a `fork` operation. We also closely examine what happens to the process identification numbers during forking.

Both the parent and the child print several lines of output to the terminal. Each line printed by the child is indented by a tab character, whereas lines printed by the parent are not indented. With no synchronization, the outputs often get garbled as they compete for the terminal.

```
Original process id = 1047
I am 1047, the parent of child 1048.
I have exclusive use of the terminal
because I have taken the semaphore
        I am the child with process id = 1048.
        I have exclusive use of the terminal
        because I have taken the semaphore
        by executing the waitsem function.
        I will now relinquish it by executing the waitsem
        function.
I will now relinquish it with the
sigsem function.
t with the
        sigsem function.
        Exiting with status = 5.
The child 1048 has finished.
Status was 500.
```

As you can see, the program first displays its process identification number before the `fork`. Next, the parent announces itself, giving its process identification number and the process identification number of its child. It then claims to have exclusive access to the terminal because it has taken the semaphore. However, this version of the program does not use semaphores, thus the child can interrupt any time. The child, in fact, does interrupt at this point. After the child prints a few lines, the parent interrupts again, actually in the middle of one of the child's lines.

Here is a typical output from a proper version of the program. The parent begins and is allowed to continue to the end of its speech until it relinquishes the semaphore.

```
Original process id = 969
Creating semaphore s1.
I am 969, the parent of child 972.
I have exclusive use of the terminal
because I have taken the semaphore
by executing the waitsem function.
I will now relinquish it with the
sigsem function.
```

```
        I am the child with process id = 972.
        I have exclusive use of the terminal
        because I have taken the semaphore
        by executing the waitsem function.
        I will now relinquish it with the
        sigsem function.
        Exiting with status = 5.
The child 972 has finished.
Status was 500.
```

It is quite possible for the child to gain access to the terminal first.

```
Original process id = 967
Creating semaphore s1.
        I am the child with process id = 968.
        I have exclusive use of the terminal
        because I have taken the semaphore
        by executing the waitsem function.
        I will now relinquish it with the
        sigsem function.
        Exiting with status = 5.
I am 967, the parent of child 968.
I have exclusive use of the terminal
because I have taken the semaphore
by executing the waitsem function.
I will now relinquish it with the
sigsem function.
The child 968 has finished.
Status was 500.
```

Now let's examine the program itself. This is the proper version of the program. The unsynchronized version is made by removing all lines that involve the semaphore.

```c
/* spawn a process */
main()
    {
    int p, x, s1;
    printf("Original process id = %d\n", getpid());
    if((s1=creatsem("s1", 0777))>0)
        printf("Creating semaphore s1.\n");
    else
        {
        printf("Cannot create semaphore s1.\n");
        exit(1);
        }
```

```
if((p=fork())!=0)
  {
  waitsem(s1);
     printf("I am %d, the parent of child %d.\n", getpid(), p);
     printf("I have exclusive use of the terminal\n");
     printf("because I have taken the semaphore\n");
     printf("by executing the waitsem function.\n");
     printf("I will now relinquish it with the\n");
     printf("sigsem function.\n");
  sigsem(s1);
  printf("The child %d has finished.\n", wait(&x));
  printf("Status was %x.\n", x);
  }
else
  {
  waitsem(s1);
     printf("\tI am the child with process id = %d.\n",
           getpid());
     printf("\tI have exclusive use of the terminal\n");
     printf("\tbecause I have taken the semaphore\n");
     printf("\tby executing the waitsem function.\n");
     printf("\tI will now relinquish it with the\n");
     printf("\tsigsem function.\n");
  sigsem(s1);
  waitsem(s1);
     printf("\tExiting with status = 5.\n");
  sigsem(s1);
  exit(5);
  }
}
```

The main program declares three integer variables: p to hold the result of the fork, x to hold a status result returned from child to parent, and s1 to hold a semaphore identification number.

The program first calls the getpid function to determine the current process identification number before any "forking" takes place. It announces this in the first line of output.

Next, we try to create a semaphore. We call creatsem much like we would call creat if we wished to create an ordinary file.

The creatsem function expects two parameters: a string containing the name of the semaphore and an integer containing the file access mode (see Chapter 7). If the result returned by this function is − 1, an error must have occurred, thus we exit the program with an error message: Cannot create semaphore s1. If everything goes okay, we print the message: Creating semaphore s1.

Next, we call fork to split off the child process. If the result of the fork is nonzero, we handle the parent, otherwise we handle the child.

The code for the parent begins with a `waitsem` function. This introduces the critical section. The `sigsem` function ends it. All statements within the critical section have been indented to make this section stand out clearly.

After the parent's critical section, we call the `wait` function to wait for the child to finish. The `wait` function returns an integer containing the process identification number of the terminating child. The argument of the `wait` is a pointer to an integer in which the status is placed. The status word contains two parts: its upper eight bits contain whatever number was placed in the argument to the child's `exit` function, and the lower eight bits contain the status of the child's exit as determined by the operating system. A value of zero here means normal successful exit by the child.

The child's program is contained within the `else` clause. The child has two critical sections, each is "bracketed" by a `waitsem` at its beginning and a `sigsem` at its end. Each statement within the critical sections is indented. Each line of output begins with a tab so that it is clearly recognizable as belonging to the child. After the critical sections the child exits, placing a value of 5 in the argument of the exit. This value was chosen arbitrarily so that you could recognize it when it was picked up and printed by the parent.

We can have as many critical sections as we please. Other processes may interrupt between them but not during them.

In this example, we have but one semaphore. If we have multiple resources, we could have a separate semaphore for each.

## Signals

Another way that processes are synchronized is through the use of *signals*.

A signal is a software device for interrupting running processes. Signals can be generated in a number of ways including: pressing special keys on your terminal keyboard, disconnecting your telephone connection to the computer, or an error condition such as a memory addressing error or a bad parameter to a system call. They also can be generated by the `kill` command or `kill` function call.

In XENIX the various types of signals are numbered from 1 to 19, although Microsoft warns that they plan to discontinue use of signals with numbers 18 and 19.

Signals can be aimed at particular processes. For example, the `kill` command sends a specified signal to a set of specified processes. The following command line sends signal number 9 to processes with identification numbers 34, 63, and 84:

```
kill -9 35 63 84
```

Signal number 9 causes processes to terminate. If you don't specify the signal number, the `kill` command sends signal number 15, which is a "more polite" request for a process to die as we will see in following text. It is interesting to note that the kill instruction is used to send all signals, even ones that are not deadly.

Some signals can be "trapped" by the processes to which they are aimed, and some cannot. For example, signal number 15 (polite request to die) can be trapped, but signal number 9 cannot (direct order to die).

# Example Program

Here is an example program that uses signal numbers 15 (software terminate) and 16 (user defined signal 1) to communicate between a parent and a child process.

Let's begin with the program's output. It consists of a series of diagnostic messages, thus, this program is purely educational rather than useful in its own right.

```
Setting the acknowledge routine.
Setting the stopping routine.
The parent 384 tries to signal the child 385 with the result 0.
The parent will now pause.
        The child acknowledges the signal.
        The child will now wait for the flag.
        The child tries to signal the parent with the result 0.
        The child will now pause.
The parent acknowledges the signal.
The parent just woke up with the result −1.
The parent tries to kill child with result 0.
        The child is stopping.
The parent is now exiting.
```

When you run this program, you first see messages generated before the birth of the child saying that an acknowledge and a stop routine have been set up. This means that routines have been set up to trap signal numbers 16 and 15. When we study the program listing, we will see how this is done.

Next you see a message from the parent indicating that it is trying to signal the child. The parent then pauses, waiting for the child.

Next messages from the child say that it acknowledges the signal and it is waiting for a software flag that is set in its acknowledge routine. These two events could happen in either order because the child may get the signal before or after it begins waiting for the signal. In either case, the child does not try to signal back until both messages have appeared. After the child signals the parent, it pauses.

The parent now responds, acknowledging the acknowledge signal from the child. It announces that it just "woke up" and that it is now trying to kill the child.

The child now says that it is stopping. The parent then signs off too.

```
/* this program illustrates signals. */

#include<signal.h>

int child, parent, flag;

main()
    {
    int acknowledge(), stopping(), status;
    if(!signal(SIGUSR1, acknowledge))
        printf("Setting the acknowledge routine.\n");
    else
        {
        printf("Cannot set the acknowledge routine.\n");
        exit(1);
        }
    if(!signal(SIGTERM, stopping))
        printf("Setting the stopping routine.\n");
    else
        {
        printf("Cannot set the stopping routine.\n");
        exit(1);
        }
    parent = getpid();
    if((child=fork())==0)
        {
        printf("\tThe child will now wait for the flag.\n", child);
        while(!flag) /* do nothing */;
        printf("\tThe child tries to signal the parent ");
        printf("with the result %d.\n", kill(parent,SIGUSR1));
        printf("\tThe child will now pause.\n");
        printf("\tThe child just woke up with the result %d.\n",
                pause());
        printf("\tNormal exit for child.\n");
        }
    else
        {
        printf("The parent %d tries to signal the child %d ",
                parent, child);
        printf("with the result %d.\n",
                kill(child,SIGUSR1));
        printf("The parent will now pause.\n");
        printf("The parent just woke up with the result %d.\n",
                pause());
        printf("The parent tries to kill child with result %d.\n",
                kill(child,SIGTERM));
        wait(&status);
```

```
        printf("The parent is now exiting.\n");
        }
    }

acknowledge()
    {
    if(getpid()==parent)
        printf("The parent acknowledges the signal.\n");
    else
        printf("\tThe child acknowledges the signal.\n");
    flag = 1;
    }

stopping()
    {
    if(getpid()==parent)
        printf("The parent is stopping.\n");
    else
        printf("\tThe child is stopping.\n");
    exit(16);
    }
```

When we look at the listing, we see a main program and two additional functions `acknowledge` and `stopping` return integers. These functions trap signals 16 (user defined signal 1) and 15 (software terminate). The listing also includes the file `signal.h` that contains the official names of the signal numbers.

The integers `child`, `parent`, and `flag` are external variables that are shared by the main program and its signal trapping routines.

The main program declares `acknowledge` and `stopping` to be integer functions and `status` to be an integer. We then use the `signal` function to redirect signals 16 and 15 (officially `SIGUSR1` and `SIGTERM`) so that they are trapped by our signal trapping routines. The `signal` function has two parameters: the first is the signal number, and the second is the address of the trap routine given by its name. The C compiler can provide this address if these functions are properly declared as we have done. If the `signal` function fails either time, we print an error message and exit.

Before "forking", we call `getpid` to get the parent's identification (placing it in the external variable `parent`). This is needed by the child to communicate with the parent.

We `fork` with an `if` statement that provides separate codes for the child and the parent. The result of the `fork` function is placed in the variable `child`. Recall that for the parent, this is the child's `pid` (process id), but for the child, it is 0.

The child's program falls directly under the `if`. It consists of a series of `printf` statement and a `while` loop with an empty action statement. The messages in the `printf` statements are all indented with a tab. The child first declares it will wait for a flag. Then the while loop waits for flag to become true. The child explains that it is trying to signal the parent and executes the kill function to do so. The first parameter of kill is the pid of the desired process (in this case for the parent), and the second is the identification number of the desired signal (in this case, user defined signal 1).

The child declares that it will pause. The next statement is a "wake up" announcement that displays the result of the pause function. The wake-up announcement should never be displayed because the parent kills the child during this pause. Thus, the final statement Normal exit for child. should never be displayed.

The parent's program follows the else. The parent first calls kill to signal the child. The first parameter is the pid of the child (as stored in the variable child), and the second is the signal number (specified as SIGUSR1). The parent executes a pause with explanation much as we saw previously for the child. However, its "wake up" announcement should execute fully after returning from the pause. The parent announces that it will try to kill the child and executes the kill function with first parameter child and second parameter SIGTERM, the software terminate signal. The parent then issues the wait command to wait for the child to terminate and announces that it is exiting. This is where the main program ends.

The acknowledge routine contains an if statement that checks the current pid against parent. If the current pid is that of the parent, it announces that the parent acknowledges the signal, otherwise it announces that the child acknowledges the signal. In either case, the last statement of the routine sets the global (external) variable flag true.

The stopping routine is structured in much the same way as the acknowledge routine. However, it concludes with an exit statement, causing the process to terminate. It becomes the programmer's responsibility to terminate a trapped software termination signal. This is why there are two levels of termination, a polite level that can be trapped and an involuntary one that cannot be redirected in this manner. You should realize that some processes refuse to die even when hit with the "hard" kill signal 9 (SIGKILL). This happens sometimes when they crash. The only way to kill these is to shut down the system.

## Pipes

Let's explore how pipes provide natural channels for communication of data between processes. A pipe is an unnamed file that can be written to by one process and read from by another.

XENIX provides a couple of levels of routines for managing pipes. At the lowest level, the pipe function allows a programmer to set up a pipe file for reading and writing. It is actually opened twice: once for reading and once for writing. The programmer must fork, then have the parent and child grab the correct ends of the pipe. An example is given in the XENIX programmer's reference manual.

A higher level function **popen** creates the pipe and another process at the other end of that pipe. We explore this function in our next example program.

## Example Program

Our example program **fsize** demonstrates how the **popen** function works. It calls the **popen** function twice, once to create a process that sends its output to our program and second to create a process that receives our output (see figure 8-1). This arrangement of processes is called a **pipeline**. You can see from the diagram that **pipe** is an apt name for the unnamed files that connect the processes.

**Figure 8-1**
**A pipeline**

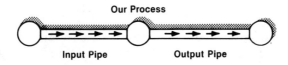

The **popen** function expects two parameters: a string specifying an **sh** shell command and a string containing either **r** for *read* or **w** for *write*. In the first case, the shell command is executed and its output can be read from the pipe. In the second case, the shell command and its input comes from what is written to the pipe.

The **popen** function returns a file pointer for the file if all goes well, and zero if not.

In our **fsize** program, we **popen** the shell command **ls [-l** in read (**r**) mode and the shell command **sort** in the write (**w**) mode. Our program takes the directory information from the first pipe, transforms it by grabbing only the size in bytes and the name of each file, then sends the results line by line to the second pipe to be sorted by the **sort** program at the other end of the pipe.

Our **fsize** program has a few extra diagnostic statements to let you know when it is opening and closing its pipes. If you examine the output, you see these statements around a directory listing with names and sizes that are ordered by increasing size from a semaphore of length zero to an executable **a.out** file.

```
Opening input pipe.
Opening output pipe.
Closing input pipe with result 0.
      0 s1
     20 a1234567890123
    111 forks.c
    330 forks.o
    913 pipe.c
    939 pipe.o
   1012 nosem.c
   1119 nosem.o
   1287 sem.c
   1287 x.c
   1364 sem.o
   1388 x.o
   1767 sig.c
   1788 sig.o
   6094 nosem
   6353 sem
   9860 a.out
Closing output pipe with result 0.
```

Notice that the input pipe (whose output we are reading) closes before the data is displayed to the screen and that the output pipe closes after the data is displayed. This is because the sort process on the end of the second pipe must get all of its input before it can output anything.

Now let's examine the listing.

```c
/* program to illustrate pipes */

#include<stdio.h>

main()
    {
    FILE *popen(), *p1, *p2;
    int status;
    char mode[11], links[6], owner[9], group[9],
        size[6], month[4], day[3], time[6], name[15];

    if(p1 = popen("ls -l", "r"))
        printf("Opening input pipe.\n");
    else
        {
        printf("Cannot open input pipe.\n");
        exit(1);
        }
```

```
if(p2 = popen("sort", "w"))
   printf("Opening output pipe.\n");
else
   {
   printf("Cannot open output pipe.\n");
   exit(1);
   }

if(!feof(p1)) fscanf(p1,"%*s%*s");
while(fscanf(p1, "%s%s%s%s%s%s%s%s%s",
      mode, links, owner, group, size,
      month, day, time, name)!=EOF)
   fprintf(p2, "%6s %s\n", size, name);

printf("Closing input pipe with result %d.\n", pclose(p1));
printf("Closing output pipe with result %d.\n", pclose(p2));
}
```

The program includes the standard I/O file stdio.h. The main program declares the following functions and variables: popen is a function returning a file pointer (see Chapter 7), p1 and p2 are file pointers, status is an integer, and mode, links, owner, group, size, month, day, time, and name are string variables. These are dimensioned to accommodate one more character (to include a terminating null character) than allowed for each variable.

First, the input pipe is opened. An if statement checks the result returned from the popen function. If the result is nonzero, we issue the message Opening input file. If not, we issue an error message and exit the program. The first argument of the popen statement is the sh shell command ls -l, which produces a "long" listing of the current directory. The second argument is r, which indicates that we wish to read this output into our program.

Next, the output pipe is opened. As above, an if statement separates success from failure. Here, the first parameter of popen is the command sort and the second parameter is w because we will write to this pipe.

Now we use the fscanf function to read the first line from the input pipe and throw it away. The first parameter of fscanf is a file pointer of the file we wish to read. We use the file pointer p1 from the input pipe. The second parameter is the format %*s%*s specifier. This indicates two strings that are to be ignored.

The main loop comes next. It consists of a while loop that calls fscanf to input a line of text. Again, we use the file pointer p1 to indicate the input file. The format specifier indicates that nine strings are expected. We list all nine variables, but we could have used the %*s notation to skip most of them. In fact, we only print two of these, size and name, to the output pipe. The while loop continues until the scanf returns a zero to indicate no more strings can be read from the input pipe.

After the main loop, we close both pipes. The pclose function ensures proper closure of the pipe. Once it is executed, it causes a wait until the process at the other end of the pipe terminates. This allows the main program to terminate last, which is a good idea if you want your shell to remain asleep until the entire job is done.

## Summary

In this chapter we have studied XENIX processes. We have examined the output of the ps command to see examples of such quantities as process priority and CPU utilization, and we have developed example C programs to illustrate process control system calls including fork, wait, signal, and pipe. Our example programs clearly display how processes are born, live in cooperation and communicate with each other, and die.

## Questions and Answers

### Questions

1. What is a process?
2. How can you tell a child from its parent process?
3. Why is it necessary to synchronize certain processes?
4. What is a pipe?

### Answers

1. A process is a running program that is managed by the operating system as a unit of work. In XENIX each command is executed by a separate process. The XENIX operating system allows many processes to exist at once. They all share the CPU, memory, and other resources of the computer system. XENIX keeps a master table of all current processes.

2. When the fork system call causes a process to split into a parent and child process, the two processes are identical except for the value returned from the fork function. This value is zero for the child. For the parent process, it is the process identification number of the child.

3. Processes have to be synchronized when they share the same resources. For example, processes must wait their turn at sharing the CPU, a terminal screen, or a printer. Otherwise, they would produce garbled results. Shared data also can be corrupted if shared in an unsynchronized manner.

4. A `pipe` is an open but unnamed file that allows the output of one process to be buffered (temporarily stored) until it is used as input by another process. Pipes can be created by XENIX at the request of users. Commands to do so are built into the shell programs and are implemented through system calls.

# 9

# Device Drivers

- Overview
- The Kernel
- System Calls
- Hardware Interrupts
- Device Driver Routines
- Block and Character Drivers
- The Device Tables
- Special Device Files
- File Operation Routines for Devices
- Routines in the Kernel Used
  by Device Drivers
- Structures in the Kernel Used
  by Device Drivers
- Block-Oriented Devices
- Example: a Terminal Driver
- Installing Device Drivers
- Summary
- Questions and Answers

# Device Drivers

Peripheral devices such as terminals, line printers, disk drives, and local area networks are connected to a XENIX system via *device drivers*. Device drivers are collections of routines and data structures in the kernel that handle the lowest levels of I/O between these devices and processes running within the computer.

Instead of presenting our own example programs, we carefully analyze a case study that is given in one of the XENIX manuals. This case study gives a device driver for a terminal. Source code for this example can be found in the chapter "Sample Device Drivers" in the XENIX *Programmers Guide* manual. However, the origin of this example dates back to a course on device drivers developed by AT&T. You should look at the source code as you read our discussion. This chapter supplies more complete and basic descriptions of the ways these routines work than can be found in the XENIX manuals.

The first part of the chapter describes device drivers and the kernel in general, the second part presents the case study, and a third part discusses how to install a device driver.

## Overview

For the purposes of this chapter, a *device* is a piece of computer hardware that generates and/or consumes data. Examples include terminals, printers, modems, and disk drives.

Each device that is to work with a XENIX system requires a device driver. These drivers consist of sets of routines and structures that handle the lowest or most device-dependent parts of the job of exchanging data between the devices and the more central parts of the computer, namely the memory and CPU.

The device drivers are connected to XENIX in the following ways: 1) their code and data structures sit within the kernel of the XENIX system, 2) they are called upon by other higher level routines in the kernel that are invoked by system calls, 3) they can call upon lower level routines in the kernel, 4) they generally have interrupt routines to handle interrupts caused by the corresponding devices, and 5) they have a special "device" file entry that sits within the file directory system.

In this chapter, we explore these concepts in great detail, but for now you should understand that the device driver routines sit inside the kernel, generally "talk" to devices via interrupts, and are referenced by programs outside the kernel through standard *system calls* on the corresponding special device file.

XENIX provides a way for sites with ordinary software licenses to install their own device drivers. This way, each XENIX system can be customized to better meet the hardware requirements of its particular site. This chapter shows how to perform customization of a XENIX system.

Although, we describe how to install your own device drivers, you should understand that a XENIX system often comes with a rather complete set of device drivers. With the SCO distribution of XENIX for an IBM XT, drivers are available to handle at least four console screens on the monochrome or color display, a printer on the parallel port, two terminals or two modems on the serial ports (or one each), two floppy disks, and two hard disks. We will see how these fit into the standard system and how to add more devices to such a system.

## The Kernel

As its name implies, the *kernel* of XENIX is the central program of the operating system. It consists of a collection of routines and data structures that are permanently housed in the computer's main memory and perform XENIX's most basic business, including allocating and scheduling resources. These resources include the CPU, the memory, and the disk, as well as performing lower level tasks such as transferring data between the computer and its peripheral devices.

Device drivers sit inside the kernel and form an integral part of its operations, providing the device-dependent parts of gateways between it and the I/O devices that it manages (see figure 9-1). The driver routines are called by other parts of the kernel and in turn, use some of the kernel's other routines and data structures. Therefore, it is helpful to have a general understanding of the organization and functioning of the kernel, especially in regard to its role as the overall manager of devices.

Although management of the memory and the CPU occupy a considerable amount of the kernel's time and space, the routines and structures that it uses to manage these internal "devices" form a permanent part of the system. That is, they are not subject to modification by sites with ordinary software licenses.

**Figure 9-1**
**The kernel and its device drivers**

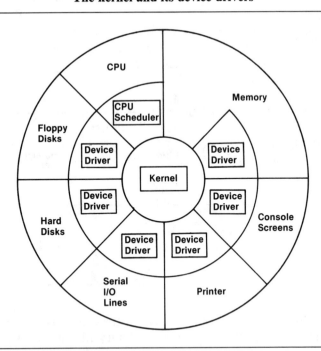

### Kernel Entry Points

One way to understand the kernel is through its *entry points* (see figure 9-2). These provide access to the majority of its functions and in some sense, define the kernel in terms of the services that it performs.

The kernel's entry points fall into three major categories: *system calls, hardware service requests,* and *error conditions.*

All three types of entry points are handled by interrupts, which make the kernel into an *event driven* or *interrupt driven* system.

Both system calls and hardware interrupts are essential to the design and operation of device drivers.

## System Calls

Let's begin with the system calls. XENIX has about 70 system calls. We have used a number of them explicitly in our C programs. For example, in previous chapters we have used `exit`, `stat`, `ustat`, `chmod`, `open`, `close`, `write`, `geteuid`, `getuid`, `getgid`, `getegid`, `execve`, `fork`, `getpid`, `kill`, `wait`, `pause`, and `signal`. Many other system calls are invoked to support the various system commands that we have used.

**Figure 9-2**
**Entry points to the kernel**

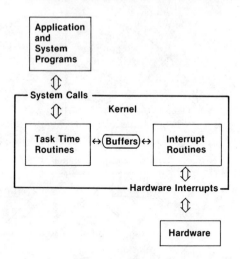

For device drivers, system calls such as: open, close, read, and write that are used to access ordinary files are also used to access devices. These calls, when applied to the special files that are associated with device drivers, cause I/O transfers to and from the devices. For example, in Chapter 7 we applied the od (octal dump) program to *read* the bytes of the file system stored on our hard disk. We also can use commands, such as cat, to *write* output to the printer or terminal. For example, the command

```
% cat myfile >/dev/lp0◄┘
```

sends myfile to the printer by *redirecting* the standard output to the special device file /dev/lp0 and writing to it.

## The System Call Interrupt

In general, each system call function performs a few housekeeping chores, then invokes a special *software interrupt* (the INT 5 instruction on the IBM XT). This provides a further level of protection, isolating the kernel from the outside world.

Before calling this interrupt, the function places the code number of the particular system call in a special register (register AX on the IBM XT).

Once this software interrupt is executed, its interrupt service routine uses this code number to dispatch to the appropriate system call routine within the kernel. You can use the debugger adb described in Chapter 3 to verify this for yourself.

XENIX uses many of the same code numbers also used by various versions of UNIX. These code numbers fall in a range between 1 and 63. For example, 1 normally means exit, 2 normally means fork, 3 normally means read, 4 normally means write, and 5 normally means open. However, XENIX has changed certain codes, deleted others, and added several new codes above 63 to handle such things as semaphores. For example, code 11 was execv, but in XENIX execv calls execve, which uses code 59. It is interesting to note that the current XENIX manuals do not mention execv or execve as system calls, although they are described along with the other library functions.

The software interrupt instruction provides the possibility of some very strong protection of the kernel from the users. On many minicomputers and mainframes, the execution of such a software interrupt changes the computer's memory, suddenly forcing the CPU to use memory "pages" belonging solely to the operating system rather than those belonging to the user. At the same time that the memory is changing, it puts the CPU into a special kernel state, allowing it to execute certain privileged instructions that give it power to change things (such as the kernel's memory and CPU priorities) that should not be accessed by ordinary users.

On the IBM XT, the hardware does not support such memory protection or CPU privilege schemes. However, the XENIX software does make a big distinction between *user* mode and *kernel* mode. The execution of this software interrupt thus really does signal "officially" the entrance of the CPU into the kernel.

### Task Time

Once the CPU has entered the kernel through a system call, it is still performing work for a particular user (running the user's process), but because it is executing code inside the kernel, it is no longer under control of the user. This "twilight zone" is called *kernel task time.*

Often, a system call results in a request for service that cannot immediately be satisfied. This may happen when a process makes a system call to transfer data to or from an external device that is not ready. In this case, rather than actively waiting, a task time routine inside the kernel (such as a driver routine) causes the process to sleep, relinquishing the CPU so that other processes may use it. Therefore, making a system call often causes a running process to lose the CPU (see figure 9-3).

## Hardware Interrupts

At the same time that processes are making system calls to the kernel, devices are interrupting the kernel to service these requests. While the inter-

**Figure 9-3**
Task time and going to sleep

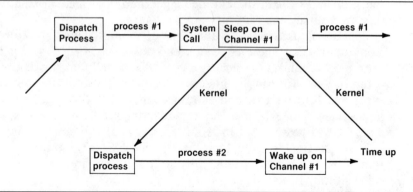

rupt is being serviced, the system is in what is called interrupt time. During this time, control has passed to the kernel but not under control of any particular user. In fact, as a rule, the process that is responsible for the interrupt is not the process that was interrupted.

Interrupt service routines normally act quickly and only when work can actually be performed. One reason why interrupt routines can proceed quickly is that the task time portions of the driver routines do much of the work. These task time routines package and unpackage the data in forms that are very convenient for the interrupt routines. Essentially, the task time routines prepare the data and hardware for interrupt time transfer by the interrupt routines.

## Device Driver Routines

Now let's study the drivers in more detail to see what they are composed of and what is required to develop them.

Each driver is really a collection of routines and structures. The addresses of many of these are listed in special device tables that we study in this section. These tables provide "entry points" to these drivers and are used by XENIX to connect the drivers to the rest of the system.

Each driver consists of a task time part, which comes into action only as a result of system calls, and an interrupt time part, which comes into action as a result of hardware interrupts (see figure 9-2).

## Block and Character Drivers

Let's begin with an organizational chart of the driver routines. In Chapter 2 we discussed two tables: one for *block* oriented device drivers and another for *character*-oriented device drivers.

These tables are stored as separate structures within the kernel and contain the addresses of certain key routines and data structures belonging to these drivers. These tables also control how the devices are interfaced to the file system through *major device numbers.*

Block-oriented device drivers are those for which data is transferred to applications and system programs in fixed-sized blocks. For example, a floppy or hard disk is normally organized as an array of *physical sectors* (see figure 9-4). Any read or write operation is physically implemented, at least at the lowest levels, as transfers of entire sectors between memory and the disk. That is, even to transfer a single byte, a whole sector must be moved.

**Figure 9-4**
**Sectors on a disk**

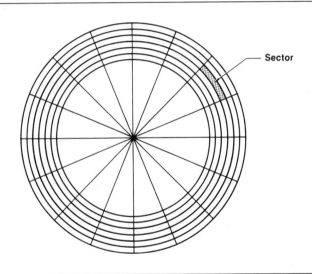

Sector

In this chapter we closely examine a character-oriented device driver for a terminal. Character-oriented device drivers allow arbitrary numbers of bytes to be transferred at one time (see figure 9-5). Character-oriented drivers are normally used for such devices as printers and terminals, but with the proper *buffering,* even disks can be handled by character-oriented drivers in addition to their more fundamental block-oriented drivers.

It is convenient to label the block-oriented drivers as: b0, b1, b2, and so on, and the character-oriented drivers as: c0, c1, c2, and so on. This numbering stresses the fact that block and character drivers are stored in separate tables.

Let's look at the device drivers installed in the kernel of version 3.0 of XENIX for the IBM XT (see table 9-1). This is a typical small system.

**Figure 9-5**
**Character-oriented devices**

XENIX System V is organized along the same lines but has more devices, including network communication drivers.

**Table 9-1**
**Device drivers for an IBM XT**

| label | name |
|-------|------|
| b0 | no device installed |
| b1 | no device installed |
| b2 | floppy disk |
| b3 | hard disk |
| | |
| c0 | console |
| c1 | tty |
| c2 | memory |
| c3 | floppy disk (as a character device) |
| c4 | hard disk (as a character device) |
| c5 | serial line |
| c6 | printer |

Our tables show four block-oriented and seven character-oriented device drivers.

The first two block-oriented device drivers (b0 and b1) are empty devices that don't do anything. The third device driver (b2) controls the floppy disks and the fourth (driver b3) controls the hard disks.

For the character-oriented device drivers: driver c0 controls the console, driver c1 controls a logical device called the *tty* , driver c2 controls the memory, driver c3 controls the floppy disk as a character-oriented device, driver c4 is the hard disk (character-oriented device), driver c5 controls the serial lines, and driver c6 controls the printer.

It is interesting to note that memory is treated as a character-oriented device. Some utilities, such as `pstat`, read this device to directly read bytes in the operating system's memory.

# The Device Tables

The addresses of the routines and data structures for the various block- and character-oriented drivers are organized in two tables inside the kernel. In addition, the kernel also contains a table of driver routines and structures designed especially for devices used as terminals.

As we mentioned in Chapter 2, source code for all three tables is provided in the file `/usr/sys/conf/c.c`. When you install a new device you must modify this file to include the names of your new routines and structures in a new "row" in one or more of these tables. We see exactly what is required in following text.

The `bdevsw` table holds addresses of certain key routines and data structures for block-oriented device drivers (see table 9-2). Each row of this table holds addresses of routines for a logically different driver. The rows are numbered starting from 0 and correspond to the labeling system mentioned above.

**Table 9-2**
**Bdevsw table for an IBM XT**

| device | open | close | strategy | buffer |
|--------|------|-------|----------|--------|
| b0 | none | none | none | none |
| b1 | none | none | none | none |
| b2 | flopen | flclose | flstrategy | &fltab |
| b3 | dkopen | dkclose | dkstrategy | &dktab |

Similarly, the `cdevsw` table holds addresses of character-oriented driver routines (see table 9-3). The `linesw` table holds further addresses for devices acting as terminals.

# Special Device Files

These tables provide the kernel direct access to these driver routines and their data structures but because these tables are "locked up" within the

**Table 9-3**
**Cdevsw table for an IBM XT**

| device | open | close | read | write | ioctl |
|--------|--------|---------|---------|---------|---------|
| c0 | cnopen | cnclose | cnread | cnwrite | cnioctl |
| c1 | syopen | syclose | syread | sywrite | syioctl |
| c2 | none | none | mmread | mmwrite | none |
| c3 | flopen | flclose | flread | flwrite | flioctl |
| c4 | dkopen | dkclose | dkread | dkwrite | dkioctl |
| c5 | sioopen | sioclose | sioread | siowrite | sioioctl |
| c6 | lpopen | lpclose | none | lpwrite | none |

kernel, there is no direct way for ordinary application programs to call them. To remedy this situation, special file entries are created (using the mknod command as described subsequently in this chapter) and placed in the /dev/ directory. We have already seen a number of these special device files.

Each such special file has permissions, an owner, a group, a date of creation, a date of modification, and so on, just like an ordinary file. However, instead of having a byte count, it has two special device numbers: a major device number and a minor device number. Also, it has file type of either *b* for block-oriented device drivers or *c* for character-oriented drivers.

The file type tells which of the two tables bdevsw or cdevsw in the kernel to use. Consistent with the table names discussed earlier, file type *b* refers to block devices and file type *c* refers to character devices.

The major number corresponds to the row position of the device driver in that table. The single letter file type and the major device number combine to form the labeling system that we used in our organizational charts.

The minor number is used by the driver routines themselves to determine which particular copy or function of the device is being referenced. For example, different serial communications lines can be handled by the same driver but differentiated from each other by a minor device number.

Looking at the /dev directory for examples as we did in Chapter 2, we see that applying the ls -l command to the path /dev/lp0 might yield the following output on the screen:

```
c-w--w--w-   1 bin     bin        6, 0 Oct 21 1985 lp0
```

The first column contains the file type and permissions. The first letter *c* indicates that this is a special file with file type *c,*. The *6* toward the middle where the byte count normally appears is the major number, and the *0* following it is the minor number. This would be c6 in our table.

Likewise, applying the `ls -l` command to the path `/dev/tty2a` might yield:

```
crw--w--w-   2 morgan   morgan    5,  8 Apr 27 20:55 tty2a
```

Here, the file type is *c,* the major number is 5, and the minor number is 8. Combining the file type and the major device number gives us the label *c5* in our organizational chart.

The system programmers or administrators who wish to create these special files must know the file type and major and minor device numbers as set up in the kernel. With this knowledge, they can execute the `mknod` command to make these files. For example, to create these files, programmers or administrators might have typed:

```
mknod /dev/lp0  c 6 0
mknod /dev/tty2a c 5 8
```

# File Operation Routines for Devices

Because device drivers are treated like files in the directory system, it is not surprising, and indeed a central part of XENIX's design ensures that, devices can be opened, closed, read, and written like ordinary files. The writing and reading represent transfers of information to and from the devices. Opening and closing are needed to initialize the device and condition the system to make and complete these transfers.

As you can see, these routines are mirrored to some degree within the `bdevsw` and `cdevsw` tables. These tables tell the XENIX kernel how to perform these functions for each device driver.

In this section we introduce the necessary routines. In following text, we describe them in detail.

## Block Routines

For block-oriented drivers, three routines are listed in the `bdevsw` table: a routine to open the device, a routine to close the device, and a `strategy` routine. The `strategy` routine handles both reading from and writing to the device, depending on what parameters are passed to it. In addition, there is a pointer to a data structure called `d_tab` that keeps track of commands currently being handled by the driver. This structure is of type iobuf, which is defined in the include file /usr/include/sys/iobuf.h. The operating system "schedules" these requests to optimize the performance of the block device (such as a disk) and the system as a whole.

### Character Routines

The list in cdevsw for character-oriented drivers consists of an open routine, a close routine, a read routine, a write routine, and a special control routine.

The device driver routines in cdevsw directly correspond to the system calls that operate on ordinary files. In fact, the system call open, when applied to a special device file, actually causes the open routine to be called for the corresponding device. Likewise, the system calls: close, read, and write indirectly call the close, read, and write driver routines.

### Terminal Routines

The c.c configuration file for the kernel also contains the linesw table, which is used in conjunction with the routines in cdevsw to control devices that are used as terminals. These consist of open, close, read, write, control, in, out, and modem routines. These routines are used in conjunction with the character-oriented device driver routines to control the corresponding devices, such as keyboards, video screens, and serial I/O communication lines, when they are used as terminals.

### Interrupt Routines

The interrupt routines for the drivers are also listed in the c.c file. They belong to a logically different part of the kernel (the interrupt time portion) than the other driver routines (which belong to the task time portion). However, all the routines for a particular driver tend to be physically grouped together in the same section of code within the kernel.

Interrupt routines usually handle the lowest level of I/O transfers. To facilitate these transfers, buffers are set up in the kernel and in user programs. Then the device driver routines help package these individual bytes into blocks that are stored in buffers for transfer between memory and hardware *ports* of the device controllers.

In general, the task time write or read routines fill or empty these buffers from and to the application or system program as they are ready to do so, and the interrupt routines empty or fill these buffers to and from the device as it is ready to do so. This smooths out the interaction between the programs and the devices, allowing them to proceed almost independently from each other, at least over the short run.

If a device does not use interrupts, it is not necessary to supply one. All the interrupt routines that are present are listed in the structure vecintsw that is defined and initialized in the c.c file.

### Initialization Routines

Some devices need initialization when the machine is first turned on or rebooted. There is a special place in the `c.c` file for such initialization routines (the `dinitsw` table). However, in the particular version that we used, only one routine was installed. Its name `initibm` implies that it initializes everything that needs initialization on a standard IBM personal computer (an XT, in particular).

## Routines in the Kernel Used by Device Drivers

Now let's discuss some routines within the kernel that are used by device drivers. A device driver can use any routine in the kernel, but these are of particular use to device drivers.

### Synchronization Routines

We begin with a discussion of routines that synchronize the driver routines with each other and the rest of the system.

### The Spl Routines

The `spl5` and `splx` routines control when interrupts can happen. They help set the "level" of interrupts. The level controls which devices can currently interrupt the CPU.

Often, it is important to "turn off" certain interrupts during certain operations. This is especially important when two independent processes have access to the same data, and in particular when there is a danger that they might access the same data in an interlocking manner. The task time portion of a driver may call an `spl` function to disable its `interrupt time` portion to prevent such an interlock.

In Chapter 8 (process control) we saw an example indicating the necessity for enforcing "mutual exclusion" between processes competing for access to the same resources. In that example, two processes were competing for the same terminal screen. Without proper synchronization they messed up each other's messages on the screen.

However, potential conflicts between the `task time` and `interrupt time` portions of a driver are a bit more subtle. In this case, both may be updating a buffer variable, such as a character count.

For example, a `task time` routine may load a count into a CPU register and be interrupted by the interrupt routine that also loads the count into a CPU register, increments it, then updates it back into memory. Later, the `task time` version takes over again and decrements the CPU register (saved from before) and updates the count in memory, overwriting the work of the interrupt routine. The result is that the count is decremented when it really should be kept the same. That is, the two actions should have canceled each other (see figure 9-6).

**Figure 9-6**
**Overlapping operations**

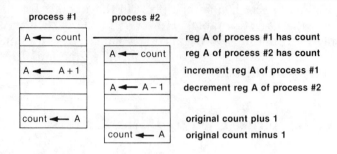

In this chapter, we describe a protection scheme using the `spl` function for the read, write, and interrupt routines of a driver, which enforces mutual exclusion for "critical sections" of driver routines in much the same way that semaphores are used to bracket critical sections of applications programs.

For driver routines, we *precede* a critical section with a statement like

```
x = spl5();
```

and *end* it with the statement:

```
splx(x);
```

There are actually a whole series of `spl` routines, starting with `spl0`, which enables interrupts from all sources to `spl7`, which disables all of them.

The `spl5` routine disables interrupts from the disk drives, the printer, and the keyboard. Thus, it could be used within the driver routines for any of these devices.

The `splx` routine at the end of the critical section is used to restore the interrupt level to what it was before the critical section. It has a single argument that should be an expression whose value is the same as the value *returned* by the `spl` function that precedes the critical section.

The real difficulty in using the `spl` functions is in judging exactly where the critical sections are and where to place the `spl` function calls. Here are some rules:

☐ A critical section should contain a *complete* operation, such as putting something into a buffer or taking something out of it. This includes updating all buffer variables such as byte counts.

☐ Critical sections should not overlap each other or contain loops.

Now let's look at the `spl` functions. Figure 9-7 shows these functions for the version of XENIX running on the IBM XT. This information is specified by the structure `splmask` in the file `c.c`.

**Figure 9-7**
**Spl routines for the IBM XT**

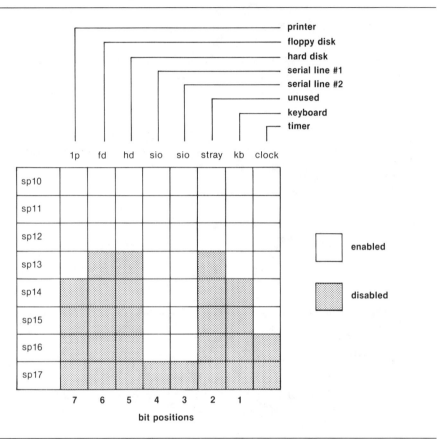

In this particular version of XENIX, `spl0`, `spl1`, and `spl2` enable all interrupts; `spl3` enables all but the floppy disk, the hard disk, and "stray" interrupts; `spl4` and `spl5` disables everything `spl3` does, plus the keyboard and the printer; `spl6` additionally disables the clock; and `spl7` disables all interrupts including both serial I/O lines.

Let's see how these routines work. This is important if you wish to understand the value returned from `spl5` and passed to `splx`. In the above example, this value was stored in the variable x.

For most machines, there is a memory location or I/O port called the *interrupt enable register* that controls which device interrupts are enabled (can be triggered) and which are disabled (ignored). Each bit in this location controls a different source of interrupts. Placing a particular bit pattern of zeros and ones in that location turns on and off the corresponding interrupts. Such a bit pattern is called an *interrupt mask.* On the IBM XT, the interrupt enable register is I/O port 33. Figure 9-7 shows how its bits are assigned.

The routines `spl0` through `spl7` are implemented as functions that return the current interrupt mask from the interrupt enable register and set a new one (chosen from the `splmask` array). Figure 9-7 shows the interrupt masks for the IBM XT.

The `splx` routine should be used in conjunction with the preceding functions to restore the previous state of the interrupt enable register (see figure 9-8). The `splx` routine expects a single integer argument, which it places in the interrupt enable register.

**Figure 9-8**
**Bracketing critical sections with `spl` functions**

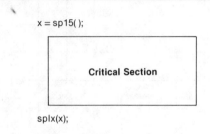

## Sleep and Wakeup

The `sleep` and `wakeup` functions also help synchronize device driver routines. These functions allow a process to become dormant once it has done all it can, thus helping to prevent it from getting too greedy or too hungry for data. The idea is that if a process is sleeping, it cannot be eating.

These functions handle a coordination problem different from mutual exclusion, which is handled by the `spl` routines.

The `sleep` function in the kernel should not be confused with the `sleep` command or the `sleep` system call, although the `sleep` command and system call normally do call this "inner" kernel `sleep` function.

Generally, when a driver routine has initiated a request for I/O transfer and has done everything it needs to do before that request is completed, it should call the `sleep` function to wait for the completion.

When the request is satisfied (normally by the driver's interrupt service routine), a call to `wakeup` (by the service routine) forces the sleeping routine to continue, starting right after its `sleep` statement.

The `sleep` function expects two integer arguments: a number called the *wait channel number,* and a number that specifies the priority at which the process sleeps.

The `wakeup` function expects one integer argument that is called the *wait channel number*. This is an integer that relates a `wakeup` to the corresponding `sleep` function. Each `wakeup` only wakes up those processes that went to sleep with that particular wait channel number.

As a matter of custom, the wait channel numbers are derived from addresses of data structures within the kernel. Usually these are data structures related to the reason for waiting. For example, the `wait` system call uses the wait channel number, which is the address of that process's entry in the kernel's table of current processes in the system.

It is interesting to note that the `ps -el` command displays the wait channel numbers (in octal) for each process in the kernel's process table. Figure 9-9 shows typical output from this command. See Chapter 8 for a description of the rest of the output for this command.

**Figure 9-9**
**Output of `ps -el`**

```
% ps − el

F S  UID  PID PPID  C PRI  NI  ADDR SZ  WCHAN TTY TIME CMD
3 S    0    0    0  1   0  20  2a40  2   47472   ?  0:00 swapper
0 S    0    1    0  0  30  20    6c 15   65566   ?  0:02 init
1 S    0   31    1  0  28  20  3c00 15   47532  co  0:04 getty
1 S    0   32    1  0  28  20  3fc0 15   47636  02  0:04 getty
1 S    0   18    1  0  40  20  3900 12   37252   ?  0:01 update
0 S   14   23    1  0  26  20    7d 26  151100   ?  0:02 lpsched
1 S    0   27    1  0  26  20  6640 26  150764   ?  0:01 cron
1 S    0   33    1  0  28  20  4380 15   47742  03  0:04 getty
1 S    0   34    1  0  28  20  5080 15   50046  04  0:04 getty
1 S  201   35    1  0  30  20  4740 22   66366  2a  0:17 csh
1 R  201   40   35 36  68  20  5440 26            2a  0:12 ps
```

The `pstat` command also lists this and other tables, but in much greater detail, showing the addresses where many of these tables are located within the kernel's memory. A user can often use this information to learn why a process is sleeping and consequently how to wake it.

Unfortunately, because wait channel numbers are 16-bit integers, they are too small to hold complete addresses. For example, the IBM XT's CPU uses addresses that consist of segment numbers and offsets (see *8086/8088*

*16-Bit Microprocessor Primer* by Christopher L. Morgan and Mitchell Waite). In general, most XENIX machines use anywhere from 20 bits to 32 bits to specify addresses. However, the kernel's data structures normally reside in an area of memory that is less than the 64K bytes that can be covered by 16-bit addressing. With this restriction, each address in the kernel yields a unique channel number by chopping off all but the lower 16 bits.

Now let's look at `priority`, the second parameter of the `sleep` function. `Priority` is used by the kernel to help it schedule processes in an equitable fashion. In Chapter 8, we saw how the `ps -el` displays the priorities of all the processes running in the system.

Priority value `PZERO` (specified in the file `/usr/include/sys/param.h`) is a kind of "zero point," in that processes that call `sleep` with lower priority values than this cannot be wakened by signals. That is, they are given "better treatment" as far as sleeping is concerned. Note that a process that sleeps so "deeply" that it won't respond to signals cannot be interrupted from the keyboard.

## The Timeout Function

The `timeout` function causes a process to sleep for a specified number of clock "ticks." The value `HZ` (as specified in the file `/usr/include/sys/param.h`) assigns the number of clock ticks that occur per second. On the IBM XT, HZ is equal to 20. Thus, a count of one causes a process on an IBM XT to sleep for 1/20 of a second. Realize that putting a process to sleep does not cause the whole system to sleep. In fact, it tends to improve the chances of other processes to get work done.

The `timeout` function expects three integer parameters: a pointer to a function, an argument code, and the number of clock ticks before the process is to wake up. In the case study for a terminal driver, we see how this routine brings about a necessary delay while a break is being sent out over the communication line.

## Transfer Functions

The kernel contains a number of low level routines for transferring information between memory and devices and between different parts of memory.

**Input and Output Functions**—The `in`, `out`, `inb`, and `outb` routines implement the absolutely lowest levels of I/O. That is, they allow a driver to talk directly to I/O ports.

The `in` and `inb` functions expect a single integer argument that specifies the hardware port number (see the aforementioned *8086/8088 16-bit Microprocessor Primer*) and returns the current contents of that port. The first function returns a 16-bit value and the second returns an 8-bit (byte-sized) value.

The `out` and `outb` functions expect two integers: a port number and the value to be sent to that port. The first sends a 16-bit value and the second an 8-bit value (the lower 8 bits).

**Memory Transfer Functions**—The copyio function provides a way to transfer blocks of memory from one location in the kernel to another. It is used by block-oriented device drivers. See the XENIX manual for more details.

# Structures in the Kernel Used by Device Drivers

Now let's investigate some structures in the kernel that are used by device drivers.

## The User Block

Each user has a block of memory in the kernel called its u area. The u area is not directly accessible to the user. Rather it is used by the kernel to manage user processes while it resides in main memory (not swapped out or logged out).

The u area can be viewed as a C structure of type user and given the name u. Some of its members, u.u_base, u.u_count, u.u_offset, and u.u_segflg, are useful for passing data back and forth between a user's program and the task time portions of a device driver.

The u.u_base is the base address in memory where the data is located. The u.u_count is the number of bytes to be transferred. The u.u_offset is the location of the data within the "file." The u.u_segflg specifies the direction of transfer.

When a process makes a system call, its "context" (contents of its CPU registers) is saved in the u area, its stack pointer is pointed to a local system stack within the u area, and the parameters of the call are placed in the u. After verifying the parameters and grabbing others from the file structures, the higher level routines in the kernel may call a device driver that uses the values in the u to do its work. When the system call is completed, the registers are restored to their original state, including the stack pointer.

For example, a write command has parameters consisting of a file identifier, a buffer pointer, and a byte count. The buffer pointer is copied into u.u_base, the byte count is copied into u.u_count, and the u.u_offset is loaded from the file structure that is set up when the device file is opened.

It is important for a device driver designer to realize that the user's process has been stopped at its u area in the manner described above. In particular, the stack in the u area is only 1024 bytes long, so a device driver must not push large amounts of data on the stack, and in fact, must make sure that the stack has room for return addresses from subroutines as well as data. Note that variables local to a subroutine are automatically pushed onto the stack, so there cannot be a lot of local data.

The kernel contains functions cpass and passc that can assist a driver's task time routines by transferring characters between it and the user.

### The I/O Buffers

Buffering is essential to the proper functioning of interrupt routines because they operate independently from the rest of the system, yet process data needed by the rest of the system.

Character-oriented device drivers have different buffering structures than block-oriented drivers. Character-oriented drivers normally use a structure called a *clist* for buffers. Block-oriented device drivers normally use a structure called *buffer*.

### The Clist

A clist consists of a collection of buffers called *cblocks*. Each cblock contains only a few characters (24 in our implementation), but they link together to form a larger structure, namely the clist. The clist structure can hold a large number of bytes (characters) of data.

Technically, a clist is a C structure consisting of a total character count, a pointer to the first cblock in the list, and a pointer to the last cblock in the list (see figure 9-10). Each cblock consists of a pointer to another cblock (the next cblock or the nil pointer if there aren't any more), a pointer to the first character in the cblock, a pointer to the last character in the cblock, and an array of CLSIZE characters, where CLSIZE is a constant such as 24.

**Figure 9-10**
**Clists**

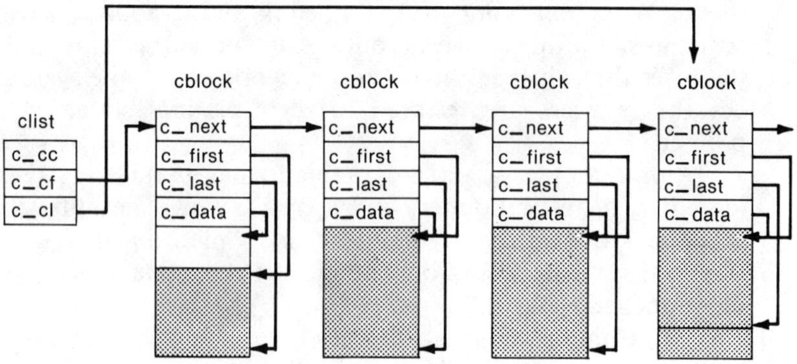

The kernel provides routines for moving data in and out of clists. The `getc` function gets a single character from the specified clist. Its single parameter specifies the clist. The `putc` function puts a single character into the specified clist. Its first parameter specifies the character and its second parameter specifies the clist. These routines can be used by both the task time and interrupt time portion of the driver, providing an easy way to use any clist as a buffer between these two portions of the driver.

Other functions act upon one cblock of a clist at a time. These include getcb, putcb, getcf, and putcf. The first two move a cblock to and from a specified clist and the last two get and put cblocks into a "free" list of cblocks.

Finally, function putchar sends characters directly to the console screen. This function is useful for sending error messages to the console when the system gets into trouble.

## Tty Structure

Associated with each device used as a terminal is a structure called a tty. This structure contains variables to manage the two-way exchange of data between a user program and the terminal that it uses.

From Chapter 5, we saw that terminals can be configured in a number of different ways, including their baud rate, parity, whether they assume the terminal is connected via a modem, whether they echo characters, whether they use XON/XOFF protocol, and how they treat the carriage return and linefeed characters. The tty structure contains bits to store these options and variables to help perform the indicated functions. They also buffer the characters as they come in and go out.

Let's examine the members of the tty structure that relate to device drivers (see figure 9-11).

The first three members are pointers to clists where characters are temporarily stored as they come in and go out of the system. The first clist is called the *raw* input queue. This is where characters are stored as they first come in from the serial line. The second is the *canonical* queue where characters are stored after they are processed (translated and expanded) and are waiting to be used by the user process. The third clist is the *output* queue where characters are stored while they wait to be sent out the serial line to the terminal.

The fifth member of the tty structure is a pointer to a part of the device driver called the tty's procedure. This function performs a variety of actions: outputting a character, starting and ending a break, and handling the XON/XOFF protocol. The particular action that it performs is determined by a command code passed to it as its second parameter.

The sixth, seventh, and eighth members of tty are 16-bit unsigned integers called *flags*, which specify how the terminal is to behave.

The t_iflag specifies input modes, such as how the driver is to respond to break conditions and parity errors from the input line, how carriage return and linefeed are handled (mapped to each other or perhaps ignored), whether or not the XON/XOFF protocol is to be used for input, and how the XON/XOFF protocol is to work if it is used.

The t_oflag specifies output modes, such as whether output is to be processed as it is sent, whether lowercase letters are to be mapped to uppercase upon output, how carriage return and linefeed are to behave for out-

**Figure 9-11**
**Tty structure**

| |
|---|
| pointer to raw clist |
| pointer to canonical clist |
| pointer to output clist |
| pointer to transmit control block |
| pointer to receiver control block |
| pointer to tty procedure |
| input flag |
| output flag |
| control flag |
| line discipline |
| internel state |
| counter |
| terminal type |
| terminal flags |
| cursor column |
| cursor row |
| variable row |
| last physical row |

•   •   •

put, and how much delay is required for such characters as carriage returns, linefeeds, tabs, and form feeds.

The `t_cflag` specifies the control modes, such as whether the interrupt and quit keys are active, whether erase (a character) and kill (a line) are in effect, and whether characters are echoed.

The `t_lflag` specifies the line discipline modes. At present this feature is ignored.

The tenth member of `tty` is a 16-bit integer called `t_state`. Its bits specify the various states that the driver can be in. It is necessary to program a driver in terms of "states" because the driver consists of a collection of routines called individually by the system when it needs to do so. That is, the driver cannot act like a regular program that starts up, goes through a series of calculations and decisions, then ends.

The states are of special concern to the `proc` routine in the driver because it performs many of the state transitions.

The integer `t_state` has the following state bits: bit 0 (TIMEOUT) tells if a delay is in progress, such as when a break is being sent out the serial line; bit 1 (WOPEN) tells if the driver is waiting for a carrier as a result of trying to open up the line for use with a modem; bit 2 (ISOPEN) tells if the driver is active (open); bit 3 (TBLOCK) tells if the driver is blocked; bit 4 (CARR__ON) tells if the carrier is on; bit 5 (BUSY) tells if the serial line is in the process of sending a character to the terminal; bit 6 (OASLP) tells whether the driver is sleeping because it is waiting for output to be sent; bit 7 (IASLP) tells whether the driver is sleeping because it is waiting for more input; bit 8 (TTSTOP) tells whether output is stopped by an XOFF (control S) condition; bit 12 (TTIOW) may be used by a process that has gone to sleep while waiting to send output; bit 13 (TTXON) tells if an XON character should be sent as the next character (as soon as the output line is ready); bit 14 (TTXOFF) does the same for the XOFF character.

Other members of `tty` include the current row and column of the cursor on the screen but are not used by the driver, at least a minimal one like the case study we discuss in this chapter.

# Block-Oriented Devices

For block-oriented devices, the system does much more of the processing than it does for character-oriented device drivers. When a user process makes a system call to read or write so many bytes from or to a block-oriented device driver, the system breaks the bytes into standard-sized blocks and calls the driver's `strategy` to process each block.

The job of the `strategy` routine is to place these blocks on a queue. This queue is allocated to the particular driver and provides a buffer between its `task time` portion (the `strategy` routine) and its `interrupt time` portion (its interrupt routine). The `strategy` routine has a single parameter that points to a structure called a *buffer*. This structure contains the block of data and the desired action to be performed on it.

The `strategy` routine normally calls the kernel's `disksort` routine to place the request in the driver's buffer queue. The `disksort` routine contains an algorithm to minimize the work that a typical disk must do to satisfy the requests on the queue. The algorithm is somewhat like that used by an elevator to minimize its travel while reaching all requested floors of a building. For example, assume there are requests for track 8, then track 40, then track 9, then track 50. The disksort routine would sort the tracks in increasing numerical order so that the disk head does not have to move back and forth so many times.

Block-oriented devices can also be served by character-oriented drivers. The kernel provides a routine called `physio` that interfaces a character-oriented driver to a corresponding block-oriented driver.

# Example: a Terminal Driver

Our case study is a device driver for a terminal. Its job is complicated by the fact that it deals with two-way communication, and, more importantly, because some of the characters have to be expanded and/or transformed as they are sent or received and others cause delays. Also XON/XOFF protocol and break conditions need to be handled.

The routines we study are given the prefix td and are associated with a particular serial communications line. Other routines, given the tt prefix (line discipline), handle terminals in general. These two types of routines work in cooperation, calling each other to get the job done.

It is interesting to note that not all terminals are connected to the computer via serial lines. In fact, for the SCO version of XENIX for the IBM XT, the first four or so terminals are implemented as the attached keyboard and screen. In this case, the tt line discipline routines would be used, but with different device driver routines.

## Externals

The terminal driver has a global area in which include files are specified and global constants and variables are declared.

The include files are: param.h, which defines the values for many of the system parameters of XENIX; dir.h, which specifies the structure of directories; user.h, which defines the u structure that the kernel has for each active user; file.h, which defines the parameters needed to manage a file; tty.h, which defines character-oriented device structures, including among other things the clist structure that is used as the buffer; and conf.h, which contains definitions of such things as the block and character tables, as well as the more specialized terminal driver routines. Note that this file is not the same as the c.c file in which these structures are actually initialized.

For this terminal driver, there are many hardware locations to define (see figure 9-12). Here, the terminal is connected to a serial communications line that has seven ports (hardware registers) associated with it. They are: 1) received data, 2) transmitted data, 3) status, 4) control, 5) interrupt enable, 6) baud rate control, and 7) interrupt identification.

The first two ports are input and output ports (hardware registers) through which the characters are passed. The third port gives various pieces of information in its eight bits. One bit tells when the input port has data to be read and another bit tells when the output port is ready to take more data. Other bits give various error conditions, such as parity error or mismatched formats. Another bit indicates whether a terminal on the serial line is ready to receive anything. Each bit is specified by a different constant in this code.

The fourth port, the control port, has a number of constants associated with it, specifying different values for control parameters such as number of bits per serial word, type of parity, and break condition.

**Figure 9-12**
**Hardware connections for serial communications**

| |
|---|
| received data |
| transmitted data |
| status |
| control |
| interrupt enable |
| baud rate control |
| interrupt identification |

The break condition needs special explanation. To understand it, you should start with an understanding of how normal characters are sent on a serial communications line. Such a data line carries a voltage of either a low value (less than $-3$ volts) or a high value (greater than $+3$ volts). Each character is sent as a string of bits, where each bit is indicated with either a low voltage for a value of one or a high voltage for a value of zero. A break consists of a constant zero bit value (high voltage) for a much longer time than just one character (perhaps a quarter to half a second or longer). On some terminals the **break** key causes this condition to be sent as long as it is held down. The break condition is used as a special signal to indicate a radical change in the way a computer is to act. For example, it may be used on XENIX or UNIX systems during login to change the attempted baud rate.

The fifth port, the interrupt enable port, has three constants that specify the bits that control (enable or disable) interrupts from the receiver (incoming data), interrupts from the transmitter (outgoing data), and interrupts generated by changes in the modem (carrier detection).

The sixth port, the baud rate control, has a constant defined for each possible baud rate. These range from 0 to 19200 baud. (Zero baud is normally a special signal to "hang up" the (phone) line.)

The seventh port, the interrupt detection port, has constants that define which of its bits correspond to which of the three sources of interrupts: transmit (ready to send), receive (ready to receive), and modem change (carrier detect or hang up).

The interrupt vectors are also defined as constants here, giving their number (2) and locations in memory.

There are two global variables: a `tty` structure (as defined in the include file `tty.h`), and an array of integers, called `td_addr`, that contains the base addresses of each of the two serial lines. Many of the driver routines have a local pointer that points to this global `tty` structure.

## The Open Routine

Now let's begin with the routine `tdopen` that opens the serial communications line for use with a terminal (see figure 9-13).

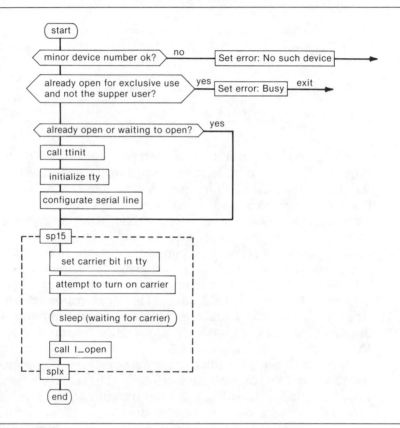

**Figure 9-13**
T`dopen` **routine**

This routine expects two integer parameters: a minor device number and a control flag.

Tdopen has several local variables: a register (temporary) pointer to a structure of type `tty`, an integer for holding addresses, and an integer `x` that is used in conjunction with the `spl` functions.

The `tdopen` routine first checks to see whether the minor device number is within range (less than the number of devices). If it is not, it calls a function called `seterror` and return. It passes the value `ENXIO`, indicating the error `No such device`. Essentially, the `seterror` function moves the error code into the `u.uerror` member of the user's u area.

The `tdopen` routine next checks to see whether the device has already

been opened for exclusive use. This information is stored in a bit in the
lflag member of the tty structure for this driver. The routine also calls
the kernel function suser and checks to see whether the process is the super
user (root). If the file is already open for exclusive use and the user is not
the super user (a system administrator) the routine sets the error code
EBUSY and returns.

If the tdopen routine continues, an if statement checks to see whether
the device is already open or is waiting for an open to complete. The reason
why it might be waiting at this point is that it might be waiting for a carrier
detect signal from the modem after initiating a telephone call. This normally takes a while, so the process often sleeps after it attempts to "turn on"
the carrier but has not gotten a carrier immediately. Later, its sleep is "interrupted" from the carrier detection circuitry. All of this is handled by
this tdopen routine as we shall see.

The tdopen routine determines the state of the open and carrier
from certain bits in the t_state member of the tty structure. As we explained in our description of tty previously in this chapter, these bits provide a standard set of states for terminal drivers.

If the serial communications device file is not already opened or in the
process of being opened, the routine attempts to open the device. To do so,
it calls ttinit to initialize the serial line, then places the address of the
driver's tdproc into the t_proc member of the driver's tty structure. Finally, it calls tdparam to configure the serial line with such things as the
baud rate, parity, etc. (according to parameters specified in other members
of tty).

The routine continues after the if with a *critical section*, which
should not be interrupted by the driver's interrupt routines. The spl5 pro-
tects the beginning of this section. As described above, this routine temporarily disables certain interrupts (including the driver's interrupt routines
that can affect the data which is being worked on in the critical section).

Within the critical section, the routine first sets appropriately the *carrier* bit in the cflag member of the tty structure. More precisely, it checks
the clocal bit of cflag to see if the line is being used with a modem rather
than for a direct connection (local mode). If so, it calls the driver's
tdmodem function to turn on the carrier. If this is successful, it sets the carrier bit in t_state. On the other hand, if the line is being used for direct
connection, it simply turns off this carrier state bit.

Next, still within the critical section, the routine waits for a carrier, if
it is supposed to. The *FNDELAY* bit of the second parameter (control
flag) passed to this open routine specifies whether a while loop waits for
the carrier.

Here, the desired condition (carrier bit on) is placed in the conditional
part of the while statement. Within the body of the loop, the *waiting to
open* bit is set in t_state, and the kernel's sleep function is called. The
parameters passed to sleep are a *wait channel number* equal to the address
of one of the driver's queues and *priority* equal to TTIPRI. This priority has
a value of 28 in our particular implementation, which is greater than PZERO

(a value of 25 in our implementation). Thus, the sleep can be broken by signals. In the case of waiting for a carrier, we want to be able to interrupt (signal) from the keyboard if there are problems.

Notice that sleeping occurs within the critical section. Recall that the process gives up the CPU while it sleeps, thus interrupts are most likely to be enabled during this time, allowing the carrier detect (modem) interrupt routine to be triggered, which then wakes up the process that is sleeping here.

Finally, still within the critical section, the l_open routine listed in the linesw table is called. Recall that this table is initialized in the c.c part of the kernel. The code for making this call involves some fancy C contortions as it looks up the address of the function in an array of structures (namely, the linesw table). The l_open routine initializes the variables associated with terminals in general (whatever device it might be connected to).

Just before returning, the routine ends its critical section with an slpx routine, returning the state of the interrupts to what it was before the critical section.

## The Close Routine

The tdclose routine in many respects has to reverse the actions of the open routine (see figure 9-14).

**Figure 9-14**
**Tdclose routine**

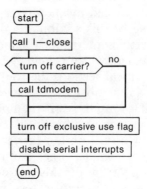

The close routine has one local variable, a pointer to a tty structure.

It first calls the l_close routine listed in the linesw table. This does the general things that have to be done when a terminal is closed. Then it continues, doing things particular to closing a serial communications line. It checks the *HUPCL* bit of the cflag member of the tty to see whether it should turn off the carrier. If so, it calls tdmodem (described subsequently) to turn off the connection to the modem (hang up the line). Next, it turns off the exclusive use bit of the lflag member of the tty structure, then it calls outb to send a zero byte out the interrupt enable port to turn off all interrupts from the serial line.

## The Read Routine

The tdread routine calls the linesw table routine l_read, passing it a pointer to the driver's tty structure (see figure 9-15). This general routine (not listed in the manual) takes characters from the input queue (canonical input queue).

**Figure 9-15**
**Tdread routine**

## The Write Routine

The tdwrite routine calls the linesw table routine l_write, passing it a pointer to the driver's tty structure (see figure 9-16). This general routine puts characters into the output queue.

**Figure 9-16**
**Tdwrite routine**

## The Param Routine

The tdparam routine sets up the serial communication line with such parameters as baud rate, parity, and word size (see figure 9-17). It is called by the tdopen and tdioctl routines.

**Figure 9-17**
**Tdparam routine**

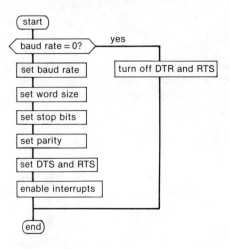

The `tdparam` routine has several local (register) integer variables: `cflag` is a copy of the byte in the `tty` structure that contains such things as the baud rate, `addr` contains the base address of I/O ports for the serial line, `speed` holds baud rates, and `temp` is just a temporary variable for manipulating bit patterns. A variable `x` is declared, but not used.

The `tdparam` routine begins with the baud rate. A baud rate of zero indicates "hang up" the telephone line. An `if` statement looks for this condition. It checks the baud rate bits in `cflag` as copied from the `t_cflag` field of the `tty` structure. If they are all zero, it calls `inb` to read the current value of the control register, does some logical ANDs to turn off just the `DTR` (data set ready) and `RTS` (request to send) bits in the control port, then `outb` to put the result back into the control register. The routine returns without setting anything more.

If the baud rate is not zero, the routine continues. It calls `outb` to send the baud rate code to the baud rate control register.

Next the routine sets the word size, stop bits, parity, DTR, and RTS values. The various bits in `cflag` are tested with `if` statements and the appropriate values are logically ORed into `temp`. The computed value in `temp` is sent out the control port of the serial line.

Finally, the enable interrupt bits for read and write are turned on in the interrupt enable register. Actually, the read interrupt is only enabled if the *read* bit in `cflag` is on.

## The Modem Control Routine

The modem control routine `tdmodem` is in charge of turning on and off the carrier on the modem by changing certain control bits of the serial lines (see figure 9-18).

**Figure 9-18**
Tdmodem routine

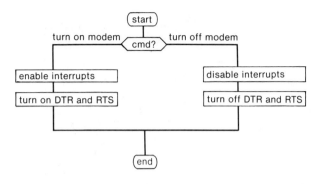

The tdmodem routine has two integer parameters: dev, which is the minor device number, and cmd, which is a command code for this routine. The two commands are: TURNON and TURNOFF.

The routine consists of a switch statement on the second parameter cmd. If the command is TURNON, the interrupt enable bits in the interrupt control register are turned on, and the DTR and RTS bits in the serial control register are also turned on. If the command is TURNOFF, all of these bits in both registers are turned off. In both cases, the inb function is used to get the original values for these registers so that other bits are preserved and the outb is used to put back modified values.

The routine returns with the contents of the status port (ANDed with SDSR). This returns the status of the carrier.

## The Interrupt Routine

The routine tdintr handles the interrupts (see figure 9-19). It has a single integer parameter vec. A value of VECT0 (defined earlier as 3) indicates device number zero and a value of VECT1 (defined earlier as 5) indicates device number one. These are the interrupt location numbers assigned to the two serial lines. If the parameter is neither of these values, the routine calls the kernel's printf routine to print an error message.

After setting the device number, a while ensures that each possible interrupt from the selected serial line is handled. The contents of the *interrupt identification* port are read into the variable iir. The while loop continues as long as any bits are set in this quantity. Within the body of the while, a series of if statements checks each of the three possible bits that indicate each of the three possible interrupts.

If the *IXMIT* bit is set, it calls tdxint, the routine to handle interrupts from the transmitter. If the *IRECV* bit is set, it calls tdrint, the routine to handle interrupts from the receiver. Finally, if the *IMS* bit is set, it calls tdmint, to handle changes in status of the modem signals.

**Figure 9-19**
**Tdintr routine**

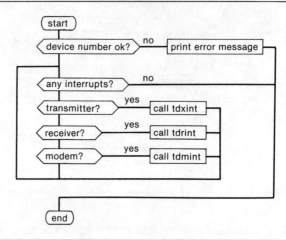

## The Transmitter Interrupt Routine

The Transmitter Interrupt routine tdxint begins by testing the status register to see whether the transmit circuits are ready to send the next character (see figure 9-20).

**Figure 9-20**
**Tdxint routine**

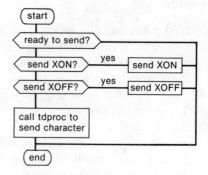

The tdxint routine calls the inb function to read the status register. If the transmit ready bit (bit number 1) is set (equal to 1), it clears the "busy" bit of t_state and executes one of three actions depending on the state of the driver.

The first possible state is *TTXON*, which occurs when the driver needs to send an XON character next. Here the TTXON bit of t_state is set (equal to 1). In this case, it sends the CSTART (XON) character out the data port and turns off the TTXON bit of t_state.

The second possible state is *TXXOFF*, which occurs when the driver needs to send an XOFF character next. The TTXOFF bit of t_state indicates this state. If this bit is set, the routine sends the CSTOP character out the data port and turns off the TTXOFF bit.

The third possible state is to send a regular character from the tty's output buffer. In this case, the driver tdproc sends the next character out from the buffer. In following text, we study how the tdproc routine does this.

### The Receiver Interrupt Routine

The Receiver Interrupt routine tdrint first calls inb to get a byte from the data port and put it into the variable c (see figure 9-21). It calls inb to get a byte from the status port and put it into the variable status. It then looks at various bits in status to find errors. For each error it finds, it sets a corresponding bit in c. It calls the l_input routine in the linesw table to put the character into the raw input queue.

**Figure 9-21**
**Tdrint routine**

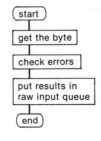

### The Modem Change Interrupt Routine

The Modem Change Interrupt tdmint routine handles two cases: when the carrier is first detected and when the carrier is lost (see figure 9-22).

The tdmint routine begins by checking the *CLOCAL* bit of t_tflag. This bit indicates whether the communications line is being used with a modem or not. If the CLOCAL bit is set, it returns without any further action (no modem control).

Next it checks the *SDSR* bit (data set ready) of the status port. This bit gives the true condition (hardware) of the carrier as it comes through the DSR signal line from the modem. This determines whether the carrier is just coming on or just going off.

**Figure 9-22**
**Tdmint routine**

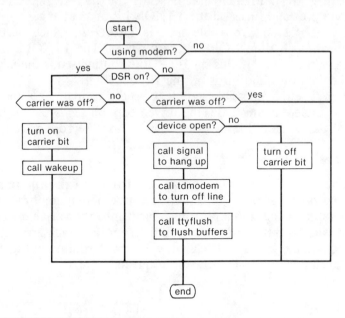

If the SDSR bit is set (equal to one), the carrier must have just appeared. In this case, it checks t_state to see whether the carrier bit (software) was off. If the carrier was off, it turns the carrier state bit on in t_state and calls wakeup to wake the tdopen routine that was waiting for the carrier.

If the SDSR bit was clear (equal to zero), the carrier must have just been lost. In this case, it checks the carrier state bit in t_state. If this is on, it checks whether the device driver is open (using the the ISOPEN bit in t_state). If all of this is true, it calls the kernel function signal to send the "hang up" signal to the process itself, the tdmodem function to physically turn off the line and the ttyflush function to empty the read and write buffers. If the device was not open, it merely turns off the carrier bit in t_state.

## The I/O Control Function

The I/O Control function allows processes to modify the parameters of the communications lines while these lines are open (see figure 9-23). It is called by the kernel when the user's process makes the I/O Control system call. This call is described in the programmer's reference portion of the XENIX manuals. It has a couple of different forms depending on the action that is specified. The actions are basically:

1. Get the parameters for a particular terminal, placing them into a particular data structure called a *termio*.

2. Set the parameters for a particular terminal from a termio structure.

3. Wait for the output queue to empty, perhaps sending a break condition for a quarter of a second.

4. Start or stop the output.

5. Flush the input and/or output queues.

**Figure 9-23**
`Tdioctl` **routine**

For this particular device driver, the I/O Control routine merely acts as an interface between the system call and the routine that actually does the work. It has four parameters: `dev`, which is the minor device number; `cmd`, which specifies the particular action required; `arg`, which specifies the arguments; and `mode`.

It calls the `tiocom` function, passing these parameters along to be processed by this routine, which places the information in the `tty` structure. If this is successful, it calls the driver's `tdparam` routine to send the corresponding information to the device.

## The Procedure Function

The driver's procedure function performs a number of miscellaneous low level functions, including ending a break condition, flushing the output buffer, resuming the output, outputting a character, suspending the transmission, blocking the I/O, flushing the input buffer, unblocking the I/O, and sending a break (see figure 9-24).

The `tdproc` function has two parameters: `tp`, a pointer to a `tty` structure, and `cmd`, which specifies the particular action to be performed.

**Time Out**—The `T_TIME` command is designed to end a break condition or other type of delay. The `tdproc` routine is called with this command parameter when the time expires from a `T_BREAK` command (another action of the `tdproc` routine).

When the `tdproc` function is given the `T_TIME` command, it clears the *TIMEOUT* bit of `t_state` and turns off the break bit in the control port for the serial line. Then it jumps to the label `start` at the beginning of the

**Figure 9-24**
**Tdproc routine**

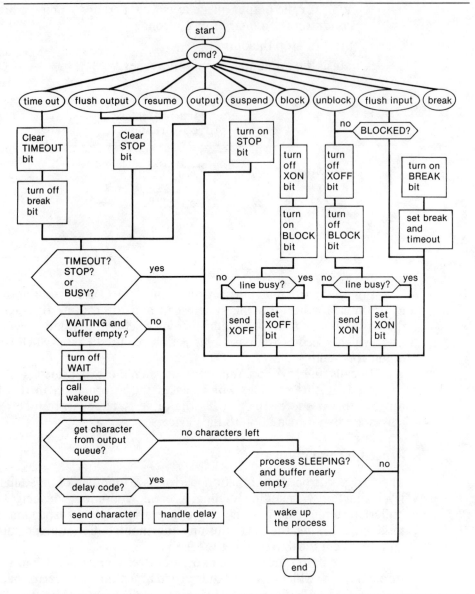

section of code to handle the **T_OUTPUT** command. Here it looks for characters to send to the device from the output buffer.

**Flush the Write Buffer and Resume**—The commands to flush the output (**T_WFLUSH**) buffer and to resume (**T_RESUME**) are handled by the same code. In both cases, the routine turns off the **TTSTOP** bit of **t_state** and jumps to **start** where it looks for characters to send.

**Output**—The `T_OUTPUT` command sends characters that are waiting in the output buffer to the serial line.

It first checks `t_state` to see whether the device driver is in TIMEOUT, TTSTOP, or BUSY states. If so, it returns without any further action.

If the routine continues, it checks the *TTIOW* bit of *t_state* and the character count in the output queue. If the *TTIOW* bit is on and no characters are in the output queue, it turns off the TTIOW bit and "wakes up" whatever process was waiting for output to drain from the output queue. It uses a "wait channel" number equal to the address of the `t_oflag` member of the driver's `tty` structure.

The routine next has a `while` loop that tries to get characters from the output queue and send them out the serial line. In the conditional part of the `while`, a character is fetched from the output queue, placed in the variable c, and checked to see whether it is non-negative. In the body of the `while`, the *OPOST* bit of `t_oflag` is examined. If this is on and the character in c has an ASCII code equal to 128 (specifying a delay), it gets the next character to determine the length of the delay. If the delay character has a negative value, the routine returns, discarding the character. If not, an `if` statement checks to see whether the ASCII code of the character is greater than 128. If so the routine sets the *TIMEOUT* bit and calls the kernel's `timeout` routine and exits.

Finally, within the `while` loop, if none of these special conditions prevail, the *BUSY* bit of `t_state` is set true, the character is sent out the data port, and the routine ends.

After the `while` loop, an `if` statement checks the *OASLP* bit of `t_state` and the relative size of the output buffer (relative to the baud rate). If the *OASLP* state bit is on and if there are "few" characters in the buffer, it turns off the OASLP state bit and wakes up whatever process is sleeping, with the wait channel equal to the address of the driver's output queue.

**Suspend**—To perform the `T_SUSPEND` command, one statement turns on the *TTSTOP* bit of `t_state`. This is one of the three conditions that cause the `T_OUTPUT` command to return without doing anything.

**Block and Unblock**—The `T_BLOCK` and `T_UNBLOCK` commands help manage the XON/XOFF protocol for the serial line.

For the `T_BLOCK` command, the *TTXON* state bit is turned off, the *TBLOCK* bit is turned on, and the *BUSY* bit of `t_state` is checked. If busy, the *TTXOFF* bit is turned on, and if not busy, the *CSTOP* character is sent out the serial port.

The `T_UNBLOCK` command turns off the *TTXOFF* and *TBLOCK* bits of `t_state`, checks the *BUSY* bit. If busy, it turns on the *TTXON* state bit and returns, and if not busy, it sends the *CSTART* character out the data port.

**Flushing the Input Buffer**—The `T_RFLUSH` command is performed by an `if` statement that checks the *TBLOCK* bit of `t_state`. If this bit is set (blocked), the routine returns with no further action. If not set, it continues into the T_UNBLOCK case where it tries to send the XON character to the device on the other end of the serial line.

**Sending a Break**—The T_BREAK command first turns on the *CBREAK* bit in the control port of the serial line, then turns on the *TIMEOUT* bit of t_state, calls timeout to cause ttrstart to occur a quarter second later (HZ/4). The ttrstart command in turn calls tdproc to end the break condition.

## Installing Device Drivers

Let's conclude the chapter by laying out the steps for installing a new device driver. Many of these steps have been discussed in preceding parts of the chapter, but this section brings all the steps together.

There are really two extreme cases under which you want to install a new device driver. One is when you acquire a new device that comes with its own driver and installation instructions and facilities, and the other is when you start from scratch with your own drivers. We are assuming the second case.

There are five major steps in installing a new device driver from scratch. They are

1. Writing the code for the device driver
2. Inserting references into certain system files that are used to make the kernel
3. Compiling a new copy of the kernel
4. Installing the new kernel on the hard or floppy disk
5. Making a directory entry for the new driver

### Writing the Code

The first step is to write the code. You would develop a file much like those discussed in the examples. This file would contain an external section in which various global constants and variables are declared, and it would have a number of functions including ones listed in the device tables, ones that serve as interrupt routines, and ones that support these.

Normally, you would start with an existing driver, such as the serial line driver given in the XENIX manual and discussed in this chapter.

### Modifying System Files

The next step is to modify the c.c file. This file contains tables, variables, and constants that interface driver routines and structures to the kernel.

Depending on the version that you have, this file might contain the tables: `vecintsw`, `intmask`, `splmask`, `bdevsw`, `cdevsw`, `dintsw`, and `linesw`. It contains constants that specify the number of available resources, such as screens, buffers, open files, and running processes. It contains variables such as: `bdevcnt`, `cdevcnt`, `linecnt`, `nblkdev`, `nchrdev`, `rootdev`, `pipedev`, and `swapdev`.

When a new device is installed, some of these tables may have to be modified. If the tables change size, some of the variables also have to be changed, but the constants should not be affected.

Let's examine the different ways that these tables might be modified.

**Interrupts**—The `vecintsw` table lists the interrupt vectors in the order in which they appear to the hardware.

For the IBM PC, the Intel 8259 Interrupt Controller (see *8086/8088 16-bit Microprocessor Primer* by Christopher L. Morgan and Mitchell Waite) handles eight possible different devices. The first two devices are the interval timer (device number 0) and the keyboard (device number 1), which are hardwired through the main circuit board. The remaining six are handled by signal lines on the IBM's main bus and can be connected to device controllers on plug-in circuit boards.

IBM has set certain standard assignments for device interrupts by providing boards that use these interrupt signal lines. Interrupt signal lines 3 and 4 are assigned to the two serial lines, number 5 is assigned to the hard disk, number 6 to the floppy disk, and number 7 to the printer.

Interrupt number 2 is not used, at least by the version of XENIX that we used. Thus, room is available for one level of interrupt customization. Currently `strayint` is installed here. If you had a board that used this line on the bus, you could replace `strayint` in `vecintsw` by the name of your routine to handle interrupts from this board.

Depending on the version of the system, the tables `intmask` and `splmask` may be in the file `c.c` or the file `primask.c`. These tables give bit patterns to be sent to the Interrupt Controller chip for disabling interrupts for various devices. The second table is used by the `spl` functions.

These tables are complicated by the fact that the devices are disabled in a certain order so that the pattern for disabling each device includes certain bits that disable others. For the IBM XT the order is: first, nothing disabled; second, just the floppy and hard disks and stray; third, add the keyboard and printer; fourth, add the timer; and fifth, add the serial communication lines.

If you installed a new device, you would have to place it somewhere in this scheme. You should, of course, place it near the most comparable device of the ones already installed. For example, if you installed a third serial line, you would treat its interrupt just like the interrupts for the first two serial lines, disabling it last.

You should be aware that "messing" with these tables can produce systems that won't work properly. Of course, you should back up your system properly before trying to install any new version of the kernel. This includes any source code files such as the `c.c` and `primask.c` files.

**Block Devices**—As we have discussed previously, the bdevsw table contains the names of routines for the block-oriented devices. If a new block device is added, a new row must be added to this table and the variables bdevcnt and nblkdev must be incremented. However, if you are merely replacing an existing driver you might have to change the names in the table. If the names are the same, you would not even have to change the names. In that case, you probably would not even have to change the c.c file at all.

**Character Devices**—The cdevsw contains names of character-oriented device drivers. Routines already discussed include open, close, read, write, and control. If you wish to add another terminal, printer, or other character-oriented device, you have to add a row to this table and adjust the variables cdevcnt and nchrdev. If you are installing a block-oriented device, it might also have a character-oriented driver that needs to be added to this table.

Again, if you are merely replacing an existing driver, you may just change some names or you may not even need to modify the c.c file at all.

## Compiling a Kernel

The make facilities in the development system allow you to automatically recompile new parts of the kernel. You may have to modify the makefile file to include the names of the new drivers. See Chapter 3 for details on how make works and how to use it.

After you have compiled your new driver file and the modified c.c file, you must relink the kernel to include these files. The file link_xenix in /usr/sys/conf is a shell script included in the Link Kit that automatically saves the old kernel and creates a new one. You probably need to add the name of the new driver to the ld command in link_xenix. It should go after the names of the other drivers, but before the −l option specifier.

## Making a Device Directory Entry

The next step is to create a new file entry in the /dev directory. You need to be the super user (root) to do this and subsequent steps.

If you merely want to replace an existing device driver with the same connections to the outer parts of the system, you may not have to perform this step.

As we discussed earlier in this chapter, you use the mknod command (in the /etc directory) to define special files for devices. This command allows you to specify its name, type (block or character), and major and minor device numbers.

You should study the names assigned to other devices already in the /dev directory to arrive at a name that is consistent with the usual conventions. For example, disks have block-oriented drivers with certain names like hd0 and character-oriented drivers in which this name is prefixed by an r, which stands for *raw*.

Recall that the major device number specifies the row position of the driver in the `bdevsw` or `cdevsw` table and that the minor device number is handled by the driver itself.

Here is an example of the `mknod` command for installing a new serial driver name `tty15` as a character-oriented device with major device number 5 and minor device number 2:

```
/etc/mknod tty15 c 5 2
```

### Testing a Kernel

The next step is to test the new version of the kernel by installing it on the floppy disk system.

First copy it from the configuration directory `/usr/sys/conf` to the root directory, giving it the name `xenix.new`:

```
cp /usr/sys/conf/xenix /xenix.new
```

Halt the system with the command:

```
# haltsys (as the super user)
```

You eventually get the **reboot or shut off** prompt. Press any key to get the boot prompt. Now type `xenix.new` and press **return**. The system should boot up with the new version of XENIX. You can test it now.

You should realize that certain commands, such as `ps` and `pstat` read the file `/xenix` and do not work properly if used as usual. For the `ps` command, the `-n` option allows you to specify a different kernel file, such as `/xenix.new`.

### Installing the Kernel on the Hard Disk

When the new kernel is thoroughly tested, the `hdinstall` command in the directory `/usr/sys/conf` saves the old kernel file and installs the new one.

## Summary

In this chapter we have studied some of the innermost parts of the system, its device drivers. These drivers consist of a number of routines and data structures that we studied in great detail. We saw how these routines and structures are connected to the kernel via device tables described in system files. We have studied the functions of these routines and structures and how they interact with other routines and structures in the kernel. We also discussed the special device files that connect these drivers to XENIX's directory system.

We saw that character and block devices are handled differently with different sets of routines and structures.

We investigated a case study of a device driver for a serial communication line that is connected with a terminal. We saw how this device driver's routines connected to special built-in terminal control routines as well as the usual device tables in the kernel.

Finally, we discussed how to install new device drivers by recompiling the kernel.

## Questions and Answers

### Questions

1. What is the role of the XENIX kernel?
2. How do you install new devices in a XENIX system?
3. How can a program send information to an installed device on a XENIX system?
4. What are some system tables that XENIX uses to manage its I/O devices?

### Answers

1. The XENIX kernel is the central part of the operating system. It contains routines to handle system calls and hardware interrupts. It contains the system's device drivers, which handle the lowest levels of I/O.

2. To install a new I/O device in XENIX, you must develop or otherwise acquire a device driver, which is a set of routines to handle certain standard transactions between the system and the device, you must modify certain system tables, you must compile a new version of the kernel that includes these routines and these changes, you must install the new kernel, and you must create a new special device file in the directory system.

3. To send information directly to a device, you can open its device file and write to it. This can be done through ordinary file utilities or from programs that use ordinary file system calls.

4. Some system tables that XENIX uses to manage its I/O devices are `bdevsw`, which contains a list of its block-oriented device drivers, and `cdevsw`, which contains a list of its character-oriented device drivers. The `vecintsw` table contains a list of interrupt service routines.

# 10

# Advanced Tools for Programmers

■ Yacc

■ Lex

■ Comparison Between Lex and Yacc

■ An English Analogy

■ Parts of a Yacc Program

■ Compiling a Yacc Program

■ How Yacc Works

■ Lexical Analysis with Lex

■ Refining Our Example of Simple English

■ A Numerical Example

■ Summary

■ Questions and Answers

# Advanced Tools for Programmers

This chapter explores two powerful XENIX programming tools, Yacc (pronounced yak) and Lex. Both of these tools are programs that make other programs according to specifications. Lex uses *regular expressions* for its specifications and Yacc uses *grammars*. In combination, these two tools can make translators, compilers, and other programs that take actions according to language that is given to them.

In Chapter 4, we introduced Lex as a means of producing stand-alone filter programs. In this chapter, we see how Lex can be used within a larger programming environment, where it provides the first level of analysis for textual input to a program.

We see how Lex helps specify the way a C program recognizes characters and how it groups them into larger units, such as words represented by tokens. Then we see how Yacc specifies the way a C program recognizes groups of tokens and arranges them in a hierarchical structure, according to some rules of grammar.

We study several examples, including a program that understands a simple subset of English. We start out small and build this into a program that can carry on a dialogue in simple English with a user.

We do not try to explain every feature of Yacc and Lex, but rather provide a sound foundation for further reading and exploration. We finish the chapter with a small example of how Yacc and Lex can handle numerical information.

## Yacc

Yacc is a program that was originally designed to make programming language *compilers*. These are programs that take input in the form of source code in some programming language and produce it as output code in some target language. It can be the basic starting point for writing your own BASIC compiler, C compiler, Pascal compiler, or a compiler for your own

XYZ processing language. It is just a tool, for not all of the work required to make a language compiler can be done by Yacc alone.

The name Yacc stands for *Yet Another Compiler Compiler*. That is, it is a compiler that makes compilers. However, Yacc is capable of making more than language compilers. It can help make language interpreters or any program that is controlled by language. This is important to the area of artificial intelligence and in modern programming in general.

## Lex

Lex is a program that makes *lexical analyzers*. These are programs that recognize character strings. However, programs produced by Lex do more. They can take specified actions based on what they find.

In Chapter 4, we saw how Lex can be used to make *filters,* programs that send textual output to the standard output which is directly determined by textual input coming from the standard input. In this case, the actions normally consist of formatted print statements.

In this chapter, we use Lex to produce C functions that return numerical values called *tokens* that depend on standard textual input given to it. Such programs sometimes are called *tokenizers*.

## Comparison Between Lex and Yacc

In many ways Yacc is similar to Lex. Both programs expect as input a file that contains a set of specifications, and both produce as output a file containing C routines that can be compiled and run (see figure 10-1). Essentially, Lex produces filters (string analyzers) and tokenizers and Yacc produces parsers (syntax analyzers). A tokenizer and a parser can be combined to form a translator program.

## An English Analogy

To understand how Yacc and Lex work, let's explore the strong similarity between the way they work and the way we understand natural languages such as English. This is the basis for the main example of this chapter.

Recognizing individual English words corresponds to Lex's job, whereas organizing them into sentences (often called *parsing sentences*) corresponds to Yacc's job. In fact, as we see in our first example, Lex and Yacc are actually powerful enough to analyze and translate English-like sentences with English-like grammar. However, a complete analysis and translation of English according to a few neat rules is currently beyond the reach of even linguists.

**Figure 10-1**
**Lex and Yacc files**

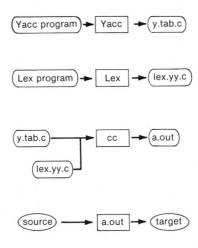

Let's begin with a simple example of what Yacc can do with a small subset of English. We see how Lex recognizes English words and Yacc puts these words together into phrases.

## Grammar Symbols

In English, grammar is built using parts of speech such as: sentences, predicates, subjects, objects, verbs, nouns, noun phrases, numerals, and adjectives. In the Yacc language, these same ideas are represented by grammar symbols.

In our Yacc example, we assign single letter names to these grammar symbols, but the names can be any reasonable length you want.

Table 10-1 shows the grammar symbols that we choose to have for our simple subset of English.

**Table 10-1**
**Grammar symbols for simple subset of English**

| symbol | name |
|--------|------|
| V | verb |
| N | noun |
| M | modifier (adjective) |
| C | count (numeral) |

**Table 10-1 (cont.)**

| | |
|---|---|
| s | sentence |
| p | predicate |
| a | subject |
| b | object |
| r | noun phrase |

The first four symbols V, N, M, and C are capitalized. These represent parts of speech, such as verbs, nouns, and modifiers that are words. These words are recognized by the routines generated by Lex and turned into tokens (integer value representations). These tokens are in turn sent to the parsing routine generated by Yacc. Grammar symbols that correspond to tokens are called *terminals* because they are at the lowest levels of syntax. By syntax we mean grammar.

The next five symbols (s, p, a, b, and r) are called *nonterminals* and reside at higher levels of the syntax. These are groups of terminals, such as sentences, subjects, objects, predicates, and noun phrases. These symbols are organized in a tree (hierarchical) structure. Sentences are at the highest and noun phrases at lower levels. We now explore how to specify this hierarchy to Yacc. For example, the sentence Thomas takes three red marbles. can be organized in the tree shown in figure 10-2.

## Syntax Rules

The grammatical specifications for Yacc are given in a tabular form as a set of syntax rules (the grammar) with corresponding action rules (how they are translated or acted on).

For English, the normal word order for a sentence is subject followed by predicate. Of course, imperative sentences (that is, commands) have only a predicate. Here is how this could be specified in the Yacc language:

```
s       :       a p
        |       p
        ;
```

Here s (standing for sentence) is in the leftmost column, indicating that it is being defined. It is followed by a : in the middle column, indicating that its definition follows. The definition consists of a, standing for subject, then p for predicate. On the next line, the definition continues with a vertical bar in the middle column, indicating that there is another possible expansion of s. This is called an *alternative* expansion. Here the alternative is given as p in the right column. This corresponds to a command sentence like Halt. made of just a predicate. On the next line, the ; indicates that the definition for s ends.

**Figure 10-2**
**Parsing an English sentence**

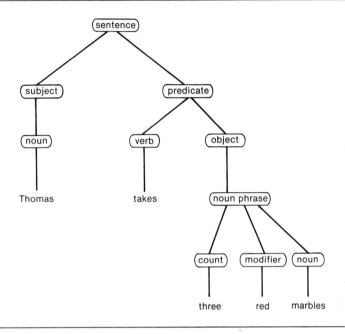

The first line of this definition corresponds to the tree structure in figure 10-3(A) and the second line corresponds to the tree structure in figure 10-3(B).

**Figure 10-3**
**Trees for sentences**

Grammar rules like this one are called *productions*. Here is how this rule might appear in a book on compiler design:

```
s -> a p | p
```

In English, we know that a predicate consists of a verb and such things as adverbs, objects, and prepositional phrases. In our simple subset, we allow it to consist of a verb followed by an object:

```
p        :          V b
         ;
```

Notice that the right-hand side of this rule has a capital letter (denoting a terminal) followed by a lowercase letter (denoting a nonterminal). The terminal (V) comes from the Lex routine (more on this later), while the nonterminal (b) is defined further within our Yacc program (next).

Figure 10-4 shows the tree structure for our simple type of predicate.

**Figure 10-4**
**Tree structure for predicates**

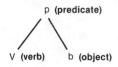

Here is how this rule would appear as a production in a grammar:

```
p -> V b
```

In English, a subject or object of a sentence consists of a noun phrase that is broken down further into nouns and their modifiers. In the Yacc language, this is written with the following three rules.

```
a        :          r
         ;
b        :          r
         ;
r        :          N
         |          M N
         |          C N
         |          C M N
         ;
```

Here, subjects (a) and objects (b) are both defined as noun phrases (r). You might wonder why we need three symbols, a, b, and r, that do the same thing. Making a and b different allows us to better determine what actions to take, and having r provides an economy in maintaining the program, in that it makes the program more compact and understandable as we shall see.

Figure 10-5 shows the trees for our subjects, objects, and noun phrases.

**Figure 10-5**
**Trees for subjects, objects, and noun phrases**

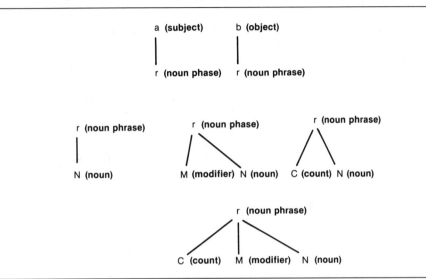

Here is how these rules would appear as productions in a grammar:

```
a -> r
b -> r
r -> N | M N | C N | C M N
```

Of course, English is more complicated than we have described here because it has more parts of speech with more rules and is filled with strange exceptions to almost any rules that have been applied to it. Thus, a complete set of rules for the English language would be huge.

## Parts of a Yacc Program

Now let's organize this grammar into a Yacc program. Such a program consists of three parts: a *declarations* section, a *rules* section, and *user routines*. Each part is separated by %% on a single line.

### Rules Section

Let's begin with the middle section, the rules section. We describe the rules section that makes our grammar rules into a working program that recognizes English sentences.

We need to place these rules in the middle section of a Yacc program. We also need to specify some actions to take as each part of speech is recognized. In a Yacc program, the actions are fragments of C code written to the right of the corresponding syntax rules in curly brackets. For example, here is a rules section with some "diagnostic" print statements for our simple English example:

```
s        :        a p '\n'    {printf(" declarative sentence\n");}
         |          p '\n'    {printf(" imperative sentence\n");}
         |          error     {printf(" erroneous sentence\n");}
         ;
p        :        V b         {printf(" predicate\n");}
         ;
a        :        r           {printf(" subject\n");}
         ;
b        :        r           {printf(" object\n");}
         ;
r        :        N
         |        M N
         |        C N
         |        C M N
         ;
```

The previous listing forms the rules portion of a Yacc program. It sits in the center of the full Yacc program. As we go along, we add the other sections to make the program run.

Notice that we have added an **error** line to the rule for sentences. This executes when the program finds a syntax error. We have also added newline characters to the end of our valid sentences.

Let's preview what these rules do. As the final program recognizes each part of speech, it prints out a message announcing that part of speech. That is, when you type a sentence, the resulting program prints an analysis of that sentence. Here is a sample of what these rules do when they are part of such a complete program:

```
? Thomas takes three red marbles.◄┘
 noun: Thomas
  subject
 verb: takes
 article or count: three
 modifier: red
 noun: marbles
  object
  predicate
  declarative sentence
```

First the program recognizes the noun `Thomas` that it says is the subject. Next the program recognizes the verb `takes`, the count `three`, the modifier `red`, and the noun `marbles`. Now that it has all of the noun phrase `three red marbles`, it recognizes that phrase as the object. Because it has a verb and an object, it acknowledges the predicate. Finally, because it has a subject and a predicate, it announces the full sentence.

Of course, the program won't do that yet. We haven't even included our word recognizer (the Lex program). Such a word recognizer would deliver the following sequence of tokens to the parser:

```
N V C M N
```

This stands for noun (Thomas), verb (takes), count (three), modifier (red), noun (marbles).

This simple set of actions doesn't do the kind of work required for a real application, but this level of action is handy for checking to see how a particular grammar works as it is being developed. This way we can test our ideas in a systematic manner as we develop them. In subsequent development, we replace these actions with more useful ones.

## Yacc Declarations

Now let's look at the first section of a Yacc program, the declarations section. Here, we can define our terminals and any global variables that we need in our actions.

In this example, the terminals are V, N, M, and C, standing for verb, noun, modifier, and count, respectively. These are integer-valued constants called *tokens* because they represent grammar symbols that are recognized by Lex and passed onto Yacc.

The `token` statement causes each of them to be assigned its own particular constant values. These values are greater than 256 so that actual characters can be passed along, too, by sending their ASCII values. No conflict arises because ASCII codes must fall within the range 0-255.

In our example, the token statement could be:

```
%token V N M C
```

The `%` introduces the `token` statement. It is followed immediately by the keyword `token`. Following this is a list of all grammar symbols that we wish to assign tokens (numerical values). When Yacc compiles this statement in a Yacc program, it assigns a separate token value to each symbol.

The programmer then can use these names throughout the program without concern for their actual numeric value. In following text we see how Lex "returns" these values to Yacc.

### User Subroutines

The last section of a Yacc program contains supporting routines such as a main program, error handling routines, and the Lex program. Let's begin with a minimal set of these routines so that our program can stand by itself.

In reality, you can leave this whole section empty if you invoke the Yacc library when you compile the program. However, these functions are easy to write and we wish to gradually gain more control over our program, so we do not use the Yacc library with our program.

**Main**—Like all C programs, the main program is called *main.* It is the starting point for the program. In the first version of our example, the main program calls yyparse the name of the routine that Yacc generates. This C function is called a *parser* because it is said to parse the grammar, meaning that it separates the incoming text into parts of speech. Here is what our main program looks like:

```
main()
    {
    printf("? ");
    yyparse();
    }
```

This particular version prints a question mark, calls yyparse, then returns. Yyparse parses the text according to our rules.

**Error Functions**—Two error functions are needed: yyerror and yywrap. The first one is invoked when a running Yacc program discovers an error, and the second is invoked to "wrap up" things at the end.

In the first version of our example, we make these empty routines:

```
yyerror()
    {
    }
yywrap()
    {
    }
```

### The Lex Function

The Lex routine can be defined in this section as well. It is called yylex. Again, its purpose is to create tokens for Yacc.

For starters, let's make this empty too.

```
yylex()
    {
    }
```

# Compiling a Yacc Program

Let's put everything we've done so far into a file **eng1.y** and compile it. Then we gradually add features until our program behaves in a responsible manner.

Here is how the Yacc program looks all together:

```
%token V N M C
%%
s           :           a p '\n'  {printf(" declarative sentence\n");}
            |           p '\n'     {printf(" imperative sentence\n");}
            |           error      {printf(" erroneous sentence\n");}
            ;

p           :           V b        {printf(" predicate\n");}
            ;

a           :           r          {printf(" subject\n");}
            ;

b           :           r          {printf(" object\n");}
            ;

r           :           N
            |           M N
            |           C N
            |           C M N
            ;
%%

main()
   {
   printf("? ");
   yyparse();
   }

yyerror()
   {
   }
yywrap()
   {
   }
yylex()
   {
   }
```

The **%%** symbols separate the program into its three sections. It is important to have a blank line after the **%%** that separates the rules from the user subroutines. Otherwise, Yacc might run right over your user routines.

To compile these programs, we issue the following Yacc statement:

```
yacc eng1.y
```

This produces a file called y.tab.c that contains over 500 lines of C code. This C code consists of a few C functions, which remain the same no matter what your Yacc program, that read some data which is also included and which depends upon your original Yacc program.

The resulting C program y.tab.c can be compiled into a binary file by issuing the following command to the C compiler:

```
cc y.tab.c
```

To run it, just type a.out. However, the results will not be spectacular. In fact the program just prints the message erroneous sentence and hangs there until you press the interrupt key (normally **delete**).

## How Yacc Works

At this point we see how the resulting C program works. This is valuable if you want to debug problems or achieve the best performance from these tools.

The command:

```
yacc -v eng1.y
```

produces a "verbose" listing in a file called y.output. This file describes the internal states that your program uses to do its job.

Here is a listing of y.output from this command:

```
state 0
        $accept :  _s $end

        error   shift 4
        V   shift 6
        N   shift 7
        M   shift 8
        C   shift 9
        .  error

        s   goto 1
        a   goto 2
        p   goto 3
        r   goto 5

    state 1
```

```
           $accept :  s_$end

           $end   accept
           . error

state 2
           s :  a_p \n

           V   shift 6
           . error

           p   goto 10

state 3
           s :  p_\n

           \n  shift 11
           . error

state 4
           s :  error_     (3)

           . reduce 3

state 5
           a :  r_    (5)

           . reduce 5

state 6
           p :  V_b

           N   shift 7
           M   shift 8
           C   shift 9
           . error

           b   goto 12
           r   goto 13

state 7
           r :  N_      (7)

           . reduce 7

state 8
           r :  M_N
```

```
                    N  shift 14
                    .  error

        state 9
                r :  C_N
                r :  C_M N

                    N  shift 15
                    M  shift 16
                    .  error

        state 10
                s :  a p_\n

                    \n  shift 17
                    .  error

        state 11
                s :  p \n_  (2)

                    .  reduce 2

        state 12
                p :  V b_  (4)

                    .  reduce 4

        state 13
                b :  r_  (6)

                    .  reduce 6

        state 14
                r :  M N_     (8)

                    .  reduce 8

        state 15
                r :  C N_     (9)

                    .  reduce 9

        state 16
                r :  C M_N

                    N shift 18
                    .  error
```

```
state 17
        s : a p \n_     (1)

        . reduce 1

state 18
        r : C M N_      (10)

        . reduce 10
```

```
9/127 terminals, 5/150 nonterminals
11/300 grammar rules, 19/550 states
0 shift/reduce, 0 reduce/reduce conflicts reported
10/190 working sets used
memory: states,etc. 86/3800, parser 6/2000
7/350 distinct lookahead sets
0 extra closures
15 shift entries, 1 exceptions
7 goto entries
0 entries saved by goto default
Optimizer space used: input 41/3800, output 23/2000
23 table entries, 1 zero
maximum spread: 260, maximum offset: 258
```

This output describes a 19-state finite state machine for analyzing token input. A finite state machine is an abstract computing machine that we can implement by a computer program. Such a machine consists of a set of states with transitions between these states that are caused by input.

We now go through our parser in detail, explaining the basic theory behind its operation and design. This explanation shows all its states and how its state transitions depend on the tokens that it receives as input.

### The Augmented Grammar

The operational basis of a Yacc program is a set of syntax rules derived from the grammar specified in the Yacc source code. The following list shows the derived rules for our English subset. We have pulled these rules from the verbose Yacc output listed previously.

```
(0)   $accept -> s $end
(1)   s -> a p \n
(2)   s -> p \n
(3)   s -> error
(4)   p -> V b
(5)   a -> r
(6)   b -> r
(7)   r -> N
```

```
(8)  r -> M N
(9)  r -> C N
(10) r -> C M N
```

Each alternative is listed separately. The preceding list presents these "productions" using the more conventional -> notation instead of Yacc's :.

This is called the *augmented* grammar because it has an extra production for accept. The accept symbol signals the end of the parsing. The parser finishes when it recognizes the $end character (ASCII code −1) at the end of this added production for accept.

You should examine carefully the verbose output to see where these rules occur. They are numbered within parentheses in this output to the right and they appear in an order according to where they are found within the finite state machine. The preceding list just reorders and reformats them. For example, look up rule number (4) in the Yacc verbose output.

## The States

Each state of the parser is defined in terms of *progress* in recognizing its grammatical productions. As the parser receives tokens from the lexical analyzer, it tries to match them with the right-hand sides of productions, using four possible operations: accept, shift, reduce, and error. Successful matching of tokens is handled by the shift operation, successful recognition of an entire production is handled by the reduce operation, and successful match of an entire sentence is handled by the accept operation. If the parser receives a token that it doesn't want, it uses the error operation. We describe these operations in detail in following text, but for now, let's continue with the states.

The parser starts out at state 0. As soon as it gets a token, the parser must try to find a matching rule, that is, a rule (production) with that token as the first symbol on its right-hand side. For example, a token C matches the first symbol of the right-hand sides of both rules (9) and (10). In that case we say that the parser has made progress in recognizing either rule (9) or rule (10).

As the parser gets more tokens, it makes more progress. If it gets an M and then an N, it progresses all the way through the right-hand side of rule (10), and thus recognizes the left-hand side of (10), which is the nonterminal r.

Recognizing the nonterminal r might mean progress through rules (5) or (6). We see exactly what it *does* do in following text, but this should give you an idea of what we mean by progress in recognizing productions.

In the verbose listing, immediately following each state's title line are some lines indicating this progress. An underscore (_) acts as a place marker, indicating *where* the parser now is in the productions. Officially, a production with such a place marker is called an *item*.

Here are some examples in the verbose listing. State 0 looks like this:

```
state 0
        $accept  : _s $end
```

```
error  shift 4
V   shift 6
N   shift 7
M   shift 8
C   shift 9
.   error

s   goto 1
a   goto 2
p   goto 3
r   goto 5
```

It has the single item:

```
$accept :  _s $end
```

The underscore before the s indicates that the parser has found nothing yet in the production

```
$accept -> s $end
```

but is expecting an s.

State 1 has the item:

```
$accept :  s_$end
```

The position of the underscore indicates that the parser has found an s and is expecting to receive a $end in that production.

State 2 has the item:

```
s :  a_p \n
```

The position of the underscore indicates that the parser has found an a in the production

```
s -> a p \n
```

but not a p.

State 5 has the item

```
a :  r_   (5)
```

which indicates that the parser has found an r in the production a -> r and thus is done with that production. This is rule number 5 (as indicated to the right of the item).

State 4 has the item

```
s :  error_   (3)
```

which indicates that the parser has found an error that it recognizes as a kind of s (rule 3—badly formed sentence).

State 9 has two items:

```
r :  C_N
r :  C_M N
```

This indicates that the parser has recognized a token C that could occur in either rule 9 or rule 10. Here, the parser "hedges its bets" by keeping all possibilities open.

Let's organize all of these states into what is called a *transition diagram* (see figure 10-6). You can see that this diagram appears to be a bit more complex than the rules that generated it.

**Figure 10-6**
**Transition diagram for simple English**

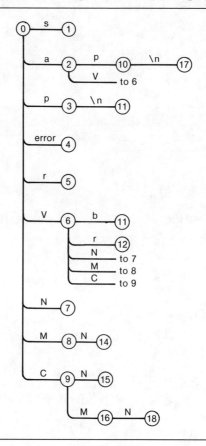

## Deriving the States

In this section we investigate how Yacc translates your Yacc program into a finite state machine. Although this understanding is not absolutely necessary, it is helpful to an overall insight into the capabilities and limitations of translation programs that can be constructed using Yacc.

We now show how to derive the states that are given in our verbose Yacc output. We use the augmented grammar rules. The method starts out with state 0 and applies repeated "closure" operations.

**The Starting Point**—We start with rule 0

```
$accept -> s $end
```

and make the item

```
$accept -> _s $end
```

which indicates the beginning of the $accept production. We call this the *primary* item. It generates the entire finite state machine by a series of closure operations that we describe next.

When the underscore is in the beginning position of an item, we call it an *initial* item. The primary item is the first initial item.

**The Closure Operations**—There are two types of closures, one to complete a state and another to get all the states. As we saw from examining our verbose output, each state is really one or more items, that is, a set of items. The first type of closure adds items to a state until we can add no more, and the second type of closure adds states until we can add no more.

**Closing Each State**—Now let's look at the first type of closure. Here we take the closures of sets of items by repeatedly including initial items for each production of any symbol that is immediately to the right of an underscore.

For example, for the first item, the symbol s is to the right of the underscore, thus we look for productions that expand s. This gives the additional items:

```
s -> _a p \n
s -> _p \n
s -> _error
```

These give rise to initial items for productions that expand a and p. They are

```
a -> _r
p -> _V b
```

Again, we take a closure, adding initial items for r. We cannot add anything due to V because it is a terminal. That is, it does not appear on the left side of any production.

Here is the complete set of items for state 0:

```
$accept -> _s $end
s -> _a p \n
s -> _p \n
s -> _error
a -> _r
p -> _V b
r -> _N
r -> _M N
r -> _C N
r -> _C M N
```

These represent all the rules that might come from state 0, depending on what the next token is.

The Yacc output only lists the first item because all the rest are generated from it, but we need them to complete our analysis. Yacc keeps these internally.

**Finding All States**—Now let's explore how to make new states. This is the second type of closure. Here, we try to move the underscore over one place. This corresponds to recognizing grammar symbols. For example, state 1 is generated by recognizing an s and thus moving the underscore over the s in the first item in state 0. This gives:

```
$accept -> s_$end
```

This set cannot be further enlarged by closure because there are no nonterminals to expand on the right of the underscore.

State 2 can be generated from state 0 by recognizing an a and thus moving the underscore across the a in rule 1. This gives the item:

```
s -> a_p
```

Because p is to the right of the underscore, we also get:

```
p -> _V b
```

No more closure is possible, thus we get the following two items for state 2:

```
s -> a_p \n
p -> _V b
```

Producing state 9 is interesting because the underscore moves in two items at once. Moving the underscore across a `C` in the last two items gives the following two items:

```
r -> C_N
r -> C_M N
```

That is all there is in state 9 because only terminals sit to the right of the underscore.

The following list shows all 19 states. Notice how each one corresponds to a different place on the diagram and how the diagram displays the rules in a pictorial form. For example, state 2 defined by

```
s ->  a_p \n
p ->  _V b
```

sits after an edge from state 0 labeled `a` and before edges labeled `p` that go to state 10 and an edge labeled `V` leading to state 6 that leads to an edge labeled `b`.

```
state 0
          $accept ->  _s $end
          s ->  _a p \n
          s ->  _p \n
          s ->  _error
          a ->  _r
          p ->  _V b
          r ->  _N
          r ->  _M N
          r ->  _C N
          r ->  _C M N
state 1
          $accept ->  s_$end
state 2
          s ->  a_p \n
          p ->  _V b
state 3
          s ->  p_\n
state 4
          s :  error_
state 5
          a :  r_
state 6
          p :  V_b
          b ->  _r
          r ->  _N
          r ->  _M N
```

```
                              r -> _C N
                              r -> _C M N
                state 7
                              r -> N_
                state 8
                              r -> M_N
                state 8
                              r -> C_N
                              r -> C_M N
                state 10
                              s -> a p_\n
                state 11
                              s -> p \n_
                state 12
                              p -> V b_
                state 13
                              b -> r_
                state 14
                              r -> M N_
                state 15
                              r -> C N_
                state 16
                              r -> C M_N
                state 17
                              s -> a p \n_
                state 18
                              r : C M N_
```

If we throw out all the items that are initial (underscore at the initial position), but keep the very primary item (even though it is initial), we get the items listed under the states in the verbose Yacc output. These restricted items form what are called *kernel items*.

In practice, the situation is a bit more complicated because the parser sometimes needs to know what comes after an item to know how to handle that item properly. Thus, Yacc might have to divide some states into smaller states that keep track of "lookahead" information. However, this is not a problem here. See *Compilers: Principles, Techniques, and Tools* by Aho, Sethi, and Ullman for a much more detailed discussion of the various methods for generating states.

## The Transitions

In the verbose Yacc output, each state has a list of possible transitions from that state according to what symbol it recognizes next. You can see what they are by examining the full set of items for that state. Any symbol that is immediately to the right of an underscore gives rise to a transition. For those items, move the underscore across that symbol (that is, "recognize" the symbol), then find the state to which these new items belong.

For example, state 0 consists of the following items:

```
$accept -> _s $end
s -> _a p \n
s -> _p \n
s -> _error
a -> _r
p -> _V b
r -> _N
r -> _M N
r -> _C N
r -> _C M N
```

Thus, the parser that Yacc generates has transitions on the symbols s, a, r, error, r, V, N, M, and C. For example, if the parser receives a token N, it, in effect, moves the underscore across the N, turning the seventh item into the item for state 7, thus leading to the transition from state 0 to state 7. This is one of the edges of the transition diagram. At this point it has recognized the entire right-hand side of rule 7 and thus the grammar symbol r, a nonterminal.

We see that the parser can recognize terminals, and from these, can recognize nonterminals. Let's look at some more examples.

Recognizing an s moves the underscore across the s, changing the first item into an item that belongs in state 1, thus it gives a transition from state 0 to state 1. This is on the first line of the diagram.

Skipping down to the transition on the symbol C, we have already seen that moving over it transforms the last two items into a total of two items, both in state 9, thus giving the transition from state 0 to state 9, which can be found toward the bottom of the diagram.

## The Parsing Operations

The parser that Yacc generates is a table-driven program which uses the same algorithm every time. When you run Yacc on a Yacc program, it generates this table and packages it with a predesigned parse function and any code that you may include in your Yacc source code program.

The parser generated by Yacc (see figure 10-7) reads input as tokens from an input queue (buffer) that is fed by the yylex function. The parser uses a stack where it stores pairs (X, s) consisting of a grammar symbol (X) and a state number (s).

The parser begins with the pair (−1, 0) on the stack, indicating an empty grammar symbol and state zero.

The parser performs four different operations:

1. accept
2. shift
3. reduce
4. error

**Figure 10-7**
**Model of the parser**

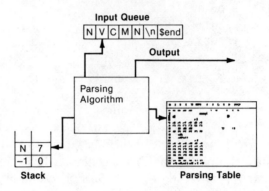

The parser stops when it finishes an `accept` or `error` operation. Let's examine how each of these works. To truly understand, you have to go through some examples, as we do in following text.

**Accept**—The `accept` operation is performed when the parser reaches the end of the `$accept` production. This signals a successful parse of a sentence. When this happens, the parser returns to the routine that called it.

**Shift**—The `shift` operation is performed when the parser recognizes a new token at the front of the input queue. It removes this token from the input queue and pushes it onto the stack with the current state. The parser then goes to a state specified by the parsing table.

**Reduce**—The `reduce` operation is performed when the parser recognizes a production. At this point the symbols on the right-hand side of the production can be found on the stack with the states where they occurred. The `reduce` operation pops this information off the stack, then goes to the state indicated by the parsing table according to the symbol on the left-hand side of the production and the state uncovered on the stack. It then pushes the symbol on the left-hand side of the production onto the stack with the new state. This rule definitely requires examples, so hold on!

**Error**—The `error` operation is performed when the parser cannot recognize what has been given to it. It that case, it pops its stack until it enters a state where the error is legal, then tries to execute the corresponding action.

## The Parsing Table

The parsing table is a two dimensional array whose rows are indexed by the states and columns are indexed by the grammar symbols. Each entry is assigned one of the four operations. Conventionally, a blank denotes the error operation. Entries in columns headed by terminals can be assigned accept, shift, reduce, or error operations. Entries in columns headed by nonterminals can be assigned either error or a state number (called a goto to that state).

For entries assigned the accept or error conditions, there are no further parameters. Entries assigned the shift operation are assigned the state number where they are to go to. Entries assigned the reduce operation are assigned the number of the grammar rule that they are to use.

The verbose output of Yacc gives the entries of this parsing table in human readable form. For terminals it gives the grammar symbol followed by an operation name and any parameter. For nonterminals, it gives a goto followed by the state that should be used by a reduce operation. When we study our example, we will see how this works.

See table 10-2 for the parsing table for our simple English example as specified by the verbose Yacc output.

**Table 10-2**
**Parsing table for simple English program**

|    | V   | N   | M   | C   | \n  | $end | s | a | b | p  | r  | error |
|----|-----|-----|-----|-----|-----|------|---|---|---|----|----|-------|
| 0  | s6  | s7  | s8  | s9  |     |      | 1 | 2 |   | 3  | 5  | 4     |
| 1  |     |     |     |     |     | accept |   |   |   |    |    |       |
| 2  | s6  |     |     |     |     |      |   |   |   | 10 |    |       |
| 3  |     |     |     |     | s11 |      |   |   |   |    |    |       |
| 4  | r3  | r3  | r3  | r3  | r3  | r3   |   |   |   |    |    |       |
| 5  | r5  | r5  | r5  | r5  | r5  | r5   |   |   |   |    |    |       |
| 6  |     | s7  | s8  | s9  |     |      |   |   | 12 |   | 13 |       |
| 7  | r7  | r7  | r7  | r7  | r7  | r7   |   |   |   |    |    |       |
| 8  |     | s14 |     |     |     |      |   |   |   |    |    |       |
| 9  |     | s15 | s16 |     |     |      |   |   |   |    |    |       |
| 10 |     |     |     |     | s17 |      |   |   |   |    |    |       |
| 11 | r2  | r2  | r2  | r2  | r2  | r2   |   |   |   |    |    |       |
| 12 | r4  | r4  | r4  | r4  | r4  | r4   |   |   |   |    |    |       |
| 13 | r6  | r6  | r6  | r6  | r6  | r6   |   |   |   |    |    |       |
| 14 | r8  | r8  | r8  | r8  | r8  | r8   |   |   |   |    |    |       |
| 15 | r9  | r9  | r9  | r9  | r9  | r9   |   |   |   |    |    |       |
| 16 |     | s18 |     |     |     |      |   |   |   |    |    |       |
| 17 | r1  | r1  | r1  | r1  | r1  | r1   |   |   |   |    |    |       |
| 18 | r10 | r10 | r10 | r10 | r10 | r10  |   |   |   |    |    |       |

Entries that are assigned the error operation are blank. Entries assigned the `accept` operation are filled in with the word `accept`. There is only one of these, namely the entry for state 1 with symbol `$end`. Entries assigned the `shift` operation are filled in with an s followed by the number of the new state. Entries assigned the `reduce` operation are filled in with an r followed by the number of the rule that is being used to make the reduction. A usual point of confusion is between the state numbers that follow the `shift` operation designator and the rule numbers that follow the `reduce` operation designator.

## A Parsing Example

The parser begins with state 0 on the stack and a string of tokens in the input queue. It executes `shift` and `reduce` operations until it encounters an `accept` or `error` operation. When this happens, it stops.

Let's follow the analysis of a particular string through the parser with this particular parsing table.

Suppose we have a sentence such as:

`Thomas takes three red marbles.\n`

A lexical analyzer should break it into the following series of tokens

`N V C M N \n`

because the first word `Thomas` is a noun, the second word `takes` is a verb, the third word `three` is a count, the fourth word `red` is a modifier, and the fifth word `marbles` is a noun.

The parser starts out with the pair `(-1, 0)` on the stack and the string

`N V C M N \n $end`

in the input queue. Here `(-1, 0)` is the pair consisting of the empty token and state 0.

The first input token is N. Looking at the preceding list in the row for state 0, under the column for token N, we see a `shift` operation to state 7. This pushes the pair `(N, 7)` onto the stack and changes the current state to 7. It also advances the input pointer past the N. The stack now contains

`(-1, 0)(N, 7)`

and the input queue:

`V C M N \n $end`

Looking in row 7, the entry under the token V contains a `reduce` operation using rule 7

`r -> N`

which reduces an N to an r. We pop the pair (N, 7) off the stack, uncovering the pair (-1, 0) that temporarily takes us back to state 0. Using the row for state 0 and the goto entry under the column for r we get the new state 5. The parser then pushes the pair (r, 5) onto the stack. The stack now contains:

    (-1, 0)(r, 5)

The first token on the input queue is still V, but the current state is now 5. Looking in row 5, under token V, we see another reduce operation. This time it reduces by rule 5, which is

    a -> r

We pop the (r, 5) off the stack, uncovering the pair (-1, 0) again. This takes us back temporarily to state 0. We use row 0 with the goto for a to determine that the new state is 2. We push the pair (a,2) onto the stack. The stack now contains:

    (-1,  0)(r,  2)

The current state is 2 and V is still on the front of the queue. Now, we are ready to shift the V. According to the preceding list, this takes us to state 6. The stack now contains

    (-1, 0)(a, 2)(V, 6)

and the input queue contains:

    C M N \n $end

The list indicates a shift to state 9. The stack contains

    (-1, 0)(a, 2)(V, 6)(C, 9)

and the queue contains

    M N \n $end

These last two symbols also are shifted onto the stack, giving us

    (-1, 0)(a, 2)(V, 6)(C, 9)(M, 16)(N, 18)

on the stack and a nearly empty input queue (just the \n and $end). We use the entry in row 16, column \n, which says to reduce by rule 10:

    r -> C M N

This pops three pairs (C, 9)(M, 16)(N, 18) off the stack, uncovering the pair (V, 6). This temporarily takes us back to state 6 with symbol r. We look this up in the parsing list and get 13 as the new state. We push the pair (r, 13) onto the stack, getting

(-1, 0)(a, 2)(V, 6)(r, 13)

on the stack. Now, state 13 with input \n gives a reduction by rule 6:

b -> r

We pop the pair (r, 13) off the stack, uncover (V, 6) again, find the new state 12, and push the pair (b, 12) onto the stack. The stack now contains:

(-1, 0)(a, 2)(V, 6)(b, 12)

According to the list, we should use rule 4

p -> V b

to reduce the V and b to p. Thus we pop the pairs (V, 6)(b, 12) off the stack, uncovering (a, 2), which returns us to state 2 with symbol p. We look up the goto for p and find state 10. We then push (p, 10) on the stack, getting:

(-1, 0)(a, 2)(p, 10)

State 10 with input token \n shifts to 10

(-1,0)(a, 2)(p, 10)(\n,17)

which allows us to reduce by rule 1

s -> a p

giving a stack

(-1,0)(s, 1)

and an input token $end. This leads to an accept operation, finishing the parse successfully.

You should realize that the preceding example only shows the steps that the parser performs as it analyzes a sentence. As we shall see later, with the proper action statements, a parser also can produce useful results as it analyzes.

# Lexical Analysis with Lex

Now let's see how to use Lex to provide lexical analysis for our program. Lex programs have rules to recognize words and return tokens.

A Lex program also consists of three parts: a *definitions section,* a *rules section,* and a *user subroutines section.* These sections are separated by the %% symbol.

The rules section consists of a table of regular expressions and corresponding actions for when they match parts of the input. (The input is a string of characters.)

## Regular Expressions

As we have seen in previous chapters, a regular expression is a string expression that is used to match strings. For example, the expression

    [A-Za-z]*

specifies any string that contains zero or more occurrences of the letters A through Z and a through z.

Table 10-3 gives some of the rules that define regular expressions for Lex.

Table 10-3<br>Rules for Lex regular expressions

| expression | matches |
|------------|---------|
| x | the character "x" |
| "x" | "x" even if "x" is a special character |
| \x | "x" even if "x" is a special character |
| [s] | any character in the string s |
| [x-y] | any character in the range from x to y |
| [^s] | any character not in the string s |
| ^x | an x at the beginning of a line |
| x$ | an x at the end of a line |
| x? | x if it is there |
| x* | 0 or more instances of x |
| x+ | 1 or more instances of x |
| x\|y | an x or y |
| (x) | an x |
| x/y | an x followed by a y |
| {s} | an expression defined by s (in declarations) |
| x{m,n} | m through n occurrences of x. |

Here is a short Lex program that finds the nouns Thomas, Elizabeth, and marble(s); the verbs give, take, and show; the colors red, green, and blue; and the numerals one through ten, and articles a and the. In each case, it returns a token signifying its part of speech. This token is used by our Yacc program. The Lex program also recognizes unknown words and other "junk," returning the appropriate token.

```
ws                [ \.\n]
%%
Thomas/{ws}       {return(noun(1, 1));}
Elizabeth/{ws}    {return(noun(2, 1));}
[Mm]arble/{ws}    {return(noun(3, 1));}
[Mm]arbles/{ws}   {return(noun(3, 2));}
[Gg]ive/{ws}      {return(verb(1, 2));}
[Gg]ives/{ws}     {return(verb(1, 1));}
[Tt]ake/{ws}      {return(verb(2, 2));}
[Tt]akes/{ws}     {return(verb(2, 1));}
[Ss]how/{ws}      {return(verb(3, 2));}
[Ss]hows/{ws}     {return(verb(3, 1));}
[Rr]ed/{ws}       {return(modifier(1));}
[Gg}een/{ws}      {return(modifier(2));}
[Bb]lue/{ws}      {return(modifier(3));}
the/{ws}          {return(numeral(0));}
a/{ws}            {return(numeral(1));}
1/{ws}            |
[Oo]ne/{ws}       {return(numeral(1));}
2/{ws}            |
[Tt]wo/{ws}       {return(numeral(2));}
3/{ws}            |
[Tt]hree/{ws}     {return(numeral(3));}
4/{ws}            |
[Ff]our/{ws}      {return(numeral(4));}
5/{ws}            |
[Ff]ive/{ws}      {return(numeral(5));}
6/{ws}            |
[Ss]ix/{ws}       {return(numeral(6));}
7/{ws}            |
[Ss]even/{ws}     {return(numeral(7));}
8/{ws}            |
[Ee]ight/{ws}     {return(numeral(8));}
9/{ws}            |
[Nn]ine/{ws}      {return(numeral(9));}
10/{ws}           |
[Tt]en/{ws}       {return(numeral(10));}

[ \.]             {/* gobble this up */}
\n                {return(yytext[0]));}
```

```
[A-Za-z]+/{ws}  {printf(" unknown word: %s\n",yytext);return(W);}
[^0-9A-Za-z \.\n] {printf(" junk: %s\n", yytext);return(J);}
%%

noun(i,n) int i, n;
    {name = i; num = n; printf(" noun: %s\n",yytext);return(N);}
verb(i,n) int i, n;
    {action = i; vnum = n; printf(" verb: %s\n",yytext);return(V);}
modifier(i) int i;
    {color = i; printf(" modifier: %s\n", yytext); return(M);}
numeral(i) int i;
    {count = i; printf(" article or count: %s\n",yytext);return(C);}
```

**Declarations**—In the declarations section, the string expression **ws** is defined. This stands for *white space*. It is a blank, period, or newline character.

**Rules**—In the rules section, most every regular expression has a corresponding action to its right that is written as C code and is inside curly brackets.

First there are a series of vocabulary words. Each word is followed by a /{ws} to indicate that it must be followed by white space. Most words (except for proper names) can begin with either a lower- or uppercase letter.

For the words that this Lex program recognizes, it returns tokens according to their part of speech. These tokens are passed to our Yacc program. The Lex program calls functions in the user subroutines section that handle the different parts of speech. For example, for nouns we call a function called noun, and for verbs, we call a function called verb. These functions set various *attributes*, such as its numerical index in a dictionary and whether a word is singular or plural. In our case, we have separate lists for the various parts of speech.

For our example, the nouns are numbered as follows:

1. Thomas
2. Elizabeth
3. marble(s)

The verbs are numbered:

1. give
2. take
3. show

The numerals are numbered according to their value. The articles **a** and the are included here also and are given the value 0. Notice that each numeral can be given either as a word or as a string of digits.

The colors are numbered:

1. red
2. green
3. blue

After the built-in vocabulary, we look for extra white space

```
{ws}
```

which it should ignore. It prints error messages when it finds unknown words given by

```
[A-Za-z]+/{ws}
```

and junk given by

```
[^0-9A-Za-z \.\n]
```

which is all the characters that it doesn't recognize.

**User Subroutines**—The user subroutines section contains the routines `noun`, `verb`, `modifier`, and `numeral` that set some variables and return token values for the various parts of speech.

This program could be modified to include a dictionary in which it could look up more words and classify them into their parts of speech. It could even add words to this dictionary in a dynamic manner so that it could gradually learn an ever larger vocabulary. This dictionary would then correspond to a symbol table in a compiler.

**Connecting the Lex Program to the Yacc Program**—If this Lex program is placed in a file `eng.l`, it can be compiled into C via the command:

```
lex eng.l
```

The result is contained in a file called `lex.yy.c`. We can include this in our Yacc program with the directive

```
#include "lex.yy.c"
```

in place of the definition of the `yylex` function that was originally an empty routine.

We must modify our Yacc program in a couple of other ways to make it run with this new Lex program. Because our Lex program generates a couple of additional tokens, namely `W` for unknown word and `J` for unrecognized junk, we must add `W` and `J` to the list of tokens. We also need to include a file in the declarations section that contains definitions of our global variables, and we beef up the main program with a do forever while loop that gives a prompt, then calls yyparse.

Here is the new Yacc program.

```
%{
#include "eng.h"
%}
%token V N M C W J
%%
s          :          a p '\n'  {printf(" declarative sentence\n");}
           |            p '\n'  {printf(" imperative sentence\n");}
           |          error     {printf(" erroneous sentence\n");}
           ;

p          :          V b       {printf(" predicate\n");}
           ;

a          :          r         {printf(" subject\n");}
           ;

b          :          r         {printf(" object\n");}
           ;

r          :          N
           |          M N
           |          C N
           |          C M N
           ;
%%

#include "lex.yy.c"
main()

    {
    while(1)
       {
       printf("? ");
       yyparse();
       }
    }
yyerror()
    {
    }
yywrap()
    {
    }
```

Notice that the include directive in the declarations section is enclosed between the symbols %{ and %}. These symbols allow us to insert C code anywhere we want in a Yacc program.

Here is the new include file for global constants and variables.

303

```
/* global variables for English Yacc program */

int    name, count, color;
int    sname, scount, scolor;
int    oname, ocount, ocolor;
int    action;
int    num, vnum, snum;
char   *where;

static char *nounname[] = {"I", "Thomas", "Elizabeth", "marbles(s)"};
static char *verbname[] = {"none", "give", "take", "show"};
static char *colorname[] = {"no color", "red", "green", "blue"};
static int   marbles[3][4] = {
                        { 0, 0, 0, 0 },
                        { 0, 8, 4, 3 },
                        { 0, 3, 7, 2 },
                        };
```

There are variables to handle values associated with various tokens, storage for the marbles, and some strings containing vocabulary needed for input and output. We won't need all of this right away, but we include it here for convenience so that we can develop our program. In general, program development begins with the data structures, so this is a natural step.

## Refining Our Example of Simple English

Now that we have prototypes of each part of our simple English understanding program, we can take a test run. In this section, we discuss how to compile, debug, and extend our program.

### Compiling

So far we have the files eng.h that contains the global variables: eng.l, which contains the Lex program, and eng2.y, which contains a second version of our Yacc program. The Lex program has been lexed with the command

```
lex eng.l
```

to produce a file lex.yy.c. The Yacc program has been yacced with the command

```
yacc eng2.y
```

to produce a file y.tab.c. We now compile this second C source file with the command:

```
cc y.tab.c
```

To run it we type:

```
a.out
```

Here is a session with this program. We end the session by pressing **delete**.

```
% a.out
? Thomas takes three red marbles.◄┘
 noun: Thomas
  subject
 verb: takes
 article or count: three
 modifier: red
 noun: marbles
  object
  predicate
  declarative sentence
```

We start by typing a sentence: `Thomas takes three red marbles.` The lexical program finds the noun `Thomas`. The parser reduces it to a subject. The lexical program finds the verb `takes`, but the parser cannot reduce it yet. The lexical program finds the numeral `three`, the modifier `red`, and the noun `marbles`. The parser reduces these to an object, then reduces the verb and object to a predicate. It finally reduces the subject and predicate to a declarative sentence.

```
? Elizabeth gives two green marbles.◄┘
 noun: Elizabeth
  subject
 verb: gives
 article or count: two
 modifier: green
 noun: marbles
  object
  predicate
  declarative sentence
```

This time the subject is `Elizabeth`, the verb is `gives`, and the object is `two green marbles`. The next example shows an imperative sentence that begins with the verb `take`.

```
? Take one marble.◄┘
 verb: Take
 article or count: one
 noun: marble
  object
  predicate
  imperative sentence
<delete>
```

We see that it is quite possible for a computer to understand simple English. This is a crucial step in developing artificial intelligence programs. Such programs could run robots that follow our commands or access vast data bases for busy businessmen. In following text in this chapter, we make this particular program more intelligent.

## Debugging

Sometimes you may need to see exactly how your parser is handling a particular thorny problem. The good news is that Yacc has built-in facilities for producing diagnostics. The bad news is that you have to go into the y.tab.c file to turn on this feature.

You must do two things. The first is to cause the manifest constant YYDEBUG to be defined, and the second is to cause the variable yydebug to take on a nonzero value. You can use the editor to insert the line

```
#define YYDEBUG 1
```

at the top of the y.tab.c file, then search for the line containing

```
int yydebug;
```

and add =1 after the word yydebug so that this declaration now reads:

```
int yydebug=1;
```

Now compile y.tab.c again and type a.out to run it. We test it with the sentence Thomas takes four blue marbles. We get:

```
% a.out◄┘
? State 0, token -none-
Thomas takes four blue marbles.◄┘
 noun: Thomas
Received token N
State 7, token -none-
```

```
Reduce by (7) "r : N"
State 5, token -none-
Reduce by (5) "a : r"
  subject
State 2, token -none-
 verb: takes
Received token V
State 6, token -none-
 article or count: four
Received token C
State 9, token -none-
 modifier: blue
Received token M
State 16, token -none-
 noun: marbles
Received token N
State 18, token -none-
Reduce by (10) "r : C M N"
State 13, token -none-
Reduce by (6) "b : r"
  object
State 12, token -none-
Reduce by (4) "p : V b"
  predicate
State 10, token -none-
Received token -unknown-
State 17, token -none-
Reduce by (1) "s : a p "
' "
  declarative sentence
State 1, token -none-
```

You should go through this output, following it around the transition diagram in figure 10-5. It should agree with our previous run through the parsing table.

## Making the Program Smarter

Let's conclude this example by replacing the diagnostic actions in the Yacc program with actions that have more meaning. We will have the program recognize what we say and respond with questions and reports on what it knows.

Here is the third version of our Yacc program. It now calls functions to perform various actions in response to recognizing each grammar rule. Rather than directly defining dummy C functions in the user subroutine section, we have used the include directive to bring it a set of routines defined in the file eng.r, which we list after we list eng3.y:

```
        /* Yacc program for simple subset of English */

%{
#include "eng.h"
%}

%token V N M C W J

%%
s       :       a p '\n'    {sentence1();YYACCEPT;}
        |       p '\n'      {sentence2();YYACCEPT;}
        |       error       {sentenceerror();YYABORT;}
        ;
p       :       V b         {predicate();}
        ;
a       :       r           {subject();}
        ;
b       :       r           {object();}
        ;
r       :       N           {nounphrase1();}
        |       M N         {nounphrase2();}
        |       C N         {nounphrase3();}
        |       C M N       {nounphrase4();}
        ;
%%
#include "lex.yy.c"
#include "eng.r"
```

The identifiers **YYACCEPT** and **YYABORT** are macros defined by the parser within the file y.tab.c. They are equivalent to return(0) and return(1), respectively.

Here is the file eng.r that contains the user subroutines.

```
/* main program and support routines for English Yacc program */

main()
    {
    while(1)
        {
        where = "beginning";
        printf("? ");
        if (!yyparse()) reportmarbles(sname, ocolor);
        }
    }

yyerror() {printf(" syntax error after: %s\n", where);}
```

```
yywrap() {printf("Thank you.\n"); return(1);}

/* Here is where action is taken according to the syntax. */

sentence1()   /* Declarative Sentence */
   {
   where = "declarative sentence";
   if (!checksvnumber()) return(0);
   if (!checksubject()) return(0);
   sentence();
   }

sentence2()   /* Imperative Sentence */
   {
   where = "imperative sentence";
   sname = 0; /* subject understood to be "I" */
   sentence();
   }
sentenceerror()
   {
   printf("  unrecognized sentence\n");
   }
sentence()
   {
   if (!checkobject()) return(0);
   switch(action)
      {
      case 1: /* Give */
              if (ocolor == 0) getcolor();
              if (ocount == 0) getcount();
              updatemarbles(sname, ocolor, -ocount);
              break;

      case 2: /* Take */
              if (ocolor == 0) getcolor();
              if (ocount == 0) getcount();
              updatemarbles(sname, ocolor, ocount);
              break;

      case 3: /* Show */
              break;
      }
   }

predicate()
   {
   where = "predicate";
```

```
                    printf("  %s: verb = %s\n", where, verbname[action]);
                    }

          subject()
             {
             where = "subject";
             reportnoun();
             checknnumber();
             snum = num;
             sname = name;
             scolor = color;
             scount = count;
             }

          object()
             {
             where = "object";
             reportnoun();
             checknnumber();
             oname = name;
             ocolor = color;
             ocount = count;
             }
          reportnoun()
             {
             printf("  %s: %s, color = %d, count = %d\n",
                    where, nounname[name], color, count);
             }
          nounphrase1()
             {where = "noun phrase with just noun"; count = 0; color = 0;}
          nounphrase2()
             {where = "noun phrase with noun and modifier"; count = 0;}
          nounphrase3()
             {where = "noun phrase with noun and count"; color = 0;}
          nounphrase4()
             {where =  "noun phrase with noun, modifier, and count";}

          checksvnumber()
             {
             if(snum == vnum) return(1);
             printf("  Subject and predicate do not agree in number.\n");
             return(0);
             }
          checknnumber()
             {
             if((num == 1) & (count > 1)) {printf(" Noun should be
                plural.\n");}
```

```
    if((num > 1) & (count == 1)) {printf(" Noun should be
        singular.\n");}
    }

checksubject()
    {
    if ((sname >= 0) && (sname < 3)) return(1);
    printf("  invalid subject\n");
    return(0);
    }

checkobject()
    {
    if (oname == 3) return(1);
    printf("  invalid object.\n");
    return(0);
    }

reportmarbles(who, what)
    int who, what;
    {
    if(who == 0) printf("\nI now have ");
    else         printf("\n%s now has ", nounname[who]);
    if(what > 0) printf("%d %s marble(s).\n",
        marbles[who][what], colorname[what]);
    else  printf("%d red, %d green, and %d blue marble(s).\n",
        marbles[who][1], marbles[who][2], marbles[who][3]);
    }
getcolor()
    {
    char str[80];
    ocolor = 0;
    while (ocolor == 0)
        {
        printf("What color? ");
        gets(str);
        if      (!strcmp(str, "red"))   ocolor = 1;
        else if (!strcmp(str, "green")) ocolor = 2;
        else if (!strcmp(str, "blue"))  ocolor = 3;
        else printf("I cannot find that color.\n");
        }
    }
getcount()
    {
    char str[80];
    int match = 0;
    while (match != 1)
        {
```

```
            printf("How many? ");
            gets(str);
            match = sscanf(str, "%d", &ocount);
            if (match != 1) printf("Enter a numerical value. ");
            }
      }
updatemarbles(whose, what, amount)
      int whose, what, amount;
      {
      if ((whose>=0) && (whose<=2) && (what>=0) && (what<=3))
         {
         marbles[whose][what] += amount;
         if (marbles[whose][what] < 0) marbles[whose][what] = 0;
         }
      else printf("Out of range, whose = %d, what = %d\n", whose,
what);
         }
```

We won't go into this code because it is really a side issue to convince you that we have the beginning of something useful. Here is a typical session using our enhanced program. The program analyzes the sentence that you type, then responds by telling you how many marbles there are. Here is our first sentence:

```
? Thomas takes marbles.◄┘
 noun: Thomas
  subject: Thomas, color = 0, count = 0
 verb: takes
 noun: marbles
  object: marbles(s), color = 0, count = 0
  predicate: verb = take
What color? red◄┘
How many? 3◄┘


Thomas now has 11 red marble(s).
```

In this example, we type the sentence Thomas takes marbles. The program analyzes and accepts this sentence but notices that you have not specified what color they are or how many there were. It asks for this information, then reports how many marbles of this color that Thomas now has. The next example demonstrates that the program understands the meaning of the word show:

```
? Thomas shows marbles.◄┘
 noun: Thomas
  subject: Thomas, color = 0, count = 0
 verb: shows
 noun: marbles
  object: marbles(s), color = 0, count = 0
  predicate: verb = show
```

Thomas now has 11 red, 4 green, and 3 blue marble(s).

You should examine the output of the rest of this session and check the marble totals.

```
? Thomas gives a red marble.◄┘
 noun: Thomas
  subject: Thomas, color = 0, count = 0
 verb: gives
 article or count: a
 modifier: red
 noun: marble
  object: marbles(s), color = 1, count = 1
  predicate: verb = give
```

Thomas now has 10 red marble(s).
```
? Show the marbles.◄┘
 verb: Show
 article or count: the
 noun: marbles
  object: marbles(s), color = 0, count = 0
  predicate: verb = show
```

I now have 0 red, 0 green, and 0 blue marble(s).
```
? Take two blue marbles.◄┘
 verb: Take
 article or count: two
 modifier: blue
 noun: marbles
  object: marbles(s), color = 3, count = 2
  predicate: verb = take
```

I now have 2 blue marble(s).
```
? Give one blue marble.◄┘
 verb: Give
```

```
article or count: one
modifier: blue
noun: marble
  object: marbles(s), color = 3, count = 1
  predicate: verb = give

I now have 1 blue marble(s).
?<delete>
```

## A Numerical Example

Let's look at a simple example of how Lex and Yacc can handle numbers and arithmetic expressions.

Suppose that the language has the following input symbols: a token denoting a NUMBER; the operator symbols *, /, +, and -; and parentheses. Suppose that the grammar consists of the following grammar rules:

```
(1) line -> expr
(2) expr -> NUMBER
(3) expr -> expr '+' expr
(4) expr -> expr '-' expr
(5) expr -> expr '*' expr
(6) expr -> expr '/' expr
(7) expr -> '(' expr ')'
```

There are only a few levels of syntax here. We will see how Yacc uses operator precedence to sort out the different levels of expressions into terms and factors.

Here is the source code for our Yacc program:

```
%token NUMBER
%left '+', '-'
%left '*', '/'

%%

line    :       expr            {printf("%d\n", $1);}
        ;
expr    :       NUMBER
        |       expr '+' expr   {$$=$1+$3;}
        |       expr '-' expr   {$$=$1-$3;}
        |       expr '*' expr   {$$=$1*$3;}
        |       expr '/' expr   {$$=$1/$3;}
        |       '(' expr ')'    {$$=$2;}
        ;
```

```
%%
#include "lex.yy.c"
main()
   {
   printf("? ");
   `yyparse();
   }
yyerror()
   {
   printf("syntax error\n");
   }
yywrap()
   {
   }
```

## The Declarations Section

The declarations section declares one token **NUMBER**. This is sent by the lexical function yylex when it finds a number (integer).

The left directive does two things. It determines the grouping of the operations among themselves and the operator precedence from operator to operator.

The left directive specifies a set of operators. These are to be grouped from the left as they are evaluated. That is, if # is a left operator, the expression

```
X # Y # Z
```

should be evaluated as follows:

```
(X # Y) # Z
```

If a number of left operators is given, the precedence of the operators is determined in increasing order. In our example, + and − are listed in the first left directive, and * and / are listed in the second left directive. This places + and − at the same level as each other, but with lower precedence than * and /.

## The Rules Section

The rules section lays out the grammar described above. In addition, it specifies actions to take.

For the production

```
line -> expr
```

we print the value $1. This represents the value on top of a value stack that runs parallel to the symbol and a state stack that we studied earlier. When the expression is completely evaluated, its value is found there.

For each of the operators +, −, *, and / we take a separate but similar action. In each case, the value of the $1 is combined with the value $3 and placed in $$. The $1 corresponds to the first expr, the $2 is skipped because it corresponds to the operator itself, and the $3 corresponds to the second expr. These values are on the value stack before the expression is reduced. They are replaced by the value $$ after the reduction.

The action for the parenthesized expression, places the value $2 into $$. Here, $1 corresponds to the left parenthesis, $2 corresponds to expr in the middle, and $3 corresponds to the right parenthesis. Therefore, $2 is what we want.

### The User Subroutines Section

In the user subroutines section we have included minimal implementations for the functions main, yyerror, and yywrap. We have also included the file lex.yy.c. Next, we give a Lex program that generates this file.

### The Lexical Analyzer for Expressions

Basically, the job of the lexical analyzer for our expression evaluator is to recognize and evaluate numbers, passing their value into the value stack and the token NUMBER as the return value. It also should pass the operator symbols as tokens to be returned, and it converts newline into the $end token.

Here is the Lex program.

```
%%
[0-9]+          {yylval = atoi(yytext); return(NUMBER);}
[-+*/()]        {return(yytext[0]);}
\n              {return(-1);}
```

The first line evaluates numbers. The regular expression [0-9]+ matches a string of one or more digits. The library function atoi converts this string (stored in yytext) into an integer that is placed in the variable yylval. The parser places the value of this on the value stack.

The second line passes the ASCII values of the operator and grouping symbols back as tokens. The characters can be found in the first entry of yytext, namely yytext[0].

The third line converts the newline character into end of file or the $end token. This has a value of −1.

### Running the Expression Evaluator

Assuming that the Yacc program is stored in the file e.y and the Lex program is stored in the file e.l, we can compile the program with the following three steps:

```
lex e.l
yacc e.y
cc y.tab.c
```

Here is a sample run:

```
% a.out◄┘
? 5*(11-1+6)+100/4◄┘
105
```

You can see that the program correctly evaluated the expression:

```
5*(11-1+6)+100/4
```

Figure 10-8 shows the transition diagram it uses for parsing. This can be derived from the verbose output (using the −v option) of Yacc.

# Summary

In this chapter, we have explored Lex and Yacc, two advanced programming tools that produce routines to help programs interpret their input.

We discussed how Lex recognized strings using regular expressions and how Yacc recognizes language specified by grammars (syntax rules). We discussed how these two tools fit together to make a complete translator or interpreter.

Our first example implemented a program that recognizes a simple subset of English, illustrating that artificial approaches work to some extent on natural languages. We saw how to specify grammars for Yacc and how Yacc converts these grammars into finite state machines, then into equivalent parsing tables. We saw how these parsing tables are packed into C programs with routines developed using Lex to form a complete translator or interpreter program.

We built our first example in three stages, first merely recognizing sentences, then printing out diagnostics, and finally taking appropriate actions that depend on the input.

Our second example was an expression evaluator, illustrating that these methods can be used to produce more traditional computer language interpreters and translators.

**Figure 10-8**
**Transition diagram for expression evaluator**

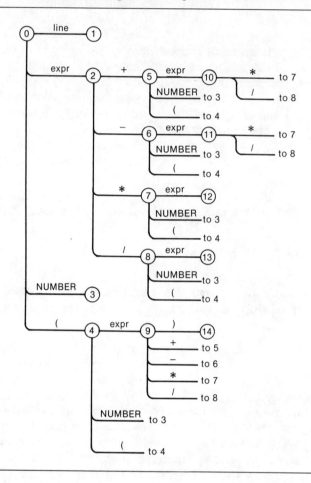

## Questions and Answers

### Questions

1. How does language translation and interpretation relate to operating systems?

2. What is lexical analysis and what kind of rules does Lex use to describe it?

3. What is syntactic analysis and what kind of rules does Yacc use to describe it?

4. What is a token?

## Answers

1. Language translation and interpretation are essential to operating systems in a number of ways. One of the jobs of an operating system such as XENIX is to provide an interface between its human users and its internal services and data. This is often accomplished through the use of language translators and interpreters that are incorporated in shell programs. A compiler, such as the XENIX C compiler, is a language translator. Also, operating systems provide support for program development of new programs. Language development tools can assist with the development of "human interfaces" for these programs.

2. Lexical analysis is the recognition of individual word-like components of a language. In programming languages, this corresponds to the recognition of individual identifiers, keywords, operation symbols, separators, and terminators. Lex uses regular expressions to describe these components.

3. Syntactic analysis is the recognition of phrase-like structures of a language. In programming languages, this corresponds to the recognition of such things as expressions, statements, control structures, and data structures. Yacc uses context-free grammars to describe these structures. These grammar rules are given as productions.

4. A token is an integer that represents an individual lexical component of a language. For example, each keyword is normally represented by a different token. The main output of lexical analysis is a stream of tokens that forms the main input for syntactic analysis.

# Index

## A

acknowledge command,
        217, 218
adb command, 20
adb debugger, 5, 49, 73, 231
        examples of, 76–83
        purpose of, 75
adb86 command, 20
adb286 command, 20
addch command, 148
Aho, A. V., 113
ar command, 20
argc variable, 132, 174, 180, 183,
        202
argv variable, 132, 134, 174,
        180, 183, 184, 202
as command, 20
asm command, 20
assemblers, 5, 7
asx command, 20
AT, the IBM, 4, 10
AT&T, 3, 4, 7, 227
        Bell Laboratories, 6
atoi command, 199
awk command, 11, 20
        as a filter, 113–14

## B

backup command, 20
banner command, 20
ba option, 73
basename command, 20
BASIC programming language,
        3, 7, 125
        compilers, 8, 271

BASIC programming—cont.
        interpreters, 8, 56
BDOS, 8
Berkeley
        C-Shell, 23, 24, 25, 49, 57,
        60, 61, 65, 95–96,
        103, 135
        enhancements to XENIX,
        4, 7, 21, 58, 143
bin directory, 20–21, 23, 173
BIOS, 8
boolean capabilities, 156, 157,
        163, 164
Bourne shell, 23, 24, 57, 103
        shell variables and the, 135
B programming language, 6
break statement, 66
breaksw statement, 68
buffer control, 102–3
buffers I/O, 246

## C

cal command, 20
calls, system. *See* System calls;
        individual calls/
        commands
cat command, 20, 30, 32, 34, 60,
        71, 184
        as a filter, 92, 107
        I/O redirection and, 25–27,
        107, 230
        purpose of, 15, 25–27
        shell scripts and, 137
cb command, 20
cb locks, 246

cc command, 20, 38
C compiler, 5, 6, 38, 70, 74, 217,
        271
        I/O redirection and, 96,
        97–98
        Lex and, 144
        programming and, 71–73,
        86, 144
        Yacc and, 144, 271
CCP, 8
cd command, 33, 34, 171
        purpose of, 15, 27–28
char variable, 146
chgrp command, 20
chmod command, 20, 40, 57, 59,
        60, 186, 187, 188, 199,
        229
        purpose of, 35–36
chown command, 20, 188, 199
chroot command, 20
ch variable, 146, 153, 202
clear command, 147,
        153–54, 199
clist, 246
close command, 40, 202, 229,
        230, 238
cmchk command, 20
cmp command, 20
comm command, 20, 115
commands, system. *See* system
        calls; individual calls/
        commands
compilers, 10, 104
        BASIC, 8, 271

compilers—cont.
  C, 5, 6, 38, 70–71, 73, 74,
    86, 96, 97–98, 104,
    144, 217, 271
  FORTRAN, 8
  Pascal, 271
continue statement, 66
control command, 238
control a, 190, 198
control b, 52
control d, 22, 26, 105, 128, 135,
    146, 202
control f, 52
control g, 52
control h, 4, 22
control j, 108
control u, 4, 22, 154, 198–99
control z, 190, 198
copio, command, 245
copy command, 20
cp command, 10, 20, 30
cpio command, 20
CP/M, 3, 5, 7–8, 9, 10, 11
  *Primer Plus,* 70
C programming language, 3, 6,
    11, 49, 67, 70–73, 83,
    84, 229
  debugging and, 73–83
  directory display program
    and, 173–74
  environmental variables
    and, 124–25, 126,
    128–32
  filters and, 91, 92, 96–102,
    103–5, 106, 108,
    115–19
  Pascal compared to, 71
  standard I/O and, 96–102,
    103–5, 144, 147, 152,
    154, 157, 163
  stat program, 181–88
  ustat program, 179–81
  *See also* Lex program
    generator, the; Yacc
    program generator, the
  *Programming Language,*
    *The,* 70
creat command, 188, 201,
    202, 213
  purpose of, 200
creatsem command, 213

crmode command, 147, 153
cron command, 208, 209
csh command, 20, 51, 57, 58,
    63, 65, 128, 208
  purpose of, 23, 24
C-Shell, 23, 24, 25, 57, 60,
    61, 65
  environmental variables and
    the, 155
  as an interpreter, 49
  I/O redirection and the,
    95–96, 103
  shell variables and the, 135
csplit command, 20
curses screen routines, 198, 200
  dialog program,
    148–54, 160
  purpose of, 143, 144
  turtle program, 143,
    144–48, 160

**D**

date command, 20
dc command, 20
dd command, 20
debuggers/debugging, 6, 7
  adb, 5, 49, 73, 75–83
  C programming language
    and, 73–83
  Lint, 73–75
  Yacc, 306–7
define statement, 146, 152
delete command, 198–99, 200
dev directory, 20, 43, 176, 177,
    236, 266–67
device, definitions of, 42, 227
device drivers, 3, 15, 41
  block-oriented, 42, 43, 44,
    232–35, 236, 237–38,
    245, 249, 266, 266
  block routines for,
    237–38, 266
  character-oriented, 42–43,
    44, 232–35, 236, 238,
    249, 266, 266, 267
  character routines for,
    238, 266
  close routine for, 254–55
  connection of, 227–28
  device numbers and,
    187–88, 233, 266–67

device drivers—cont.
  externals of, 250–51
  file operation routines for,
    237–39
  IBM XT, 233–35
  initialization routines for,
    239
  installation of, 264–67
  interrupt routines for, 238,
    257–60
  interrupt time of, 232, 239,
    247, 249
  I/O control function for,
    260–61
  modem change interrupt
    routine for, 259–60
  modem control routine for,
    256–57
  open routine for, 252–54
  param routine for, 255–56
  procedure function for,
    261–64
  purpose of, 42, 227
  read routine for, 255
  receiver interrupt routine
    for, 259
  routines for, 232–45,
    250–64
  special files for, 235–37
  system calls and, 228
  tables for, 235
  task time of, 232, 239, 245,
    247, 249
  terminal, 250–64
  terminal routines for, 238,
    250–64
  transmitter interrupt routine
    for, 258–59
  write routine for, 255
  *See also* I/O; kernel, the
df command, 20, 178
dialog program, 160
  compilation of, 149–52
  data structure of, 152–53
  initialization of, 152
  main program of, 153–55
  purpose of, 143, 148–49
diff command, 20
diff3 command, 20
Digital Equipment Corporation
    (DEC), 7, 8

dircmp command, 20
directory(ies), 170
    bin, 20–21, 23, 173
    dev, 20, 43, 176, 177, 236,
        266–67
    display program for a,
        173–75
    etc, 155, 266
    home, 15, 18, 28, 33,
        65, 123
    i-nodes and, 172–73,
        174, 175
    mail, 15
    MS-DOS and, 171, 172
    organization of, 172–73
    PC-DOS and, 171, 172
    root, 18, 19–20, 65–66, 171,
        172, 208
    security, 33–35
    *See also* file(s); path(s)
dirname command, 20
disable command, 20
disksort routine, 249
dItem variable, 152–53
dList variable, 152, 153, 154,
    197, 198
doit command, 75
done variable, 153, 154, 175, 198
DOS. *See* MS-DOS; PC-DOS
doscat command, 30
doscp command, 10, 30–31, 72
dosls command, 10, 30
dos option, 72
dTitle variable, 152
dtype command, 20
du command, 20
dump command, 20
dumpdir command, 20
dup command, 202

**E**

echo command, 20, 59, 60, 69
    shell scripts and, 137
ed command, 20
edit command, 20
editors/editing, 4, 6, 7, 10
    ed, 50, 113
    ex, 50
    vi, 5, 24, 49, 50–56, 57, 59,
        60, 71, 113, 143, 144,
        146, 155, 158, 160

ed line editing program, 50, 113
egrep filter, 20, 106, 108–11
*8086/8088 16-Bit*
    *Microprocessor*
    *Primer,* 78,
    243–44, 265
else statement, 62–63, 214, 218
enable command, 20
endif statement, 62, 137
end statement, 137
endsw statement, 68
endwin statement, 148, 199
env command, 15, 20, 125–26
    purpose of, 17–18, 127–28
    run program and, 128–32
environments/environmental
    variables, 18–19, 21–24
    C programming language
        and, 124–25, 126,
        128–32
    C-Shell and, 155
    exec command and, 128,
        133, 134
    home directory and, 123
    inheriting, 126–27
    insertenv command and,
        132, 133–34
    processes and, 123
    purpose of, 123–24
    run program and,
        128–32, 133
    scripts and, 124
    shell, 126–28
    structure of, 124
etc directory, 155, 266
ex command, 20, 55, 56
exec command, 128, 133
    purpose of, 134
execv command, 231
execve command, 40, 132, 134,
    229, 231
exit command, 40, 218, 229, 231
ex line editing program, 50
expr command, 20
external file commands, 24–29

**F**

false command, 20
fclose command, 175, 200
fcntl command, 202
feof command, 103, 174, 175

fgetc command, 100, 101
fgets command, 100, 101
fgrep filter, 20, 106, 108–11
fid variable, 202
file(s)
    accessing, 169, 171
    block information of,
        176–81
    definition of a, 169
    device drivers and, 235–37
    device numbers and, 187–88
    external commands, 24–29
    group, 185, 197, 199
    group IDs, 188, 197,
        198, 199
    IBM PC and physical
        organization of, 176
    IBM XT and physical
        organization of,
        175, 176
    i-nodes and, 176–200
    I/O routines, 3, 11, 169,
        200–202
    logical organization of, 170,
        171
    modes, 184, 197, 198
    modifying attributes of,
        188–200
    owner IDs, 197, 198, 199
    password, 185, 197, 199
    physical organization of,
        170–71, 175–78
    security, 15, 33–35, 169,
        185–87
    size, 188
    stat program and, 181–88
    types, 184–85
    user IDs, 188
    ustat program and, 179–81
    vm program and, 188–200
    *See also* directory(ies);
        path(s)
file command, 20, 65
filter(s), 30, 70
    C programming language
        and, 91, 92, 96–102,
        103–5, 106, 108,
        115–19
    combining, 114–15
    examples of, 92

filter(s)—cont.
    I/O and, 91–102, 103–5,
      106, 111, 114–15
    Lex program generator and,
      115–19, 272
    purpose of a, 91–92, 93
    redirection and, 93–103,
      105, 107
    standard, 106–14
    standard error streams and,
      91, 94, 99–100
    standard input and, 91, 94,
      99–101
    standard output and, 91,
      94, 101–2
find command, 20, 98
fopen command, 174–75, 200
foreach statement, 65–66,
    68, 137
fork command, 40, 229, 231
    example program for,
      209–10
    if statement and, 210, 217
    piplining and, 218–19
    processes and, 209–10, 211,
      213, 217, 218–19
    purpose of, 209
for loop, 66, 76, 132, 133,
    154, 164
    insertenv command
      and, 134
    stat program and, 184
    ustat program and, 181
    vm program and, 198, 200
FORTRAN compiler, 8
fprintf command, 101, 102, 174,
    217, 257
fputc command, 101, 102
fputs command, 101, 102
fscanf command, 100, 101, 221
fsck command, 20, 178–79

**G**

getc command, 99–100, 101,
    174, 175, 200
    purpose of, 100
getcb command, 247
getcf command, 247
getchar command, 103, 104, 202
    purpose of, 100–101
getch command, 148

getegid command, 40, 229
getenv command, 133, 163, 164
geteuid command, 40, 229
getgid command, 40, 229
getgrgid command, 183,
    184, 197
getgrname command, 197
get … id command, 199
getopt command, 20
getpid command, 40, 213,
    217, 229
getpsuid command, 184
getpwnam command, 197
getpwuid command, 183, 197
gets command, 20, 100, 101
getuid command, 40, 229
getw command, 100, 174, 175
    purpose of, 101
Graphics Development
    Laboratories, 156
grep filter, 20, 106, 108–11
    shell scripts and, 137
group(s), 32–33
    files, 185, 197, 199
    IDs, 188, 197, 198, 199
grpcheck command, 20

**H**

haltsys command, 267
hardware interrupts, 41–42,
    231–32
hd command, 20
hdinstall command, 267
hdr command, 20
head command, 20
hi command, 72–73
HOME variable, 18–19, 123, 129
home directory, 15, 28, 33, 65
    environmental variables and
      the, 123
    purpose of, 18–19
HZ variable, 23, 123, 244

**I**

IBM
    AT, 4, 10
    PC, 9, 10, 155, 176, 265
    XT, 4, 5, 9, 10, 16, 42, 101,
      175, 176, 228, 230,
      231, 233–35, 239, 242,
      243, 244, 250, 265

id command, 20, 163
if statement, 62–65, 137, 181,
    199–200, 218, 221, 256,
    257, 263
    fork command and,
      210, 217
if else statement, 164
if then statement, 63
if-then-else statement, 70, 137
ignoreeof variable, 134–35
inb command, 244
in command, 238, 244
init command, 208, 209
initscr command, 146, 153
I-nodes
    device numbers and, 187–88
    directories and, 172–73,
      174, 175
    files and, 176–200
    group IDs and, 188
    number of links and, 188
    stat program and, 181–88
    times and, 188
    user IDs and, 188
    ustat program and, 181–88
input/output. *See* I/O
insert command, 199, 200
insertenv command, 132
    purpose of, 133–34
Intel 8088 microprocessor
    chip, 9
Intel 8259 Interrupt
    Controller, 265
interpreter(s), 7, 10
    BASIC, 8, 56
    CCP, 8
    C-Shell as an, 49
interrupt(s), 40
    definition of an, 39
    enable register, 241–42
    hardware, 41–42, 231–32
    mask, 242
    software, 230–31
interrupt routine, 249
I/O
    BIOS, 8
    buffer control and, 102–3
    buffers, 246
    C programming language
      and, 96–102, 103–5,

I/O—cont.
   *C programming language*
      144, 147, 152, 154,
      157, 163
   file routines, 3, 11, 169,
      200–202
   filters and, 91–102, 103–5,
      106, 111, 114–15
   redirection of, 9, 15, 25–27,
      69–70, 93–103, 105,
      107
   scripts for, 69–70
   standard error streams, 91,
      94, 99–100
   standard input, 71, 91, 94,
      99–101
   standard output, 71, 91, 94,
      99–100, 101–2
   terminal routines, 7, 11,
      124, 143–64
   *See also* device drivers;
      kernel, the
ipcrm command, 20
ipcs command, 20
i variable, 132, 133, 153, 154,
      163, 164, 174, 180, 184
   vm program and, 197, 198

**J**

join command, 20
j variable, 153

**K**

kernel, the, 10, 11, 15, 23
   entry points to, 39–44, 229
   hardware interrupts and,
      41–42, 231–32
   interrupt time of, 232, 238
   purpose of, 39, 228
   routines for, 239–45
   sleep function and, 242–44
   software interrupts and,
      230–31
   spl routines for, 239–42,
      252, 254, 265
   structures in, 245–49
   synchronization routines
      for, 239–44
   system calls and, 3, 40–41,
      228, 229–31
   task time of, 231, 238

kernel—cont.
   timeout function and, 244
   transfer functions and,
      244–45
   tty structure of, 247–49,
      252, 253, 254, 255,
      256, 261
   user block of, 245
   wakeup function and,
      242–44
   *See also* device drivers; I/O
Kernighan, Brian W., 70, 113
keyboard I/O. *See* terminal I/O
   routines
kill command, 20, 40, 214–15,
      218, 229

**L**

Languages, programming. *See*
   name of
l command, 19, 20, 173
lc command, 19, 20, 173
ld command, 20, 38, 266
Lex program generator, the, 5,
      11, b70, 279
   C compiler and, 144
   declarations section of, 299,
      301
   description of, 272
   example program for,
      300–301
   filters and, 115–19, 272
   lexical analysis with,
      299–304
   make program and, 83,
      84, 85
   Ratfor programming
      language and, 117
   regular expressions of, 271
   routines section of,, 302
   rules section of, 117, 299,
      301–2
   Yacc compared to, 117,
      271, 272–73
   Yacc connected to, 302–4
   *See also* Yacc program
      generator, the
lf command, 20, 173
lfile variable, 137
line command, 20, 69, 137
link command, 188

linkers, 5
links. *See* I-nodes
Lint debugger, 73–75
list variable, 137
ln command, 20, 173
logging in, 16–17
logname variable, 137
lr command, 20, 173
ls command, 19, 20, 30, 33, 34,
      44, 173, 175, 177, 209,
      219, 221
   pipelining and, 184
   purpose of, 10
   special device files and,
      236–37
lseek command, 201
lx command, 18, 19, 20, 26, 28,
      30, 34, 85, 173
   purpose of, 15

**M**

mail directory, 15
MAIL variable, 24, 124
make command, 20, 83, 85, 86
make program, 5, 49, 266
   example of the, 83–86
   Lex program generator and,
      83, 84, 85
   Yacc program generator
      and, 83, 85, 86
markit command, 147, 148
Martin, Donald, 70
masm command, 20
microcomputers, background of,
      7–9
Microsoft, 8, 9
   enhancements to Xenix,
      4, 214
mkdir command, 20, 28–29, 34
mknod command, 188, 236, 267
   purpose of, 237, 266
modifier routine, 302
more command, 42, 96, 128,
      160, 184
   purpose of, 15, 21–22
modem command, 238
Morgan, Christopher L., 78,
      244, 265
move command, 81, 148, 154,
      200, 290
moveto command, 198, 200

MP/M, 8
MS-DOS, 4, 5, 9, 10
    directories and, 171, 172
    programming and, 71
mvaddstr command, 153–54,
        198, 200
mv command, 20, 185

**N**

name variable, 134
ncheck command, 21
newgrp command, 21, 185
nice command, 21, 208–9
nl utility, 21, 73
nm command, 20, 40–41
noclobber variable, 134–35
noecho command, 147, 153
nohup command, 21
nonl command, 147, 153
noun routine, 301, 302
numeral routine, 302

**O**

od command, 21, 176–77,
        208, 230
open command, 40, 229, 230,
        231, 238
    purpose of, 201
operating system, function of
        an, 4–6
outb command, 244, 256
out command, 238, 244

**P**

Pascal programming language,
        3, 67, 99
    C compared to, 71
    compilers, 271
passwords, 15, 16–17,
        31–32, 177
    stat program and, 183, 185
    vm program and, 197, 199
passwd command, 21, 183, 185
path(s), 15, 18
    purpose of, 169, 172
    symbols used with, 172
    *See also* Directory(ies);
        File(s)
PATH variable, 123, 124, 133
    purpose of, 21, 24
    run program and, 128,
        129, 130

pause command, 40, 218, 229
PC, the IBM, 9, 10, 155
    interrupts and, 265
    physical organization of
        files and, 176
PC-DOS, 3, 4, 9, 11, 30, 31, 95
    directories and, 171, 172
    programming and, 71–73
pclose command, 222
physio routine, 249
pipe command, 160, 188, 218
pipes/pipelining, 15, 30, 185
    example program for,
        219–22
    fork command and, 218–19
    purpose of, 9, 185, 218
popen command, 219, 221
Prata, Stephen, 70
pr command, 21
printenv command, 21
printf command, 71, 75, 101,
        157, 163, 164, 181
    purpose of, 102
printw command, 154–55, 199
proc command, 249
process command, 75
processes, 11, 15, 185
    control table for, 208
    environments and, 123
    fork command and,
        209–10, 211, 213, 217
    ps command and, 36–39,
        207–9
    purpose of, 36
    semaphores and,
        210–14, 219
    shell, 123
    signals and, 214–18
    superuser and, 208, 209
programming
    advanced tools for, 11
    automating program
        development, 83–86
    C compiler and, 71–73,
        86, 144
    MS-DOS and, 71
    PC-DOS and, 71–73
    vi and, 71
    writing shell programs,
        56–70, 124, 135–37

programming—cont.
    *See also* names of individual
        programming
        languages and program
        generators
ps command, 21, 38, 243, 267
    output of, 36–37, 207–9
    processes and, 36–39, 207–9
    purpose of, 15
pstat command, 21, 243, 267
putcb command, 247
putc command, 101–2
putcf command, 247
putchar command, 101, 102, 104
    purpose of, 247
puts command, 101, 102
putw command, 101, 102
pwadmin command, 21
pwcheck command, 21
pwd command, 15, 21, 25, 28

**R**

ranlib command, 21
Ratfor programming
        language, 117
raw command, 147
read command, 188, 230,
        231, 238
    purpose of, 201
red command, 21
redirection, I/O, 9, 15, 69–70
    cat command and, 25–27,
        107, 230
    C compiler and, 96, 97–98
    controlling, 95–96
    C-Shell and 95–96, 103
    filters and, 93–103, 105, 107
refresh command, 154, 155, 198
    purpose of, 147, 148
regcmp command, 21
restor command, 21
Ritchie, Dennis M., 6, 70
rm command, 21
rmdir command, 21
root directory, 18, 19–20, 65–66,
        171, 172
    as superuser, 208, 253, 266
routines, libraries of, 5
rsh variable, 21, 23
run command, 132, 133

run program
    environmental variables
      and, 128–32, 133
    PATH variable and, 128,
      129, 130
    showenv command and,
      128, 130
    TERM variable and, 128,
      129, 130

**S**

Santa Cruz Operation (SCO)
    enhancements to
      XENIX, 4, 10, 146
    IBM XT and, 42, 228, 250
scanf command, 71, 100,
    102, 221
    purpose of, 101
screen I/O. *See* terminal I/O
    routines
script(s), 24, 30, 49, 114
    controlling I/O, 69–70
    environment and, 124
    expressions and control
      structures for, 61–69
    passing parameters to a,
      59–61
    shell, 3, 10–11, 57–70, 124,
      135–37
sddate command, 21
sdiff command, 21
security, 5–6
    directory, 33–35
    file, 15, 33–35, 169, 185–87
    group files, 185, 197, 199
    group IDs, 188, 197,
      198, 199
    groups, 32–33
    passwords, 15, 16–17,
      31–32, 177, 183, 185,
      197, 199
    superuser, 15, 35, 36, 176,
      186, 187, 208, 209,
      253, 266
sed command, 21, 113
semaphores, 231
    example program for,
      210–14
    processes and, 210–14, 219
    rules for using, 210
setbuf command, 103

set command, 58–59, 135, 137
seterror command, 252
setkey command, 21
settime command, 21
shell(s), 15
    Bourne, 23, 24, 57, 103, 135
    C-, 23, 24, 25, 49, 57, 60,
      61, 65, 95–96, 103, 135
    environment, 126–28
    process, 123
    purpose of, 56–57
    scripts, 3, 10–11, 57–70,
      124, 135–37
shell programs, writing
    binary operators and, 61–62
    expressions and control
      structures for, 61–69
    pathname modifiers and, 62
    purpose of a shell, 56–57
    scripts, 3, 10–11, 57–70,
      124, 135–37
    selecting the shell, 58–59
    unary operators and, 62
SHELL variable, 123
shell variables
    Bourne shell and, 135
    C-Shell and, 135
    purpose of, 134–35
    scripts and, 135–37
shift statement, 66
showenv command, 125, 126
    run program and, 128, 130
showterm program
    compilation of, 160–63
    display of, 159–60
    purpose of, 143
sh variable, 21, 51, 57, 58, 59,
    219, 221
    purpose of, 23
signals
    example program for,
      215–18
    processes and, 214–18
    purpose of, 214
signal command, 40, 217, 229
sigsem command, 214
size command, 21
sleep command, 231,
    242–44, 253
software interrupts, 230–31

sort command, 21, 92, 106,
    219, 220
    as a filter, 111–12, 114
spl routines, 239–42, 252,
    254, 265
sprintf command, 198, 199, 200
sscanf command, 199, 200
standard filters, 106–14
standard I/O. *See* I/O
stat command, 40, 183, 184,
    197, 229
stat program
    compilation of, 183
    contents of, 182–83
    file attributes and, 184–87
    for loop of, 184
    main program of, 183–84
    output of, 181–82
    passwords and, 183
status variable, 137
stderr stream, 94, 100, 103
stdin stream, 94, 100, 103
stdout stream, 94, 100, 102
stopping routine, 217, 218
strategy routine, 249
string processing, 11
strings command, 21
strip command, 21
stty command, 21, 147
substitute command, 113
su command, 21, 36, 177, 185
sum command, 21
superuser, 15, 35, 176, 186, 187
    process control and,
      208, 209
    purpose of, 36
    root as, 208, 253, 266
suser command, 253
swapper command, 208, 209
switch statement, 67–69, 118,
    199, 200, 257
    errors and, 164
    while loop and, 148,
      154, 198
symbols
    &, 38, 96, 133
    *, 56, 67, 78, 98, 107,
      110, 118, 125, 221
    @, 4

symbols—cont.

\, 56, 107–8, 110–11, 112, 114, 118, 137, 156, 157, 158, 172, 199

{}, 110–11, 137, 174, 278, 301, 303

[], 56, 107, 110, 125

, 9, 114, 156, 185

^, 25, 65, 110, 111, 118, 137, 158

:, 113, 118, 133, 137

$, 24, 51, 55, 65, 110, 111, 118, 135, 137

=, 81, 128, 134, 157

!, 24, 181

>, 9, 26, 95, 102, 104

>>, 95

-, 33, 154

<, 9, 26, 81, 95, 100–101, 104

<<, 69

., 110, 116, 118

(), 111

%, 24, 38, 51, 116, 118, 157, 221, 277, 279, 281, 299, 303

+, 56, 154, 157

#, 4, 58, 84, 97, 156

?, 79, 80, 81, 209

', 137

;, 112

/, 18, 19, 25, 56, 98, 113, 172, 301

sync command, 21

system calls, 3, 40–41, 228

  examples of, 40, 229–30

  purpose of, 40

  software interrupts and, 230–31

  *See also* individual calls/commands

system libraries, 4

system variables

  environmental, 18–19, 21–24, 123–34

  shell, 134–37

  *See also* individual variables

**T**

tail command, 21

tar command, 21

T_BLOCK command, 263

T_BREAK command, 261, 264

tdclose routine, 254–55

tdintr routine, 257

tdioctl routine, 255

tdmint routine, 257, 259–60

tdmodem routine, 256–57

tdopen routine, 252–54, 255, 260

tdparam routine, 255–56, 261

tdproc routine, 259, 261–64

tdread routine, 255

tdrint routine, 257, 259

tdwrite routine, 255

tdxint routine, 257, 258–59

tee command, 21

TEMP variable, 127

termcap routines, 146

  function of, 143, 155

  sample entry for, 155–59

  showterm program, 143, 159–64

TERMCAP variable, 21, 124, 128, 134, 155

terminal I/O routines, 4, 7, 11, 124

  curses screen routines, 143, 144–55, 298, 200

  termcap routines, 143, 146, 155–64

  vi screen editor and, 143, 144, 146, 155, 158, 160

TERM variable, 21, 123, 164

  modification of, 135

  run program and, 128, 129, 130

test command, 21

textcopy command, 105, 106

Text processors, 3

Thompson, Ken, 6

time command, 21

T_IME command, 261

timeout routine, 244, 263, 264

tiocom command, 261

tmodem routine, 254, 256–57, 260

token statement, 279

touch command, 21, 85–86

T_OUTPUT command, 262, 263

T_RESUME command, 262

tr filter, 21, 70, 106–8

T_RFLUSH command, 263–64

true command, 21

tset command, 21

tsort command, 21

T_SUSPEND command, 263

ttrstart command, 264

tty command, 21

ttyflush command, 260

tty structure, 247–49, 252, 253, 254, 255

T_UNBLOCK command, 263, 264

TURNON command, 257

TURNOFF command, 257

turtle program, 160

  clearing the screen with, 147

  compilation of, 145–46

  initialization of, 146–47

  main program of, 148

  marking character position with, 148

  purpose of, 143, 144

T_WFLUSH command, 262

TZ variable, 23, 123

**U**

uname command, 21

uniq command, 21, 114

University of California at Berkeley, 3, 4, 6, 7, 23, 143

  *See also* Berkeley

UNIX, 97, 251

  background of, 6–7

  features of, 9

  System V, 3, 4, 7

  versions of, 6, 7, 156

  XENIX code numbers and, 231

unmask command, 34–35, 202

update command, 198, 199, 208, 209

ustat command, 40, 179, 229

ustat program, 179–81

utime command, 188

**V**

variables, system. *See* system variables

vedit command, 21

verb routine, 301, 302

vi command, 21, 128, 184
vi screen editor, 5, 24, 49, 57, 59
    editing text with, 52–53
    entering, 50
    command modes, 50, 51, 53
    cursor commands, 51–52
    ex command mode, 50, 51,
        55, 56, 113, 143
    exiting, 51
    insert mode, 50, 51, 53
    programming and, 71
    purpose of, 50
    reading and writing to other
        files with, 55, 60
    removing and copying text
        with, 53–55
    screen command mode, 50,
        51, 53, 54
    searching and replacing
        with, 56
    terminal I/O routines and,
        143, 144, 146, 155,
        158, 160
view command, 21, 38
vm program
    contents of, 190–97
    for loop of, 198, 200
    i variable and, 197, 198
    main program of, 197–99
    purpose of, 188–89
    while loop of, 198, 199
vsh variable, 23, 155

**W**

wait channel numbers, 243–44
wait command, 40, 214,
    218, 229
Waite, Mitchell, 70, 78, 244, 265
waitsem command, 214
wakeup command, 242–43, 260
wc command, 21
Weinberger, P. J., 113

while loop, 66–67, 71, 104, 125,
    133, 202, 217–18, 221,
    253, 257, 263
    directory display program
        and, 175
    switch statement and, 148,
        154, 198
    vm program and, 198, 199
who command, 21, 64
whodo command, 21
write command, 40, 188, 202,
    229, 230, 231, 238, 245
    purpose of, 201

**X**

xargs command, 21
XENIX
    advantages of, 9–10
    background of, 3–4, 6–7
    Berkeley enhancements to,
        4, 7, 21, 58, 143
    Microsoft enhancements to,
        4, 214
    SCO enhancements to, 4,
        10, 42, 146, 228, 250
XENIX Development System
    Reference Guide, 134
XENIX *Programmers Guide*
    manual, 227
XT, the IBM, 4, 16, 101
    advantages of, 9, 10
    device drivers for, 233–35
    disadvantage of, 5
    HZ variable and, 244
    initialization of, 239
    interrupts and, 242, 265
    physical organization of
        files and, 175, 176
    SCO enhancements to
        XENIX and, 42,
        228, 250
    software interrupts and,
        230, 231

XT—cont.
    wait channel numbers
        and, 243
x variable, 146, 148, 152

**Y**

Yacc program generator, the, 5,
    11, 70
    C compiler and, 144, 271
    compilation of a program
        for, 281–85, 304–6,
        316–17
    debugging with, 306–7
    declarations section of, 279,
        315
    description of, 271–72
    expression evaluator of,
        316–17
    grammars of, 271, 273–80,
        285–86
    handling numbers with,
        314–15
    Lex compared to, 117, 271,
        272–73
    Lex connected to, 302–4
    lexical analyzer of, 316
    Lex routine of, 276, 280
    make program and, 83,
        85, 86
    making the program
        smarter, 307–14
    parsing operations of,
        293–98
    routines section of, 280, 316
    rules section of, 277–79,
        315–16
    states of, 286–92
    transitions of, 292–93
    *See also* Lex program
        generator, the
yes command, 21
y variable, 146, 148, 152

*Tape 5.25 Backup    WKY*

*# Tar -Cv6f -/usr/Abies/Persons /BFW.ALL*